YELTAW

By

R. Jermaine Schex

ISBN: 1-4107-9726-0 (e-book)
ISBN: 1-4107-9725-2 (Paperback)

Library of Congress Control Number: 2003096883

This book is printed on acid free paper.

Printed in the United States of America
Bloomington, IN

1st Books - rev. 10/03/03

1

The Last Thanksgiving

Gordon Exbrook, president of the Exbrook movie theater chain, was at his large, luxurious Boston home on Thanksgiving morning preparing dinner in the kitchen. Gordon, at seventy-seven years of age, became the president of Exbrook Cinemas during the late 1950's, nearly three decades after his father, Irving Exbrook, purchased a small downtown Boston opera house and converted it into a movie theater. Since then, especially under Gordon's leadership, Exbrook Cinemas grew into a chain of over eight hundred movie houses in the eastern United States—with locations as far east as Portland, Maine; as far west as Chicago, and as far south as Richmond, Virginia.

Although Gordon was very old, he was still a very active businessman with an unusually vibrant personality. Since he was a widower (his wife died nine years ago), he did all of his cooking and cleaning by himself.

Back in the kitchen, Gordon had just finished putting a huge turkey into the oven, and now he was laying out an hors d'oeuvre tray on the dining room table, next to the centerpiece. Later he set down five place settings on the table—one for himself and one for each of the four guests he had invited.

"Whew!" gasped Gordon. "All that hard work, for only five people!" He settled down on a recliner in the living room, grabbed a remote control, and turned the television set on.

Sitting like the proverbial "couch potato," Gordon decided to take in what seems to be an American tradition on Thanksgiving Day. No, not a big turkey dinner. He was watching two gangs of men—some as big as turkeys—brawling on an Astroturf field over a prolate spheroid. In other words, Gordon was watching a football game. The game that Gordon watched was a college game: the University of Nebraska at Omaha Twisters versus the University of Pennsylvania at Sellecca Valley Firebirds.

It was almost four o'clock, and Gordon sat idly watching the halftime show, when he heard somebody knocking on his door. He opened the door, and there was his oldest son Lester, his wife Jamie, and their teenage son, Jeremy.

"Happy Thanksgiving!" said both Lester and Jeremy, in unison.

"Come right in! I've been waiting for you," responded Gordon.

Lester, Jamie, and Jeremy took a seat on the living room couch. Lester, at seven feet tall, was a social studies teacher and basketball coach at his son's high school. Jeremy was following in the footsteps of his father—a one-time center for an NBA team—and was becoming a superstar on the hardwood just as well. Jamie, a certified public accountant, operated an income tax preparation office.

"How's business at the head office?" Jamie asked her father-in-law.

"Best in more than a year," said Gordon. "People on the board of directors keep asking me when I'll be retiring. At the pace I'm going, I'll probably be with the company for one more century!"

Moments later, everybody was watching the second half of the game. The Firebirds of Pennsylvania-Sellecca Valley were leading by a score of 16 to 3.

"Sellecca Valley?" asked a puzzled Jeremy. "Never heard of the place."

"Neither have I," said Gordon.

"I have," said Lester. "Sellecca Valley is a real *powerhouse* on the collegiate football scene. Some of the NFL's best draftpicks came out of that small school in central Pennsylvania. One of them—I forgot who; it was so long ago—even won the Heisman Trophy."

As the game progressed, Lester and Gordon heard one more knock on the door. Lester jumped up to answer it.

"Hey, Corey!" shouted Lester as they threw themselves around each other. "How's my little brother been doin' these days?"

"As usual. Uncertain."

"Just like me, sometimes," replied Lester.

Corey, the second and youngest son of Gordon, was an employee at a movie theater—an Exbrook Cinema, at that. Considerably shorter than Lester, Corey had what could be described as movie-star looks. Corey was not married; he shared an apartment with a female roommate.

Everybody sat down at the dining room table. There was plenty on the table—turkey, mashed potatoes, stuffing, cranberry sauce, pumpkin pie, and an antepasto tray. There was so much food on the table that Gordon thought nobody might go hungry.

"Perhaps," said Jamie, "shouldn't somebody say 'grace' before the very special meal?"

2

"Grace! Amen!" shouted Jeremy.

"Well, he did as you suggested," Corey reminded Jamie.

"Makes no difference to me," said Gordon. "All I can say is 'Let's eat'!"

So dinner began without another word spoken. Gordon, always a heavy eater (although his waistline never showed it), took a monstrous portion of turkey, then began to pass the Thanksgiving bird around the table. Everybody then began helping himself to servings of the potatoes, stuffing, pie, and cranberry sauce.

(Except that Corey had no cranberry sauce, since cranberries gave him skin rashes.)

For a while, all was perfectly silent at the table. Then Lester let out a belch. Next, Jeremy began choking on a piece of turkey. When Jamie tried to get it jarred loose, her chair slid out from under her, and she fell to the floor on her spine.

"Ow!" moaned Jamie. "My aching back!"

"Here, Jamie," said Corey, lending a hand to her, "let me help you up."

Just as Corey reached down to pick up Jamie, he too slipped and fell to the floor.

But as all this happened, Gordon just kept on eating as if nothing had been going on.

Finally, around seven-thirty, everybody was finished with dinner. Jamie was left to clean up the table and wash all the dishes, while all the men—Gordon, Corey, Lester, and Jeremy—went back to the living room and watched another football game.

(Incidentally, in the previous game, University of Pennsylvania at Sellecca Valley won by a score of 38 to 15.)

Lester watched this game very closely, because the home team, New Haven University, was his alma mater.

"Lester," said Jamie, "does New Haven have a chance to win?"

"During my days at New Haven, the football team seemed to be almost—*unbeatable!*" Now if only I could say the same thing about the basketball team."

"But that doesn't really mean anything," Gordon added, "except to you."

Three and a half minutes into the game, New Haven fumbled the ball, leading to a 62-yard touchdown by the opponents.

"Ow! That hurts!" shrieked a frustrated Lester as he put his hands upon his head.

3

During a timeout, Corey asked Gordon if there was any beer in the refrigerator.

"Got almost a whole six-pack; maybe even a five-pack," answered Gordon.

Corey searched the refrigerator, then took out a bottle of dark beer.

"First a glass of wine with dinner, and now a *beer*?" asked Jamie, who was watching Corey closely.

Corey didn't say anything. Instead, he went back to the living room, sat down next to Lester, screwed the cap off the bottle, and took a few sips of beer.

"Lester," he said, "you look—perplexed!"

"I can't help it. My favorite team, my *alma mater*, nonetheless, is getting blown out by 28 points!"

"Aw, c'mon! New Haven is a tough team. It's just that they're playing a slightly tougher team."

Meanwhile, Jeremy had gone into another room. He sat in the dining room reading George Orwell's *Animal Farm*, for a report that was due in his English class on Monday.

After watching his favorite team go down in defeat by a rather wide margin, Lester's eyes opened widely as he got up to go to the bathroom.

Looking up briefly from his reading, Jeremy wondered what the weird sound that he heard was. He went right into the bathroom, and saw his father, bent over the toilet, heaving.

"Dad? Is something wrong?" asked a highly concerned Jeremy.

"I...think..." stuttered Lester, "the t-t-t-turkey didn't agree w-with m-m-me..."

Even Jamie came in to see what the commotion was.

"Here. Let's go get your jacket," she said. "We gotta get you home."

Jamie, Jeremy, and a sickly-looking Lester went out the door into a cold, nippy Boston November night. Lester lay down in the back seat of their car, with Jeremy in the shotgun seat and Jamie driving.

Corey remained in the living room. "Well [hic] I g-guess that [hic] it's time for me to be getting [hic] home.

"Corey!" yelled Gordon. "You're drunk! You can't drive! Here, let me take you to the guest room."

Corey lay down on the bed in the guest room, and almost instantly fell asleep. Soon thereafter, Gordon, feeling stuffed, went to bed.

Morning had broken. Corey woke up, completely sober. "Where am I? How did I get here?"

"You got drunk last night," answered Gordon from another room.

4

"Oh, now I remember. I had just one beer too many."

"I'll make breakfast," said Gordon. "But I'm so full I still can't eat."

Corey, who had eaten about one-third of what Gordon had, was certainly hungry enough for breakfast. After a very short morning meal, he went to the bathroom for a very short shower.

It was a Friday morning. Since it was the day after Thanksgiving, it was the second day of a four-day weekend for many people, with Lester and Jeremy being no exception. Jeremy woke up about an hour later than he usually does on school days, and Lester got up at the same time. But this morning, Lester showed no signs of illness whatsoever. His only malady the night before was simple stomach discomfort.

"How's your book report coming along?" Lester asked his son eagerly.

"Just have to read chapter ten, then start writing my report."

Suddenly Jeremy remembered something.

"Dad, have you seen my book anywhere? I looked all over this morning for it but could not find it."

After thinking it over for a moment, Lester eventually remembered. "I think…"

"Uh, oh!" mumbled Jeremy. "I left it at—Grandpa's!"

Lester and Jeremy hurried over to Gordon's house. Jeremy knocked on the door. Gordon told them to come in.

"Grandpa," said Jeremy, "I left a book here last night."

"You mean—" gasped Gordon, "*Animal Farm*?"

"Yes. That's it."

"It's on the dining room table."

"I remember!" said Jeremy. "I was distracted by my father puking. That's why I left it here. Good thing I found it. It's due back at the library tomorrow."

Just after Jeremy stopped speaking, he and Lester heard something fall to the ground in the living room. Then in walked Corey, just out of the shower, dripping wet, and stark naked with a towel wrapped around himself.

"What was that I heard?" he asked in fright.

Just then everybody heard a low, unintelligible moan. Everyone went into the living room, and everyone was frightened stone cold! There lay Gordon, curled up on the ground, trying to get up but unable to.

Jeremy ran to a telephone in the hallway and dialed 911.

"A man has fallen down and he can't get up!" said Jeremy frantically. "Send an ambulance to 2425 Essex Court!"

Paramedics arrived at the door within two minutes. Corey, still wet with a towel draped around himself, guided them to where his father was lying. Gordon was then taken out of the house on a stretcher.

"What a way to spend Thanksgiving vacation!" sighed Lester. "I get sick at the stomach; you get drunk, and my son forgets his library book. Now, *this* has to happen!"

"I'm worried," Jeremy told everybody. "Will Grandpa be all right?"

"I sure hope so," said Corey. "I'm even more worried!"

2

Must the Show Go On?

Before not too long, Gordon was inside an emergency room at a Boston hospital. Several doctors were standing beside him, with all of them making a serious effort to help Gordon regain consciousness. One of the physicians was checking his pulse.

"His heart has stopped beating! Send him to intensive care! We don't have very long!"

Jeremy, Lester, and Corey were waiting somewhat impatiently at Gordon's house just in case the telephone were to ring.

"Could it have been a heart attack?" wondered Corey.

"Very possibly," said Lester, moaning. "But I wonder—just *how*? Our father was always very active. He exercised just about every single day!"

"I think he overate," responded Jeremy. "Did you see how much food he ate last night?"

"I'm—not so sure," replied Corey. "Your grandfather was *always* a very heavy eater. I remember Easter of thirteen years ago, when he ate much more than he did last night."

"But he was much younger then," said Lester.

"How could it be?" asked Corey. "Our first thanksgiving with our father in several years. Now it appears that it was our last."

"Maybe, maybe not," said Lester. "Just like you two, I'm still in suspense. It's killing me!"

The telephone rang, and Corey answered it.

"Hello?"

"This is Boston Memorial Hospital. Are you related to Mr. Gordon Exbrook?"

"Yes. I am his son, Corey."

"Your father has a very weak heart. He had a heart attack last night, but he is still alive, in guarded condition. We're going to have to perform bypass surgery."

"Oh, my!" gasped Corey.

"We'll have to start the operation within five minutes. May we proceed?"

"Go right ahead!"

Corey hung up the phone.

"Dad will be all right, as far as I know," said Corey. "In less than five minutes, they'll do bypass surgery."

"He absolutely must make it," said Lester. "Exbrook Cinemas has absolutely no chance of survival without him. No one has done more for the company than he has."

Lester and Jeremy went home for lunch, but Corey stayed at his father's house. Uneasy about his father's condition, Corey decided to remain near the telephone. He turned on the television set in the living room, and figured he'd try to relax with a soap opera.

Then Corey's female roommate came by.

"Corey!" she said. "Where *have* you been all night?"

"I got drunk—too drunk to drive home. So my father asked me to stay overnight. When I was about to come home this morning, he fell to the floor, suffering a heart attack. Now, at Boston Memorial, he's lying underneath the scalpel."

"So why are you still here?"

"I am waiting for the telephone," replied Corey. "I'm just waiting to hear what his condition is."

"Unbelievable! Your father is so active! How could he get a heart attack?"

"We think he may have overeaten last night."

Almost two hours had passed. It was almost two o'clock, but the telephone had never rung. Corey and his roommate decided to go home. But when they got home, who else should be waiting there but older brother Lester!

"Les!" shouted Corey. "You waiting for me?"

"I felt there was no other choice. With our father's life in question, I just didn't want to be alone."

At the same time, Jeremy was at a park playground, on the basketball court. Three of his friends were with him, standing and talking on the edge of the court.

"Jeremy," said one of his friends, "You've missed six shots today. Is something not up to speed?"

"I guess so. I keep having flashbacks of last night."

"What exactly happened?" asked someone else.

"Today, my grandfather is having a—eh, I don't know the word for it."

"But what about last night? What does your grandfather have to do with this?"

"He fell down, and his heart stopped."

That night, Corey was lying in bed, alone. (His roommate slept in another room.) He wasn't asleep, however. He was too tense to sleep. Sometimes when he closed his eyes, he could see terrible images, some of them almost nightmarish. This would keep him lying down with his eyes open, staring at the ceiling.

But Lester, on the other hand, had been able to fall asleep more easily, since he had Jamie by his side. Yet Jamie had a little trouble falling asleep, since Lester frequently has a tendency to snore.

"Lester!" she whispered. "I can't sleep! Could you turn down the volume on your snoring?"

Just then Lester woke up, rolling over to his side. "Oh, Jamie," he groaned. "Why did you have to wake me up in the middle of such a beautiful dream?"

"Beautiful?" asked Jamie. "What was so beautiful about it?"

"Oh, I was in a fairy-tale land, riding a unicorn, when an ultimately beautiful woman, far more beautiful than thou, came up to me. Right when you woke me up, she was putting her lips right up to mine."

"More beautiful than *me*? How could any woman be more beautiful than me? Unicorns? What a wild imagination."

Lester didn't answer. Instead, he rolled over again and went back to sleep.

The next morning, at about six o'clock, Corey was finally sound asleep, but his roommate had just woke up. She went right into the kitchen, and started to make breakfast. About fifteen minutes later, she went back into the bedroom, where Corey was still fast asleep.

"Corey," she said, "I just made breakfast."

"Oh, it's too early," grumbled Corey. "I don't feel so good. And I didn't get much sleep last night."

"But I made just what you like—a tall stack of pancakes, with bacon, eggs, and French toast."

Slowly, Corey got up, groped his way to the bedroom door, and stumbled over to the kitchen table. With slight difficulty (he had lost plenty of sleep, and was still tired; fortunately it was only a Saturday) he pulled out a chair and sat down. Within two minutes, Corey began to eat. His roommate then sat down to join him.

9

"Is it good?" she asked.

"Best you've ever made!" he answered. "Maybe the best thing you have ever done for me."

"I see that you're eating just like—your *father*!"

"Uh, oh!" said Corey, with some food in his mouth. "We forgot about him."

"Just one question," asked Corey's roommate. "Did he get through his surgery?"

"I don't know. I haven't heard anything about it since yesterday afternoon. Let's go down to the hospital around ten o'clock."

Ten o'clock came by quickly. Corey and his roommate arrived at the main entrance to the hospital. In the distance, who else should be there but—*Lester*? Corey approached cautiously.

"Lester!" Corey said, sounding a bit uncertain. "What made you come by?"

"You were right," said a poker-faced Lester, with an emotionless voice.

"Right? About what?"

"Yesterday you said that it might have been our last thanksgiving dinner together. It was indeed," said Lester.

"Our father is DEAD?" shrieked Corey.

"Yes. It happened at about 5:35 this morning. According to the head doctor, it wasn't the heart attack; it was complications from the anesthesia."

"I just thought of something. When did he have his last operation?"

"I think," said Lester, "it was around March of 1980. Or was it 1981? It was so long ago I don't even remember."

"Whenever it was, he was able to make it through *that* operation," commented Corey.

"One doctor," said Lester, "believed that the operation may not have been necessary. I don't know what to say about that."

Lester slowly walked away and went home. When he arrived at home, there was Jeremy sitting on the couch.

"I guess you heard," said Lester.

"Yes, I heard. Grandpa finally croaked."

"That wasn't really a good choice of words. He didn't really croak; he just wandered off slowly into the distance…"

"I got a phone call from the hospital about 5:40 this morning."

"Why didn't you tell me?"

"You were still asleep. After getting off the telephone, I went back to bed. You must have left while I was still in bed."

Corey, meanwhile, was at home with his roommate.

"What happens now?" he asked with a lump in his throat.

"I guess, we just go on with our own lives."

"But who will get his house?"

"Only time will tell."

"And who will now be president and CEO of Exbrook Cinemas Corporation?"

"There's only one way to find out," said Corey's roommate. "We need to look for his will."

"That's right! I just remembered! But what I can't remember is— where did he hide it?"

"Let's go find it," said Corey's roommate, a bit overly eager.

"But where do we start?" asked Corey.

"There's no better place than the beginning."

3

Where, O Where, Art Thy Will?

It had been three days since Gordon's death. On that Tuesday, a somewhat impromptu funeral service was held at a Boston mortuary. The service was attended not only by members of the Exbrook family, but also by many top-ranked employees of Exbrook Cinemas Corporation. Most of Exbrook's theaters in the Boston area had closed for the day, likewise.

During services, Lester, Jamie, and Jeremy seemed rather calm, but Corey felt very shaky about the future of his job. All his life, since he was sixteen years old, Corey had held only one job—he had worked at several locations of Exbrook Cinemas, usually behind the ticket window. On several occasions, Corey had worked behind the concession stand as well.

It so happened that the next day, Wednesday, was Corey's day off. He was now more determined to find his father's will. He hoped, in a way, that he'd be the one who would inherit the corporation, since it would be a promotion from the job he had been stuck will all those years. Sometimes, however, he hoped that Lester would inherit the company, since Corey had no entrepreneurial experience.

Lester, on the other hand, hoped Corey would be the heir. Lester enjoyed his job as a teacher (and basketball coach), and was afraid that being a corporate executive would cause him to lose touch with his friends and family, and would make him abandon the life he loved.

On Wednesday, Corey decided to go to his late father's house to try to find the will. He opened the front door (he had a key), and let out an "Anybody there?" down into the hallway, just to scare off any spirits that may be occupying the house.

First he started looking in Gordon's desk. The drawer had plenty of pencils, pens, paper clips, staples, and other office supplies, but there was no will, nor anything that even looked like a will. He observed the drawers in Gordon's bedside dresser. No will there—just a bunch of clothes! Looking through the kitchen cabinets was to no avail, either.

"I give up!" he murmured. "Someone will have to tear this whole place apart, just to find that thing!"

Meanwhile, Lester was on lunch break, but found it very hard to eat, since nearly everyone on the school's faculty knew about Gordon, and the possibility that Lester may have been the lucky heir. Everybody was talking about Lester's fortune—and fate. Some hoped he would be the new president of Exbrook, many of them asking silly questions like "Can I share in part of your millions?" or "Will you appoint me to a top management position?" What he would not say was that he was hoping *not* to get it.

At the same time, Jeremy was also on lunch break. He, however, felt that he was unaffected by the will, seriously doubting that he'd end up the heir. Unlike his father, Jeremy was able to have lunch without being disturbed by others.

That evening, Corey was at home watching a movie on television. During a commercial break, the telephone rang. Picking it up, he instantly recognized the voice on the other end. It was Lester.

"Lester?" asked Corey into the mouthpiece of the phone.

"Yes, it is I," said Lester. "I've found a new development. Remember yesterday, at the funeral, you asked me who the lawyer was who helped Dad prepare his will?"

"I remember."

"His name was Samuel Katzman. I found a business card of his in my wallet. I forgot it was there."

"*Your* wallet? How did it get there?"

"I also remembered that he helped me out on my own will."

"I'll go see him one of these next few days," said Corey. "Finally, the mystery will be solved once and for all."

"Tell me what you find tomorrow evening."

"I'll tell you. Goodbye."

As Corey hung the telephone up, he gasped a sigh of relief. "Just what I've been pursuing. The 'McGuffin'."

"McGuffin?" asked Corey's roommate, who was listening.

"That's Hitchcock slang. A 'McGuffin' is his term for the one element in the story that eludes the heroes of the film, and gives the film its suspenseful edge."

"So your dad's will is causing all the suspense?"

"Very much so," said Corey, convincingly. "It's been causing me to lose sleep these past few nights."

"Incidentally," said his roommate, "there's a Hitchcock movie on TV tonight."

"No, thanks. Life itself is a mystery to me."

13

The next afternoon came somewhat slowly. Corey had woke up shortly after four in the morning, riddled with anxiety. An hour or so after he had lunch, Corey found himself waiting in the office of Mr. Katzman. Then Mr. Katzman came into the waiting room, and asked Corey to come with him.

"Lester Exbrook?" asked Mr. Katzman.

"No, I'm Corey. Lester is my older brother."

"What is it you came to see me about?"

"My father."

"You mean Gordon Exbrook?"

"Yes. He died last Saturday. I was wondering if you have the will."

Mr. Katzman got up from his chair, and walked over to a file cabinet with the word "Wills" printed across the top. He opened the second door down from the top, which was labeled "E to I."

"E," Samuel murmured to himself. "Eastlack, Edwardson, Eldridge, Estes, Everett…But I see no—wait a minute! Here it is. Exbrook."

Corey felt relieved. "Is that it?"

"No," responded Mr. Katzman, "it's Lester's. It's the only one I've found with the 'Exbrook' name."

"Didn't my father even leave a will with you?" asked Corey, feeling disappointed.

"Yes, he did. I specifically remember the moment. But it was more than three years ago."

"What happened three years ago?" inquired Corey.

"My office burned down. It was an electrical fire. All my files, including wills, were destroyed."

"How long ago did Lester write out his will?"

"Two years ago. Almost a year after I moved into this new office."

Mr. Katzman went back to the file cabinet, took out the envelope with Lester's will, and observed the seal on the back.

"Does the name 'Dan Sanger' sound familiar?"

"Dan Sanger?" asked Corey. "Who's he?"

"He's a notary. He put his seal on the envelope that contains your brother's will. Also, I seem to recall, he did your father's as well."

Mr. Katzman took out a small piece of paper, and wrote down an address.

"Here," he said, "this is his address."

Corey later went to the office of Mr. Sanger, which was just a few blocks down the street.

"Good afternoon," said a female receptionist, when Corey walked up to the desk. "May I help you?"

"Is this the office of Dan Sanger?" asked Corey.

Then, a man walked up next to Corey.

"You looking for Mr. Sanger?" he asked.

"Yes, I am," said Corey.

"I'm Dan Sanger," said the man.

Dan led Corey into his office. Apparently, Mr. Sanger may have been the notary who signed and sealed Gordon's last will and testament, thought Corey, since there was a sign on his door that said "Notary."

After Corey sat down in the office, Mr. Sanger asked, "What may I help you with?"

"Do you remember signing and sealing the last will and testament of a Mr. Gordon Exbrook?" Corey asked.

"No, the name doesn't sound familiar," Dan said.

"Were you working here three years ago?"

"No, only two. Before that my father was working here."

"So you must be Dan Sanger, *Junior*, said Corey.

"True. Dan Sanger, *Senior* was my father."

"Where may I reach your father?" asked Corey.

"It'd be easier said than done," said Mr. Sanger. "My father is dead."

"Just like mine," said Corey. "By the way, do you keep records of wills that you sign?"

"No, I don't, and neither did my father."

Corey's heart sank. Surely his father *had* written out a will?

"But suppose there isn't any will," said Mr. Sanger.

"I know there was," said Corey. "Mr. Katzman, who filed my father's will, said that Gordon came into his office four years ago. He also remembered seeing the seal of Dan Sanger, Sr. on the envelope."

A whole week had elapsed since Gordon died. Nobody had ever found the will, and Corey and Lester were about to give up trying. It was a Saturday, and nobody was working. Jamie, however, had to take both her own and Lester's paychecks to the bank. Luckily, the Exbrooks bank at Cape Cod National Bank, which has most of its branches, including the one near Lester's home, open on Saturdays.

"Going to the bank, Jamie?" asked Lester.

"Yes, I am."

"One very quick question," said Lester, "When I wrote out my will, where did you stash the copy that I gave you?"

"I believe," said Jamie, "I put them into the safe deposit box at the bank."

"Do you have the key to the safe deposit box?" asked Lester.

Jamie held her key ring in her hand, and held up the safe deposit box key. "This one," she said.

"Let's go do some banking," said Lester, feeling very excited. "But first, let's pick up Corey, and stop by Dad's house."

Just then, Corey rang the doorbell. Lester jumped up to answer the door.

"Corey! *Still* searching?" asked Lester.

"I've just about given up," said Corey.

"I think I have a new lead," said Lester. "First we'll go to Father's, then to the bank."

"Bank?" asked Corey in curiosity. "Why the bank?"

"You'll see when we get there. C'mon, let's go!"

Jamie, Lester, and Corey went to their father's house together. Right away, they went into the kitchen, where hanging near the end of the cabinets, there was a wooden board with keys hanging from hooks.

"Jamie," said Lester, "bring me the safe-deposit box key."

"Here," said Jamie, as she walked up to Lester with the key in hand.

One by one, Lester looked at each of the keys, until he was able to find one that had a design matching that of their safe-deposit box key.

"Aha! I've found it! Box number 817. Let's get to the bank!"

Within minutes, the Exbrooks had arrived at the bank. Jamie went straight to the teller, with the paychecks in hand. Corey and Lester went to the security guard at the vault, and signed in. The guard opened box number 817, then Lester placed the other key in. The box was opened, but all that was inside was an envelope with the name GORDON JOSEPH EXBROOK typed on the front, with a seal on the back.

Corey looked at the seal. "That's the seal of Dan Sanger!"

Lester looked at the fine print around the seal. "It was four years ago—just one year before the fire at Katzman's office."

"Take it to Katzman on Monday morning," said Corey. "Then, just maybe, the suspense will end."

That afternoon, when Lester got home, he hung the envelope on the refrigerator. Suddenly Jeremy came out of his bedroom and into the kitchen.

"Dad," said Jeremy, "you seem to be so excited."

"I am! Your Uncle Corey and I finally found the will!"

"Where was it?" asked Jeremy.

16

"We found it in a safe-deposit box at the bank," said Lester with a wide smile.

"So now who's the owner of Exbrook Cinemas?" asked Jeremy.

"Either Corey or I," said Lester, "but hopefully Corey."

"How could you say that?" asked Jeremy, not quite knowing the reason.

"To be honest, it's because Corey's hoping that *I'll* get it."

"What if there's a third party no one knows about?"

"That could happen," said Lester, "but I don't know why."

Finally, it was Monday morning. Corey woke up at six-thirty, as he usually does on Mondays. He put on a sweater, started out the front door, and proceeded to go around the block. As he went by, he stopped to chat with some of his neighbors. Somehow, he managed to avoid talking about the will, or the possibility of his inheritance.

As he came back inside, he saw his roommate, sitting on the living room couch, painting her fingernails.

"Corey," she said, "are you still worried?"

"I am. But I really shouldn't be. I know that *somebody* will be in the black as of tomorrow morning, but who?"

"Do *you* want to be the one?"

"Yes, and no," replied Corey.

His roommate was baffled. "Yes *and* no?"

"Well, it goes like this. I *would* like to be a billionaire, and I don't know of anyone who doesn't, but I've been too much of a playboy all my life."

"Yeah. I should know. I'm the third woman you've lived with this year!"

"And with a playboy lifestyle, I could never be a company president! The Exbrook Cinemas Corporation would be doomed! May even go out of business!"

"So you want your brother Lester to inherit the business?"

"Maybe."

"Maybe? What kind of answer is that?"

"I really wouldn't mind. But Lester would. He loves his job, and doesn't want to leave it behind."

Just after the stroke of noon, Corey found himself punching the time clock at the local Exbrook Cinema where he worked. He went directly to the box office, and in no time, the first lines had formed outside for a matinee movie. Even though their parent corporation was in disarray, the theaters owned by Exbrook were still profiting.

17

About a half-hour later, the show sold out. Finally, Corey could sit down and take a rest. He sat down calmly, but was jittered by a "beep-beep-beep-beep" coming from his pager. He reached for a telephone, and dialed the number on his beeper.

"Hello?"

"Corey? This is Mr. Katzman. Your brother Lester brought the will to me this morning. I carefully analyzed and scrutinized it."

"I'm starting to get anxious. Who got what?"

"I was getting to that. First, the house and its adjoining land go to your brother, Lester Exbrook. As for Exbrook Cinemas Corporation, which is privately held, the presidency and majority ownership go to one certain person with the name 'Cornelius Vanderbilt Exbrook'."

"Cornelius Vanderbilt Exbrook? That's—me!"

After Corey got off the telephone, he went into the main office to speak with the manager of the theater, Mr. Hodgson.

"Mr. Hodgson, I've just had a strange twist of fate," said Corey.

"What could that be?" asked Mr. Hodgson.

"I've inherited the company!"

"Are you serious?"

"Absolutely! I just got off the phone with my lawyer. He read the will."

"Well what do you know? I'm standing in front of our new chairman of the board!"

Corey fainted and fell to the floor.

"Are you all right?" asked Mr. Hodgson.

4

Strangers on a Train

Corey lay on the floor of the theater's main office, still out cold. Mr. Hodgson, the theater manager, knelt down on the floor and shook Corey's arm. Mr. Hodgson's secretary, who happened to be educated in CPR classes, put her finger just to the right of Corey's Adam's apple.

"His heart is still beating," she said.

"But is he breathing?" asked Mr. Hodgson.

Then she felt Corey's chest, and put a finger close to, but not quite covering, his nostrils. "Still breathing," she responded. "I think it's just a fainting spell. In his situation, I would have fainted too."

Just then, Corey's eyes opened. He came up from the ground, and staggered as if he were intoxicated.

"Where am I? How did I get here?" were some of the questions he asked.

"You're at work, at Exbrook Cinemas," said Mr. Hodgson. "You just fainted, that's all."

"Oh, yeah. That's right. I was so aghast at becoming the new company president."

"What do you plan to do when you're at the helm?" asked Mr. Hodgson's secretary.

"I haven't had the time to decide that yet."

"Well," commented Mr. Hodgson, "hurry up. Too much time has passed. The company is still in despair. If too much more time slips away, the company will probably fold, and we'll all be out of jobs."

Corey was back to working within an hour. At eight o'clock, when his workday ended, Corey came home immediately. Tonight, he felt a bit tired, and planned to go to bed early, maybe at nine o'clock, or fifteen minutes thereafter. When he walked up to the door of his apartment, he heard something bizarre inside. Hesitantly, he opened the door. What did he see? Balloons. Streamers. Confetti. His roommate was wearing a pointed hat with a pompon on top, like the hat of a circus clown. A party was going on inside his apartment. But why? It surely wasn't his birthday (Corey's

19

birthday is on February 17; today was the first of December), nor was it his roommate's. (She was born in April.)

"Surprise!" yelled the crowd.

"Hey, hey," said Corey, scowling at his roommate, "what's the special occasion?"

"Take a look at the cake," she said as she led him to the kitchen table. On the cake was a design like that of a theater marquee, with the words COREY EXBROOK, HEIR TO THE FAMILY FORTUNE on the marquee in red icing.

"How did you find out?" asked Corey, as if he were about to faint again.

His brother Lester stood up. "I got a phone call today. Mr. Katzman told me that you inherited the ownership and presidency of Exbrook Cinemas," he told Corey. "After I heard that, I breathed a sigh of relief. Now I can keep my job, and live in a bigger, better house, since that's what my father left me. With some of the profits I make when I rent out my present house, I could get rid of that old pickup truck I've been driving the past nine years, and buy a luxury car, perhaps a Lincoln or Lexus."

"Whose idea was this?" asked Corey.

"Mine," answered Jamie. "I ordered the cake from the bakery at the supermarket. Do you like it?"

"I...am...flabbergasted!" responded Corey.

"Join in the party!" everyone said together.

For the next two hours, the atmosphere inside the apartment was festive. Lester left rather early, however, since he had to return to work the next day. In a matter of minutes, everyone was gone except for Corey and his roommate. She was cleaning up the mess left by all the guests, while Corey went to bed and fell asleep quickly.

Corey woke up at ten the next day. After he turned the alarm clock off, he started pacing around in his bedroom, wearing only his pajamas and bedroom slippers. "I still don't know what to do," he said to himself. "I'm completely *un*experienced in business management. Theater management, especially. What will I do? What *will* I do?"

Slowly, Corey walked into the kitchen, and picked up the newspaper from the table. Right away, he took out the back section of the paper, which had the classified advertising, and he observed all the items people were trying to sell. The majority of the ads were for used cars, and homes for sale or rent.

"Hmmm," mumbled Corey. "Maybe I could sell the company that way. It would surely take a load off my mind!"

Shortly afterward, he walked over to the apartment of his next-door neighbor, Wally Beasley. Mr. Beasley opened the door just before Corey was about to ring the doorbell, because Mr. Beasley knew Corey so well that even the sound of Corey's footsteps was familiar.

"Corey!" said Mr. Beasley. "Come right in."

Corey sat down in an easy chair in the living room.

"I read about you in the newspaper today," said Wally. "I heard all about your fortune and fate."

"Which newspaper do you get?" asked Corey. "We get the *Register*, and I saw no such story."

"We get the *Independent Times*," said Mr. Beasley, as he took the newspaper off the coffee table. "Read about yourself on page 5A."

After Mr. Beasley handed the *Independent Times* to him, Corey immediately turned to page 5A. There he saw the headline, EXBROOK CINEMAS EMPLOYEE PROMOTED TO CORPORATION'S HIGHEST RANK. "It has to be me," he said to himself.

"I'd say so," said Wally. "since the name listed is Corey V. Exbrook. Now that you own the corporation, what do you plan to do?"

"If it is possible, I'd like to sell it. I have absolutely no business experience."

"I think it is possible," said Mr. Beasley. "It so happens that my brother-in-law is on the board of directors of a theater company like yours."

"Really?" asked an astonished Corey.

"Yes, it's true! My brother-in-law, Harry Castormeier, is with CinemaStar Incorporated."

"I remember them!" said Corey. "Several times in the past few years, they tried to buy out Exbrook. My father refused everytime."

"But that's not the end of it," said Mr. Beasley. "CinemaStar still has eyes on Exbrook. After I read the article this morning, I called Harry. He said he would like to talk to you at any convenient time, hopefully today."

"Would right now be a good time?" asked Corey.

"I'm sure it would be. He should be in his office right now, waiting to hear from you. The number is area code 303, 555-STAR."

Wally picked up the telephone and dialed Harry's number.

"Hello?" he said. "Is Mr. Castormeier in?"

Mr. Beasley sat and waited for a few minutes while he was placed on hold.

"This is Mr. Castormeier," he finally heard. "How may I help you?"

"Harry, this is Wally. I just finished speaking to Corey Exbrook. He's here right now if you'd like to speak to him."

"Put him on the phone," said Harry.

Wally handed Corey the telephone.

"Hello?" asked Corey.

"Is this Corey Exbrook?" asked Mr. Castormeier.

"Yes, sir! I'm Corey Exbrook."

"I'm speaking to you concerning your ownership of Exbrook Cinemas Corporation."

"I found out the hard way that I'm now the owner of all my father's privately held stock. But I don't know what to do with it."

"That's why I wanted to speak to you. Several times in the past we had tried to buy out the stock, and the corporation, from your father, but have never had any success. From the way you spoke to me, it might seem as if you are interested in selling it to us."

"I most certainly am!" said Corey.

"We have men here, ready to get your signature, and purchase all the stock from you, after we sign a little paperwork. Would it be possible for you to be here in Denver tomorrow afternoon at about three o'clock? The address is 8 Mile High Road. Will you be there tomorrow afternoon?"

"I'm afraid not," said Corey. "I feel very leery about flying these days. Could you give me until Tuesday? I'm going to take the train."

"I understand," said Harry. "I also get jittery when I board a plane. I'll make sure we're ready to meet with you on Tuesday. Thanks for your time. Remember the address, 8 Mile High Road."

Corey hung up the telephone, finally feeling relieved. He finally knew just what he wanted to do. And he knew how he would do it. Through what seemed to be a miracle, he found a buyer for the stock he now held—stock potentially worth millions of dollars. But he was still uncertain what he'd do with all that money. Still, Corey felt it should be first things first, and he decided not to worry about his wealth until he actually had it.

"How'd it go?" asked Wally.

"I've finally found myself a buyer," said Corey, grinning. "I don't think I could have done it without you."

"Isn't that what neighbors are for?" asked Wally, giggling.

"Tuesday," said Corey, "I have to be in Denver, at 8 Mile High Road. This evening, I must get on a train to Denver."

"I guess you'd better get going," said Mr. Beasley. "It won't be too long until Tuesday."

Corey went back home, quite eager to tell his roommate of his good fortune. At the last minute, however, he remembered that his roommate had already left when he woke up that morning. He did not know when she would be coming back home, so he wrote a small note explaining his last minute trip, and put it on the refrigerator.

He went into his bedroom, took out a suitcase from under the bed, and carefully put a week's worth of clothing into the suitcase. Then he set it aside, and quickly went over to Lester's house.

"Hello, Corey," Lester said when Corey arrived. "What's going on now with Exbrook Cinemas?"

"A sale is pending," Corey said. "CinemaStar, of Denver, has offered to buy out all the stock in Exbrook, which is what Father left me. Tuesday afternoon I have to be at their headquarters to sign the papers."

"Tuesday afternoon," commented Lester, "that's only a few days away."

"But I have to leave today," said Corey. "I'm a little too afraid to fly, especially during snowy weather, so I decided to take the train. It should take about three days to get to Denver from here that way."

"Sounds about right," said Lester. "I once took a train from here to L.A. We stopped in Rochester, Pittsburgh, Cleveland, Chicago, St. Louis, Tulsa, and yes, Denver, en route to Los Angeles. I got to see some very beautiful countryside. That train leaves here at about six o'clock. I'll drop you off at the station at about four."

"You're not working today, are you?" asked Corey.

"No, not today. I have an appointment with my optometrist early this afternoon. But I should be out by four o'clock, to pick you up."

At four o'clock, Corey was waiting in the living room for his brother Lester to arrive. Lester came within minutes, and Corey stood up with his baggage packed and ready to go.

"Are you ready?" asked Lester.

"Just as ready as you are."

Lester and Corey walked out to the apartments' parking lot, where Lester parked his old, beat-up pickup truck. Corey put his baggage into the back, while he got into the passenger seat, and Lester got into the driver's seat. Lester started the ignition, and drove off.

"Here, let me take that in," said Lester, as he and Corey approached the entrance to the station. Corey then went over to the ticket window.

"Round trip to Denver, please."

"That'll be five hundred twenty dollars," said the ticket seller.

"Here's my credit card."

Corey gave the man behind the window his card. Then the man gave Corey back his card, along with tickets and an itinerary.

Corey looked at the timetable. "Next train to Rochester, the first stop, arrives here at six. Could you wait with me?" he asked Lester.

"Only until five," said Lester. "I have to be back home by five-thirty."

Lester left at five, just as he said he would. For a half hour afterward, Corey sat and waited alone on a bench. He was later joined by a man, about his age, who sat down right next to him.

"Hello," the man said. "Where are you headed?"

"Denver. What about you?"

"I'm going back home to Chicago," the man said. "Actually, I don't live in the city, but in a small suburb called East Hazel Crest, which is around 175th Street and Halsted."

"I wouldn't know," said Corey, "I've never been to Chicago. I'm a native of Boston."

"You know somebody in Denver?" asked the man.

"Not quite. My father was the owner of Exbrook Cinemas Corporation. When he died last Saturday, I became majority holder of the corporation's stock. This morning I brokered a deal to sell it to CinemaStar of Denver. By the way, my name is Corey Exbrook."

"And my name is Jevon Dandridge," said the man. "I'm the owner of a gourmet jelly-bean shop in Chicago. Like you, I've come upon hard times financially. As a matter of fact, I came to Boston just to sell it to a company that owns a similar store here in 'Bean'-town."

"You mean—you're selling a business, just the way I'm selling mine?"

"Exactly. I've already signed the paperwork."

After the two men had been conversing for about an hour, they heard the public address system churn out the familiar "all aboard!" for the train from Boston to Rochester. Corey and Jevon boarded the train, took seats next to each other, and settled themselves down. After taking his seat, Corey placed his tickets in the inside pocket of his coat.

"I just can't wait until we get to Rochester," commented Jevon shortly after the train took off.

"Why's that?" asked Corey.

"Between Rochester and Pittsburgh lies the town of Sellecca Valley. I have a cousin living there. Beautiful woman, she most certainly is!"

Corey's mouth was about to water. "How does this woman look?" she asked.

"I really couldn't describe her now, because I haven't seen her for a few years. She's a nurse at a hospital in Sellecca Valley."

Minutes later, Corey began feeling very hungry. "I think I made a mistake," he said. "I left home without anything to eat."

"Here," said Jevon, as he reached into his pocket and took out some jelly beans.

"Jelly beans," commented Jevon. "Take some with me everywhere I go. I especially like the purple ones."

"My favorites are the orange ones," said Corey. "Here, I'll trade you my purple ones for some of your oranges."

Jevon and Corey sat for a little over an hour, talking about their plans for the future. Corey decided that with the money from the sale of Exbrook Cinemas, he would retire to a home by the Boston harbor—near the spot where the famous "tea party" occurred, Corey joked.

Later, the train made its first stop along the way to Denver, at Rochester, New York.

As passengers were boarding the train at the Rochester station, Corey was starting to yawn.

"Getting tired?" asked Jevon.

"Yes, but I forgot something very important—my pillow."

"You can use me instead. Lean over, and lay your head down beside me."

Corey lay his head down, and soon after the train had left Rochester, he fell asleep, with Jevon's right arm holding him up close.

Minutes later, Jevon was also asleep, but somehow his arm was still around Corey. By now, the train was crossing southbound into Pennsylvania. Two and a half hours later, the train was scheduled to arrive in Pittsburgh.

That night was cold and blustery. A blizzard had struck in central Pennsylvania. The tracks were icy, and extremely slippery.

"Oh, no!" yelled the conductor. Immediately he groped for a rope hanging overhead, and pulled it down. Along the track, the front wheels skidded for about a hundred or so yards. Then the wheels of some of the middle cars started to jump. The car in which Corey and Jevon were riding shook from side to side, and bounced along the icy track, but Jevon and Corey were still asleep. Jevon's arm was still around Corey, and Corey's head was still on Jevon's shoulder.

After reaching a grade crossing, on a steep downhill section of Pennsylvania State Route 12, the cars in the middle of the train jumped off the track. Soon, the entire train went down the hill about twenty yards.

Jevon and Corey were still inside the train, even after it had derailed. Jevon's body was lying on top of Corey's. Corey and Jevon were no longer asleep, however. Now they were unconscious.

5

Tragedy on Route 12

After the train settled on the hill, where it blocked off part of Route 12, the conductor, who was slightly bruised, but not otherwise injured, got out of the train, to look at the wreckage.

At that moment, a newlywed and his beautiful new bride were driving back home along Pennsylvania State Route 12 from a honeymoon at Niagara Falls. Off in the distance, a pair of red lights was flashing. Their car stopped right in front of the railroad tracks. They waited a few minutes. Where was the train? From inside the car, they could not see any train; or anything else, for that matter.

Since there were no gates at this crossing, the man drove past the tracks. He looked out the window on both sides, but there wasn't any visible headlight, so he drove on downhill.

"Look! Down there!" said his bride, feeling frightened.

The man turned on his high-beam headlights, and saw something eerie: a derailed train, with several bodies scattered around. One man, the train's conductor, was standing among the bodies, feeling uncertain and a bit guilty.

"Can you help me?" asked the conductor, desperately. "My train has derailed, and I have no way of calling for help.

"Get me my cellular phone," said the newlywed to his bride. "It's in the glove box."

Within minutes, a helicopter flew over the accident scene. Then ambulances came from the other side of the wreck. Of the men lying on the ground (all of whom were thrown from the train), all but two of them were pronounced dead on the scene. Rescue crews then went into the train, where a dozen or so passengers, including Jevon and Corey, still lay. Luckily, none of them were dead. But all the men, alas, were unconscious. Without causing any additional injuries, crews were able to remove every one of them. One by one, all the people were loaded into ambulances, and the ambulances traveled in a caravan beyond the accident scene and into the lights of a town three miles away.

The town was Sellecca Valley. It was a medium-sized place, of about thirty thousand people, located along the western bank of the Sellecca River, bordered by mountains on the north, and forest on the south. Small, and little-known during the fifties, Sellecca Valley started to become a boom town in 1961, when a university opened its doors in the then sleepy town. The university came to be known as the University of Pennsylvania at Sellecca Valley.

The caravan of ambulances came to a stop on the university campus, at the UPSV Medical Center. The hospital at the medical center had plenty of emergency rooms—enough to accommodate all the passengers of the ill-fated train trip.

The ambulance carrying Corey and Jevon was the last one to arrive. The two men were admitted into an emergency room, with a brilliant, young, and somewhat handsome staff physician working the late-night shift.

The physician's name was Dr. Kendall Grayer. A graduate of University of Pennsylvania at Sellecca valley seven years before, Dr. Grayer was skilled in nearly all branches of medicine, with a few exceptions, most notably neurophysics.

Immediately Dr. Grayer walked over to Jevon, who had one of the two beds in that particular room. Jevon was still breathing, and his heart was still beating. Dr. Grayer then went a few feet away, to the bed where Corey was laying. Corey had a pulse, but it was unusually slow. He was still breathing, but his breaths wee short and raspy.

Into the room a few minutes later came Dr. Francis. Francis, a veteran doctor, took Jevon off to an X-ray room. Once inside the room, Dr. Francis put on a mask and an apron. Jevon was placed under the X-ray machine. With a few clicks of a switch, five different X-rays were taken.

In minutes, a woman came out of the darkroom, with the exposed film of Jevon's X-rays. Dr. Francis looked closely at the X-rays.

"He's very fortunate," said Dr. Francis. "Only two bones fractured—his right arm and his right collarbone."

Jevon was then taken into another room, and he had a cast put on his right arm.

In the meantime, Dr. Grayer was still working with Corey. Kendall tried still to revive Corey. But nothing worked.

Just then, Dr. Francis came back into the emergency room.

"Dr. Grayer," he said, "One of our derailment patients, Jevon Dandridge, has just been X-rayed. He has two broken bones."

"But what about the other patient?"

"We don't know yet," replied Dr. Francis. "We must take *him* in for a few X-rays."

Dr. Francis was puzzled. "What is the other patient's name?" he asked.

"I can't tell. He has no identification on him, only a set of round-trip train tickets."

"Take him in for some X-rays," Dr. Francis told Kendall.

"Yes, Dr. Francis. I'll get them the first available moment."

In haste, Dr. Grayer rushed Corey into an X-ray room—the same room in which Jevon had been X-rayed. Dr. Grayer put on a mask and an apron. Five X-rays were taken, just as Jevon had the same five X-rays.

"This doesn't look very good," said Dr. Grayer to Dr. Francis. "Seventeen bones fractured."

Dr. Francis was shocked. "Seventeen? That's nearly one-seventh of the bones in the human body!"

"Good thing we have plenty of Plaster of Paris," remarked Dr. Grayer.

"Anything crucial?" asked Dr. Francis.

"Yes. Absolutely. There is a small chip in his skull. Maybe that is why he can't seem to be revived."

"Get him into surgery. *Quick!*"

Faster than Dr. Kendall Grayer could say his full name ten times, he had rushed Corey into an operating room.

"Is this the 'mystery patient'?" asked one of the surgeons in the room.

"Yes. We don't know his name. But I know his condition. We've got to get a chip in his skull fixed."

"We could use your help. Would you help us to perform the operation?" one of the surgeons asked Dr. Grayer.

"I suppose so. I'm the one assigned to treat this patient. He's one of them found in that nearby train accident."

"Put him on an IV," said one of the doctors.

In mere seconds, the other doctor inserted an IV into Corey's left arm.

"Careful!" admonished Dr. Grayer. "He has a fracture very close to there."

Dr. Grayer took a tank of anesthetic, and placed a hose over Corey's nose and mouth. Although Corey was unconscious, the anesthetic was to prevent him from regaining consciousness during the surgery.

Two hours passed. The surgery was successful. Corey was still out cold, however. Dr. Grayer started to yawn.

"It's a long night," he said to his colleagues, somewhat tired. "It's not quite fair. I have to be back at work at eight."

Dr. Grayer walked out of the emergency room. He didn't go home, however. He went into the lounge, sat down on the sofa, and went to sleep.

While Kendall was sleeping, Jevon's eyes opened. A nurse was standing beside him.

"What happened? Where am I?" Jevon asked the nurse.

"You're in the town of Sellecca Valley, Pennsylvania, at the University of Pennsylvania at Sellecca Valley Medical Center."

"Sellecca Valley? Hmmm….I seem to remember. I have a cousin living in this town. Last time I saw her, she was an extremely beautiful woman."

"What's her name?"

"I forgot her last name. It's somewhat unusual. Her maiden name was Starke. She married some man whose last name began with a 'Y.' But they're no longer married. He's dead."

"I see. What's her first name?"

"Connie."

"Wait. Connie…. 'Y'….Could 'Yeltaw' be her last name?"

"Yeltaw? Yes! That's it!"

"She works here. But she's not here right now. She's a nurse, like me. She works in pediatrics."

"Will I still be here tomorrow? Tell her I'm here."

"Yes. Tomorrow afternoon, you will be discharged. But before then, I'll see that she meets with you."

Back in Boston, a local television station, WCBV-TV, had a report on the early morning news, stating that Corey Exbrook, the heir to the Exbrook Cinemas fortune, was missing.

"Missing?" wondered Lester, biting his nails. "Hopefully he isn't *dead*!"

Jeremy was worried too. "What could have happened to Uncle Corey?" he asked his father. "Was he abducted? Was he murdered? Is he alive? Is he all right?"

In Sellecca Valley, at eight the next morning, Dr. Grayer had just woke up (his watch had an alarm), and went back to the room where Corey was being kept.

Several doctors were in Corey's room.

"Any luck?" asked Dr. Grayer.

"Nope. Still out cold."

"How successful was the operation?"

"We relieved some of the tension on his head," said one of the doctors. "He didn't suffer any brain damage."

Jevon was in his room, with the same nurse with him the night before. He just woke up, and was having breakfast. Meanwhile, the beautiful young nurse, Connie, who just happened to be Jevon's cousin, came into the room.

"Connie!" Jevon said holding his left arm out. "Haven't seen you in a while!"

Connie leaned over, and she and Jevon were kissing and hugging, as he held his left arm around her.

"What brought you out here?" asked Connie.

"I got derailed on my way back home from Boston."

"Why'd you take the train?"

"Much cheaper. Have you seen the price of air fares recently?"

"I know what you mean. How did your arm and your collarbone get broken?"

"It was late at night. A man I traveled with felt sleepy. But he forgot his pillow. So I let him rest on my shoulder. I was holding him up to me. Eventually, I fell asleep too. The train derailed while we were sleeping."

During the conversation, Dr. Grayer came into the room.

"Connie?" asked Kendall. "What are you doing here?"

"I asked her to report here," said the other nurse.

"This man is my cousin," said Connie, pointing to Jevon.

"Jevon," said Dr. Grayer, "today you are going to be released."

"But—where will I stay?" asked Jevon.

"You can stay with me until your casts are ready to come off," said Connie.

"Thanks. I feel good about that."

Eventually, the afternoon came, and Dr. Grayer came back to discharge Jevon.

"It's time for you to go back home," said Kendall.

"Already?" asked Jevon.

"Yes. Connie is waiting in the parking structure. She'll take you to her home. But first, you and I have some unfinished business to take care of."

Dr. Grayer put Jevon into a wheelchair, and took him down the hallway into a waiting elevator. When Kendall went to the control panel, Jevon observed him pushing a button marked "5."

"Why are we going to the fifth floor?" asked Jevon.

The elevator stopped on the fifth floor, and Dr. Grayer took Jevon down the hallway, toward room 508.

"Jevon," said Dr. Grayer, "there is a man in room 508. I would like for you to see what you remember about him."

"Who is it?" asked Jevon.

"I don't know. He has no ID," said Dr. Grayer.

Dr. Grayer opened the door to room 508, and brought Jevon inside.

"Remember him?" asked Kendall. "You were on the same ambulance with him, and the same emergency room."

"Let me see….I also remember we were on the train together."

"Do you know his name?"

"I can't remember his last name, but his first name, I think, was Corey. He told me that he was heir to a movie-theater company. I believe the company name is the same as his last name."

"As soon as you remember," said Dr. Grayer, "tell me."

Jevon put his hand to his head, and tried to concentrate.

"Wait. I believe his last name began with the letters E-X. But I can't remember *exactly* what it is."

Dr. Grayer brought Jevon to the front entrance, where Connie was standing, waiting for him. Kendall followed Connie and Jevon to the parking structure, where Connie put Jevon into the passenger seat, then put herself in the driver's seat, started the ignition, backed out of the space, and drove away to her home.

6

The Inseparable Interns

After Connie drove away with Jevon, Dr. Grayer slowly walked a few feet away, as another car was pulling into that same space. Kendall was puzzled. He'd never seen that car there before. Obviously, he thought, the person *had* to be an employee, since that floor of the parking garage was reserved for doctors, nurses, and hospital employees. Dr. Grayer looked at the driver, to see who it was.

"Lamar," he said as the man came out of the car. "I didn't recognize the car. Is it new?"

"Not really," Lamar said. "I've had it a few weeks. I've just never driven it here. Normally Reno and I come together, and he drives."

The man with whom Dr. Grayer was speaking was Dr. Lamar McCormick, an intern in his second year, supervised by Kendall.

"About Reno," asked Dr. Grayer, "Will he be back today?"

"Yes," said Lamar. "He told me his injured knee is almost completely healed. He's walking again."

Just then, another car drove nearby, and came inches close to bumping into Dr. Grayer. As the car pulled into the space next to Lamar's car, the driver came very close to sideswiping it.

Out of this car came Dr. Reno Simmons, the partner and best friend of Lamar. Like Lamar, Reno was in his second year of internship with Dr. Grayer.

"Reno, are you all right?" asked Dr. Grayer in concern. "Is your knee healed?"

"Just about," answered Reno.

"What do you mean by 'just about'?" asked Lamar.

"I can walk, but I still have a little difficulty driving. I find myself having to do left-foot braking. That's why I almost ran over you, Dr. Grayer. And it may explain why I nearly scratched the paint job on your new car, Lamar."

"Don't worry about it," said Lamar. "It feels so good to have you back. I was wondering if you'd ever be here again."

"And it feels so good to be back with you two again," replied Reno happily. "Did anything unusual happen while I was out? How'd everything go, Lamar?"

"I was all right," said Lamar. "While you were out, Dr. Grayer let me out early to take care of you."

"This past night was hectic," said Dr. Grayer. "Hear about the train wreck on Sellecca Boulevard?"

"Yes. There were bodies all over," commented Lamar.

"And one of those bodies is still unconscious. His name is Corey, but that's all I know. I'd like for you two to try to bring him back from this coma he seems to be in."

Reno and Lamar walked with Kendall into the lobby of the hospital, where they signed in at the front desk.

"Well," said the receptionist, "I see that McCormick and Simmons, the 'Tweedle-Dee' and 'Tweedle-Dum' of the medical center, are back together."

"Tweedle-Dee and Tweedle-Dum?" asked both Lamar and Reno.

"It seems that you two are so inseparable, like the Tweedle-Dee and Tweedle-Dum characters of *Alice in Wonderland.*

Lamar and Reno may have been almost completely inseparable for nearly fourteen years. Lamar, a straight-A honors student, first met Reno when he was a freshman in high school. Reno was in his science class. Reno seemed to be somewhat of an outcast, since he was younger than the other students in his class—he was such an intelligent student that he was advanced from kindergarten to third grade. Reno had very few friends, but did plenty of studying and reading.

It was on the first day of high school that Lamar met Reno for the first time. Other students had been making fun of Reno, because he was so young. In class that day, Reno, who sat right next to Lamar, lay his head down on his desk and started to cry.

"Is something wrong?" asked Lamar, with his hand on Reno's shoulder.

"Nobody likes me," sobbed Reno. "I'm just so young. I'm three years younger than everybody else here. What am I doing here?"

"Don't cry, now," said Lamar, sympathetically. "I kinda like you, even though I don't really know you. You've got a friend. You'll never be alone."

Since that time, Lamar and Reno completed high school, getting closer to one another as the days went by. Both men were able to get scholarships for the same college—University of Pennsylvania at Sellecca

Valley. Then after graduating from UPSV, they went to medical school together. After completing medical school, they both became interns at the same medical center.

"Lamar, Reno," said Dr. Grayer, "Come along with me to room 508. Our patient is in there. See what you can do. I've tried everything. I still can't wake him up."

"We'll try everything," said Lamar.

"Yeah, everything," added Reno.

Reno and Lamar then walked into the hallway, and went to an open elevator.

After they stepped off the elevator on the fifth floor, Lamar opened the door to Room 508, where Corey still lay unconscious. Reno walked right up to Corey, and held his arm up.

"He's out cold," said Reno, shaking the arm. "No doubt about it! I wonder, I just wonder, if he is still alive."

"He is," said a doctor, who was watching the two interns.

"How do you know?" asked Lamar.

"He's still breathing. And his heart still beats."

"Please," pleaded Reno to Corey, "don't die on us. I hate it when a patient dies on me. I just know I could have done something to save him."

"Be careful around the head," said the doctor. "He had to have brain surgery. "That's why he's in bandages."

"I suppose," said Lamar, "Maybe we will need to take some X-rays."

"Let's do that!" answered Reno.

Lamar and Reno then took Corey down to the ground floor, and into an X-ray room.

"Well," said an X-ray technician, "who else but Mr. Bonebreak?"

"Mr. Bonebreak?" asked Reno, with a scowl.

"Yes. Dr. Grayer brought him in here to be X-rayed."

"Really?" asked Lamar.

"Yes. We have his X-rays right here. I'm surprised that nobody has him plastered up yet."

The technician reached into a file cabinet and took out a file folder of X-rays. Lamar and Reno walked up to the X-ray viewer, and made observations about Corey's X-rays.

"Wow! Seventeen fractures!" commented Lamar.

"We need to get crackin'!" said Reno. "And, please pardon the pun."

Reno went into a storeroom to get some gauze and some plaster of Paris, while Lamar went with Corey back to his room. In minutes, Reno came back to join Lamar.

Within the course of minutes, Corey looked less like a human being, and more like a mummy—he had a cast on nearly every part of his body! Somehow, the interns were able to put a cast on his left arm without having to remove the IV that kept Corey alive.

Dr. Grayer then came in to look at Corey.

"Eek!" shrieked Kendall. "What have you done?"

"Sixteen fractures," said Reno.

"Seventeen," said Lamar.

"Okay, seventeen," said Reno. "But one of them didn't quite look like a break, but more like a bruise."

"Twelve o'clock. Time for lunch," said Dr. Grayer.

"We've had a very busy day," said Reno. "After hard work like this, we need a break."

"Let's go out today," said Lamar. "We'll take my new car."

Lamar got into the driver's seat, Reno took the front passenger seat, and Kendall in the back seat, behind Lamar.

"I see that you finally got a new set of wheels," said Dr. Grayer.

"Good thing *you're* not the one driving it today," Lamar told Reno.

"How could that be?" asked Reno in curiosity.

"If you had your knee problems," said Lamar, as he shifted into second gear, "you'd have a *terrible* time driving this."

"So you bought a car with stickshift transmission," Reno said. "Couldn't you have bought one with an automatic?"

"Well," said Lamar, "this was the only one I could find in the low price range."

"So," said Reno, "you finally got rid of that old Volkswagen Rabbit convertible, the one you'd driven since high school."

Lamar had driven into the parking lot of Harland's Fried Chicken. As he turned the ignition off, everybody started to feel hungry, because of the smell of chicken.

"What do you plan to order?" asked Kendall. "I'd like the Classic Blue-Ribbon Recipe."

"So would I," responded Lamar.

"I go more for Double-Crispy," said Reno.

"Why don't I just get some of each," said Lamar.

The threesome went inside, and Lamar stepped up to the counter.

"I'll have a medium bucket of Classic Blue-Ribbon Recipe, and one of Double-Crispy, please."

"Why, Lamar, my old friend," said the cashier, "how's Reno doing?"

"His injured knee is almost completely healed now. He's back to working with me and Dr. Grayer once again."

A few minutes later, Lamar had taken two buckets of chicken to the table.

"This bucket has the Double-Crispy," he said, putting the bucket on the table, "and as you see here, this has the Classic Blue-Ribbon Recipe."

All three men sat down and began eating lunch, while Dr. Grayer was listening to some people talking at the next table. One of those people at the next table just happened to be from Boston, and was talking about a favorite topic of many Bostonians: Whatever had happened to Corey Exbrook?" Dr. Grayer raised his eyebrows when he heard the first name Corey, since that was the name Jevon had told him.

"Pardon me," said Dr. Grayer to one of the men, "who is this Corey Exbrook you're referring to? I think I may know him."

"Corey Exbrook," said the man, "is the heir to the fortune of Exbrook Cinemas Corporation. He's been missing since December 2, and is presumed dead."

"Well, they've presumed wrong," said Dr. Grayer. "Corey Exbrook is in Sellecca Valley right now, undergoing treatment at UPSV Medical Center. He's still alive, but comatose."

When lunch was nearly over, Lamar's pager beeped. The number on the pager's readout was the telephone number of UPSV Medical Center's front desk.

"We've been paged," said Lamar, frantically. "We've got to get back to the hospital—*fast!*"

Lamar, Reno, and Kendall all got into Lamar's car, and drove away quickly.

"Lamar," said Dr. Grayer, "Watch the speedometer!"

"I'm only doing 45," remarked Lamar.

Lamar slowed down as he entered the parking garage, and then everyone ran straight toward the entrance, stopping only at the front desk.

"So good you got here," said the receptionist. "We have an emergency in room 508."

"Room 508!" gasped Reno. "That's—Corey Exbrook! Our 'mystery patient'!"

Everyone ran up four flights of stairs (it would have taken too long to wait for an elevator; by the time an elevator would reach the ground floor, it may have been too late) and directly down the fifth floor hallway to room 508, where a nurse was waiting.

"Oh, no!" gasped the nurse. "The patient has stopped breathing!"

"How so?" asked Dr. Grayer.

"He came down with pneumonia," said the nurse. "And he's still comatose! We've got no time to lose! We *must* do something! The question is, *WHAT?*"

7

Signs of Life

"Go get an oxygen mask," said Dr. Grayer to Reno. "And be quick."

A few minutes later, Reno had connected Corey to the oxygen mask.

"Listen, gentlemen," said Dr. Grayer to his two interns, "this is a life-or-death situation. Corey has pneumonia. And it seems nothing we can do will help him come to. If he isn't treated immediately, he will die."

Moments later, a nurse placed Corey into an oxygen tent, right over his bed.

"Bring up some penicillin," said the nurse.

"But," responded Lamar, "suppose he's allergic to it?"

"Right, Lamar," said Reno. "There's always that possibility."

"Let's try it anyway," said Dr. Grayer.

Lamar left the room, then came back with a vial of penicillin and a syringe.

"Where do we inject it?" he asked. "He has casts over both of his arms, as well as this IV."

"Here," said Dr. Grayer, "I'll take care of that. I'm an expert, you know. I've been through situations like this before."

Dr. Grayer took the vial and the syringe, and was able to find an opening in Corey's "mummy case," and inject Corey with the penicillin. Meanwhile, Reno closed his eyes, almost afraid to watch.

"Reno," asked Lamar, "why were you so afraid to look?"

"Oh, seeing Dr. Grayer inject our patient right there on his tush gave me a sudden flashback."

"Flashback?" asked Lamar. "About what?"

"It reminds me of when I was three or four," said Reno.

"What happened then?" asked Lamar.

"It was about how afraid I was to go to the doctor's office."

"That's not unusual," said Dr. Grayer. "Can you think of a little child who wasn't?"

"Guess not," said Reno. "But it was a spirit—a *ghost*—who used to scare me."

"You believe in ghosts?" asked Lamar.

"I did then. When I got terribly sick one time, and found myself in the doctor's office sitting on the examining table, that's when the ghoul came out."

"What did it look like?" asked Dr. Grayer.

"I couldn't see it. But I sure could feel it. Right on my other end. Ow! Did this ghost hurt me, or what?! I thought I'd never be able to sit down again!"

"One more thing," asked Lamar. "Did your ghost have a name?"

"Oh, yes," said Reno. "It was known as 'gamma goblin'."

"Gamma goblin," said Dr. Grayer, "like 'gamma globulin'. Now you've given out a few of them yourself. Does that scare you?"

"I don't think so," said Lamar. "Reno just *loves* to give GG to women. He likes getting mooned."

Reno started giggling at this remark.

"When did you two decide to enter the medical business?" asked Dr. Grayer.

"Actually," replied Lamar, "that wasn't our original intention. Reno had originally planned to be a musician, and I planned to become an actor. It was at semester break, in our freshman year of college, that we decided to go to medical school."

"And it's a good thing," said a nurse who had just walked in.

"What brought you here?" asked Reno.

"Your patient will be needing another X-ray," said the nurse.

"Not so fast," insisted Dr. Grayer. "We're going to wait until he overcomes his pneumonia, and this oxygen tent comes off."

"But how will we know when to remove the head bandages?" the nurse asked.

"Just give us a little time," said Lamar, taking a glance at Corey. "He seems to be breathing a little right now. A little more time, and his pneumonia will have remitted."

"By the way," said Dr. Grayer as he was watching Corey, "he is trying to cough up. I think it could be a matter of minutes now."

"Any signs of consciousness?" asked Lamar.

"No, still not."

As Corey was overcoming his bout with pneumonia, a nurse from UPSV Medical Center, Lisa Kettering, was at home putting her makeup on, preparing for work.

"Lisa," said her husband Todd, "it's getting a little late."

"Yes, Todd," she responded, "I know. I have been asked to work on a very special patient today. So I want to look my best."

Just then, Reno had asked Dr. Grayer when Nurse Kettering would be arriving.

"Just a few minutes," said Dr. Grayer.

In just a few minutes, Lisa came hobbling in to the lobby with her husband Todd.

"Did something happen?" asked the receptionist.

"Lisa tripped and fell while coming down the stairs," said Todd. "She thinks she may have broken a few bones."

"How far down did she fall? And how hard?" asked the receptionist.

"About four feet," said Lisa, wincing in pain. "I lost my footing on the edge of the step. Now I know how Gerald Ford must have felt."

"You mean," said the receptionist, "the time he tripped on the stairs of *Air Force One*?"

"Exactly."

In the parking garage Nurse Yeltaw was driving up to what was normally her parking space. But in the space, she noticed a car she'd never seen before.

"Somebody took my space!" she mumbled to herself. Then, she gazed at the license plate of the car, which read "LAMAR."

Finally, she found a place to park. She then headed for the receptionist's desk, where she would be surprised at what would happen next.

"Connie, how's Jevon doing?" the receptionist asked Nurse Yeltaw.

"He'll be back later today, to have his casts taken off."

"Do you remember much about the other man who was with him on the train?"

"Nothing at all," said Connie. "What is there for me to know?"

"Nurse Kettering," said the receptionist, "is injured and will be out for a little while. She's asked for you to fill in for her. The patient is in room 508."

Connie then went directly to room 508, where she was greeted by Kendall, Lamar, and Reno.

"Connie," asked Lamar, "what brings you back?"

"I've been temporarily reassigned. Miss Kettering has a broken leg."

"At least she's doing better than Corey," said Reno. "He has seventeen fractures."

41

Connie then walked up to where Corey was lying. She took a glance at Corey, and then turned to Lamar and Reno.

"He looks like a mummy," she told them.

"Connie," asked Reno, "is there any chance that you could make this man conscious?"

"Why ask me?" Connie asked Reno.

"Lamar and I tried," said Reno, "and so did Dr. Grayer. None of us were successful.

"Then maybe I won't be successful, either."

"I wouldn't say *that*," added Dr. Grayer. "My interns at least were able to save his life."

"But how?" asked Connie.

"He came down with pneumonia, and while he was unconscious at that. It was an urgent situation. The oxygen and the penicillin saved him."

"I looked at his charts," said Connie, "and I believe it's time for another X-ray."

"I wouldn't advise it," said Reno. "It's been only two days since he got his last X-ray. He's about to glow in the dark."

Connie chose not to take Reno's advice, and sent Corey to get another X-ray. This time, Corey's rib, which had been broken, was nearly healed.

In a few minutes, she and Corey were back in Room 508, to find Lamar and Reno waiting.

"Don't bring him so close to me,"said Reno. "He's radioactive!"

"Don't be so silly,"said Connie. "Modern X-ray technology requires very little radiation."

"How's the outlook?" asked Lamar.

"His rib fracture is about to heal, just give him about five more days."

"Will he regain consciousness by then?" asked Reno.

"Hopefully so," said Lamar. "This man is worth a few million, remember?"

"What do you mean by a few million?" asked Connie.

"He's the heir to Exbrook Cinemas Corporation," said Reno. "He was on last night's TV news, reported missing."

"So he'll be a rich man soon," said Connie to herself. "I've found my new love!"

"Oh, really?" asked Lamar.

Connie went to Corey, reached into a pocket in her gown, and took out a thermometer. She put the thermometer into Corey's mouth, but there was no display on the readout. (It was an electronic thermometer with an LCD display.)

"Kendall," she said to Dr. Grayer, "the batteries in this thermometer are dead. Do you have any spare batteries with you?"

"No," said Dr. Grayer, "but I have an old-fashioned mercury thermometer."

Connie took the thermometer from Kendall's hand, and set it into Corey's mouth, under his tongue. While she was waiting, she put her hand down on his forehead, and was stroking his face gently. Then his eyes slowly started to open. Connie gasped and stepped back.

"What happened?" asked Reno.

"His eyes opened!" said Connie, in excitement. "Could he be regaining consciousness?"

"Possibly," said Lamar. "Let me take another look."

Connie and Lamar took another look at Corey, and Connie gazed into his eyes.

"His eyes are open," said Lamar, "and I think he's starting to move them."

"Really?" asked Reno. "I just have to see this!"

Reno then walked up next to Connie and Lamar, and looked directly into Corey's eyes.

"Yes, he is most definitely alive," said Reno.

Meanwhile, Dr. Grayer was walking down the hallway, right up to Corey's room. He stood in the doorway, and his eyes were opened wide.

"Did I miss anything?" he asked.

"Not much," said Lamar. "All that happened was that Corey began to move his eyes."

"He did?"

"Yes. His eyes were open, but he said nothing, made no other movements, and appeared to be emotionless."

Dr. Grayer then walked up to Corey, standing opposite Connie and the interns.

"Corey," whispered Dr. Grayer, "do you see me? Do you know who I am?"

Corey didn't say anything.

"When did it happen?" asked Dr. Grayer.

"It happened while you were in the lavatory," replied Lamar.

"I was feeling him with my hands as I took his temperature," Connie told Dr. Grayer.

43

"This is amazing!" the doctor said. "It took a nurse, from the pedIatrics department, to do what my interns and I couldn't do—revive Corey."

"So I saved a life, possibly," commented Connie. "What comes next?"

"You could start by attending to Corey until he's released," said Dr. Grayer.

"Hopefully," Connie said, "he'll be released before Nurse Kettering gets back."

"That'll be in about three weeks," said Dr. Grayer. "It shouldn't be too long before Corey is released, however. We plan to let him out as soon as he is completely recovered from his injuries."

"How long do you figure that to be?"

"I'm not so sure. A broken rib of his will heal shortly. After that, there will be sixteen more bones. Could take anywhere from two to five weeks."

For a few seconds, it was all silent. Then Reno stepped up to Connie and put his arms around her. Lamar then put his arms around the two of them. Later, Dr. Grayer joined in. It looked almost like a football huddle. But Corey just lay there, unaware of what was going on.

8

Do You Remember Me?

Thirty-six hours had passed since the Corey opened his eyes for the first time since he had fallen asleep on the train. Corey was able to see, but could not quite comprehend what he was seeing. He still could not speak, nor was he able to move any muscles. It was obvious that Corey could not eat solid food, therefore, because he was unable to move. All this time an IV had been keeping Corey from starvation.

Dr. Grayer had just given Corey another X-ray. This time, the fracture on his skull was almost fully healed. A few more hours, thought Dr. Grayer, was the time that the bandages could be removed.

When the time came to remove the bandages, Connie was asked to do it. Slowly she began to pull each of the bandages loose, lest there should be skin stuck tightly to the bandages.

As Corey was having his head bandages taken off, he let out a small sigh. Then, he made a series of moans and grunts, apparently trying to say something.

"Corey?" said Connie softly. "Can you see me? Can you hear me?"

"W-W-Who are you? Wh-Where am I?" gasped Corey, with some difficulty.

"You are in a hospital," said Connie. "You're at the University of Pennsylvania at Sellecca Valley Medical Center."

"Pennsylvania? Sellecca Valley?" asked Corey, breathing heavily. "Something sounds familiar about the name."

"Ever been to this town before?"

"I really don't remember. But I have heard of the town. How did I get here?"

"You were injured in the train derailment. Only yesterday, you were nearly dead."

"Who are you?"

"My name is Connie Yeltaw. I am a nurse here."

"Yeltaw?" asked Corey. "What kind of name is that?"

"It was my ex-husband's last name. But that's all I know."

"What was I doing on a train?"

"Apparently, you were traveling to Denver. I just know."

"How did you know?" asked Corey, feeling both puzzled and annoyed.

"My cousin told me. He traveled with you on the train. His name is Jevon Dandridge. Remember him?"

"No. Wait. Yes. He rode right next to me. It's starting to come back to me now."

"And you leaned upon him and fell asleep."

"You know something? That's the very last thing I remember. I just remembered that I was going to Denver to sell the movie theater company I had inherited."

"I heard all about that too. For the past few days, Jevon has been wondering how you've been doing."

"I'd like to know how *he's* doing."

"He's almost healed," said Connie. "This afternoon, he will be here to have his casts taken off. He broke his right arm and his collarbone. It's so fortunate that you're back to consciousness now. He's going back home to Illinois tomorrow. But he'll stop by your room after his casts come off.

At that moment, Dr. Grayer came into the room. He put an ear close to the door, wondering whom Connie was speaking with.

"Connie," asked Dr. Grayer, "is our patient back to life yet?"

"Oh, yes," she replied. "I'm getting to know him."

"Who are you?" asked Corey, when Dr. Grayer walked up to him.

"My name is Dr. Kendall Grayer. I am a staff physician here. You are Corey Exbrook, is that right?"

"Yes, I am," said Corey. "As soon as I get healed, I've got to get to Denver. I have a company to sell."

"Let me guess," said Dr. Grayer, "you own a movie theater company. You inherited it from your late father."

"Where did you find that out?"

"Two friends of mine heard about it on TV. You were reported missing, and even presumed dead."

"Who are your two friends?"

"These two friends of mine are interns. They'll be attending to you while you're here."

"How good are they? I wouldn't want to file a malpractice suit."

"They're two of the best that I've ever worked with," said Dr. Grayer. "This fall, they'll be graduating, and go into practice for themselves."

As Dr. Grayer was speaking, Lamar came in.

"Oh," said Dr. Grayer, "this is my senior intern, Dr. Lamar McCormick."

"How do you do, Lamar—is it all right for me to call you by first name?" asked Corey.

"Perfectly," said Lamar. "I like to get close with my patients."

"And who's that young kid, dressed like a doctor, that just came into the room?" asked Corey. "Is he Doogie Howser, M.D.?"

"No," said Lamar, "that's no young kid, that's my partner, Dr. Reno Simmons. He's a few years younger than I am."

"Corey," said Reno, "how do you feel?"

"Oh, I feel some numbness, and I ache all over at the same time. I can't move any muscles because I feel so stiff."

"Corey," said Connie, "you're gazing into my eyes. Do you think I'm beautiful?"

"Beautiful? Indeed. How many hours did you spend doing your hair and your make-up?"

"One and a half," said Connie. "I work very hard on how I look, in fact, sometimes I have to get up rather early some mornings. But you didn't answer my question: Am I the most beautiful woman you've ever seen?"

"Yes," said Corey, Lamar, and Reno.

Connie nearly collapsed, because she was so overcome with ecstasy.

"So we have three men who think I'm beautiful. I do that mostly because I work in pediatrics, usually. The children just love me. Many of them just can't take their eyes off of me. Sometimes, I admit, I tend to get a little carried away, such as by getting too affectionate with the children, especially with the kisses. I always get them too wet. It seems that the babies stop crying as soon as I pick them up and hold them."

"So," asked Reno, "why aren't you in pediatrics today?"

"I was asked to substitute for Nurse Kettering."

"What happened?" asked Lamar.

"Yesterday morning," said Connie, "she fell and broke her leg. She'll be out a little while."

"At least it isn't as serious as Corey's condition," said Dr. Grayer.

Inside the lobby, a news crew from Boston television station WCBV-TV had arrived. One of the people on the camera crew asked where Corey was staying. The crew was directed to room 508. One member of the crew then knocked on the door to Corey's room.

"Who is it?" asked Dr. Grayer.

"We come from WCBV-TV in Boston. We're with TV-6 News. May we throw in an interview with Mr. Exbrook?"

47

"He's the one lying in the bed. I'm sure he'd be willing to give an interview or two."

A reporter walked up to Corey's bedside. A cameraman was following not far behind. Connie, Lamar, and Reno stood back.

"Mr. Exbrook," said the reporter, "are you doing all right right now?"

"Just about," said Corey. "I am definitely alive, but I can't move a muscle. I still wonder how long I will be here, and when I'll be able to get to Denver."

"Does this have to do with the proposed sale of Exbrook Cinemas?" asked the reporter.

"Yes, that's the reason, the only reason," said Corey.

"What made you want to sell it?"

"I don't have business experience."

At this time, Lester was watching live reports from his home in Boston, and he nearly fainted. Jamie was sitting there with him to keep him from falling down.

"Well," Lester said, "that solves another mystery. This weekend, I'm taking a trip to Sellecca Valley. Could you and Jeremy do all right without me?"

"We suppose so," said Jamie.

The very next morning, Jevon came to Corey's room as he'd promised. Jevon had his casts off, and showed almost no signs of injury. Corey tried to extend his arms, but found that he could not.

"Jevon," said Corey, "it feels so good to see you again."

"Oh, yes, Corey. Seeing you again has put a light in my eyes, on that hasn't shone there before."

"What do you think of this town of Sellecca Valley?"

"Brings back a few memories," said Jevon. "It reminds me so much of the city of Tempe, Arizona, where I lived as a teenager."

"How's it going with you and Connie? How's she treating you?"

"Oh, she's one of the nicest, kindest women I've ever known. I've known her since I was four."

"Four?" wondered Corey. "Now I remember. She's your cousin. And she's quite a beauty at that."

"All along, that's what I'd been thinking," said Jevon. "But I had no need to tell her. She knew all along."

"Where did you sleep?" asked Corey.

"She set up a guest room for me. It's big and beautiful. And the house is big and beautiful as well."

"And does she cook for you too?"

"Sometimes," said Jevon. "And sometimes she took me out for dinner as well."

"How much longer will you be here?"

"Unfortunately, I'll only be in Sellecca Valley a few hours more. I'm taking tonight's first flight out to Chicago. I've got a family waiting for me there."

"Yeah," said Corey. "I remember you were from a small suburb— East Hazel Crest, to be exact. Aren't you the owner of a business—a belly jeans shop, is it?"

"Close," said Jevon. "You just threw in a spoonerism on me. It's *jelly beans*, not *belly jeans*. I think you did that intentionally," joked Jevon.

"Maybe," said Corey, "just maybe."

"How many bones did you break?" asked Jevon.

"Seventeen. And you?"

"Only two. My right arm and right collarbone."

"I think I know how they got broken. I forgot to bring a pillow, so you let me lean on you."

"Yes, yes. But I have no regrets. And I just might do it again, should I ever get the opportunity."

"You mean," said Corey, "that you care that much for me?"

"That much and more. And Connie cares for me just as much as I do you, if not a little more."

"Really?" asked Corey. "What does she do?"

"Look closely at my face," said Jevon. "Do you see any lipstick marks?"

"I'm looking closely, and I see a lip mark on you. I think she loves you."

"Oh, yes. Right before going to bed at night, as well as on certain special moments, she plants one on me."

"Kissin' cousins, eh?" asked Corey.

"Guess so."

Just then Connie came into the room.

"I see that you've become very close," she said. "What is all this about 'kissing cousins'?"

"It's about you and me," Jevon told her. "Corey wonders what goes on between us."

"How could you feel about her the way you do?" Corey asked Jevon.

"Once you really know someone," said Jevon, "it just happens."

"What just happens?" asked Connie, as she had her arms around Jevon, kissing and hugging him one more time.

"That," said Jevon. "That's what happens."

"I knew Jevon when he was just a small child," said Connie. "He was an only child. I was one of the first people he came to know well. He and I spent so much time together. We really loved each other, or so it seemed."

"I remember so well," said Jevon. "Time has passed, we've both grown and changed, but there still is, and always will be, a special bond between us."

"Bond?" asked Corey. "What kind?"

"It's a very special kind," said Connie. "It occurs when you've known somebody for a very long time."

"A long time?" Corey asked. "It wasn't very long—seems like only yesterday—that I've known you, Jevon. But you've developed a bond for me, one I never thought anyone could. I've had many friends come and go over the years, but none have I been able to hold on to for a long time. I wonder if you'll be the next."

"I sure hope not. Friends were made to last forever, you know."

"Actually," said Corey, "no, I didn't know."

"But it's something everyone should know," said Connie. "Jevon, sometimes I think that there's no one else in the world like you. You've been the best thing to ever happen to me."

Jevon almost blushed. "Right now," he said, "I'm standing by the *two* best things to ever happen to me. One of them I've known all my life; the other I've just met only recently."

For the first time since his fateful train ride, Corey began to giggle. He felt like putting his hand in front of his mouth, but he was still unable to move his arms. He just went on giggling, feeling somewhat embarrassed.

"Let's get back to an earlier subject now," said Jevon.

"Which subject?" asked Corey.

"The movie theater company."

"Oh, yes. Exbrook Cinemas Corporation. What about them?"

"How much is the company selling for?"

"That I will have to find out. We have nearly eight hundred locations."

"Yes. And I know there are several in the Chicago area."

"And just what do you plan to do when you make all this cold, hard cash?"

"Most likely," said Corey, "I'd go into retirement. Maybe even before I reach the age of twenty-seven."

"When is that?"

"On the seventeenth of February."

"Where would you like to live?" asked Jevon.

"I never really thought about that," said Corey. "Where should I live?"

"I have an idea. Find yourself a home here in Sellecca Valley. But a home big enough for three or four."

"Why three or four?" asked Corey.

"You, me, and maybe my beautiful bride-to-be. By then, even you may find the love of your life."

Corey started to yawn. "I'm beginning to feel a little tired. I gotta get some rest."

"Yes," said Jevon, "And I got to get going. My flight out will be in less than two hours."

"Flight?" shrieked Corey. "Please don't say that word. It frightens me."

"Anyway, I must go now. One of these days, I'll come back to Boston to meet with you again. Goodbye..."

As Jevon finished talking, he bent over Corey's head, and gave him a small kiss just between the eyes.

"You love me?" asked Corey.

"You can think of it that way if you want to. Friendship is actually a form of love. Let those kind words guide you for all the rest of your days. And please do get well soon."

"Jevon," said Corey, "I guess I could say that I love you too, though sometimes I'd feel a little silly saying that. Anyway, I'd like to hear from you when you get back to Illinois."

Jevon was just walking out of the room. Connie was now walking up to Corey, noticing a red blotch between his eyes.

"Connie," asked Corey, "do you have a mirror on you?"

"Let me see. I usually carry one in my handbag," she said, as she started searching through her bag. "Ah, ha! Here it is," she said as she found the mirror, and put it in front of Corey's eyes.

"Connie," said Corey, feeling surprised. "I've got some of *your* lipstick on me!"

"Mine?" asked Connie. "How could that be?"

"Yes, yours. I guess you must have kissed Jevon right after you put your lipstick on."

51

Connie started to feel embarrassed. So did Corey, having some of Connie's lipstick on him, as is she had planted it there herself.

9

Back from the Deep Freeze

That evening, Jevon had just flown back home to Chicago, and was safe and sound, in spite of a slight amount of snow on the runways at O'Hare Airport. During the evening, Connie received a phone call from the airport from Jevon.

"Hello? Is this Jevon?" she asked after she heard a familiar voice on the other end of the line.

"Yes, this is Jevon. How's Corey doing?"

"He seemed to be all right when I got off work," answered Connie.

"Has he moved a muscle?"

"Still not. I can remember when everyone was wondering if he ever would snap out of his coma."

"Will he still be in the hospital tomorrow?"

"Indefinitely. At least until he can move his muscles, and especially his hands. Dr. Grayer said that we'll need to keep him until he can start feeding himself, and can move about somewhat."

"When you get back," said Jevon, "tell him I'm back at home, and I'm thinking about him."

"I will. It'll make him breathe a sigh of relief."

"And also, you might want to give him another kiss right between the eyes, just as I did."

"I'm not so sure of that."

"You can do it. Just say I told you to."

"I may as well, I guess. I'll tell you a little secret. I think I'm in love with him. I dreamed about someone like him last night."

"That would be oh so nice," said Jevon. "Then he could be a part of my family."

"Just one more question," said Connie. "Why *do* you like him so much?"

"I just met him that evening, because I was all alone at the station. He seemed such a neat person."

"Oh, yes. I think he is."

"I've got to go now. I'm expecting a cab any minute now. Goodbye."

"Goodbye, and I love you too," Connie said, and then hung the telephone up.

An hour later, Connie got undressed, went into the bathroom to take her makeup off, and got into bed. She was tired enough to fall asleep immediately. Somehow, she managed not to dream about Corey, or any man who looked like him. She was nonetheless dreaming, but she did not quite know what it was about. Her dream seemed somewhat abstract (as most do), and she was changing locations for what seemed to be every three seconds.

In the morning, Dr. Grayer's senior intern, Lamar, woke up a few minutes before his friend Reno, who lived in Lamar's house and slept in a bedroom right next to Lamar's. When Reno woke up, he took a seat at the kitchen table, next to Lamar, who was drinking a cup of coffee and reading the *Valley Pennsylvanian* newspaper.

"Good morning, Reno," Lamar said, with a jingle in his voice.

"And good morning to you too," said Reno.

"Lamar," asked Reno after taking a sip of coffee, "could today be the day?"

"For what?" asked Lamar.

"Is it possible for Corey to begin moving his muscles? How long will it be?"

"Don't worry, Reno. He's perfectly all right. Remember a few days back, when we were worried about his chances of survival?"

"I can't help it," said Reno. "I'm just not quite the person to take things easy."

"Don't be so hard on yourself," said Lamar. "Everything has gone right so far. What could go wrong now?"

"Corey isn't paralyzed, is he?" asked Reno with deep concern.

"No, he isn't. If he were, the X-rays would have said so."

Lamar and Reno got up from the table, and went to their bedroom closets. The twosome then put their uniforms on, and came out of their bedrooms at the same time.

"Let's roll," said Reno.

"Good idea," said Lamar, agreeingly.

Just as Reno and Lamar had come out of their bedrooms simultaneously, they started their cars and began driving, within a split-second. Lamar followed Reno all the way to work, staying so close together that they drove like a caravan.

Likewise, they came up to the front desk at the medical center at the same time, and walked together to room 508.

Corey had just woke up from a restless night's sleep. He lay still, like a log, trying to move his arms, but as before, he was completely stiff. The only bone Corey could move was the bone that he used while he was talking with Connie, Jevon, Kendall, Lamar, and Reno—his jaw bone. He was able to speak and remember, but still tended to have some difficulty in doing so. Even though his head bandages were removed, he still felt a throbbing in his head on occasion.

Lamar was now standing by Corey's bedside, and held Corey's hand up to his eyes. Lamar was feeling Corey's wrist, which had been broken, and felt no fracture now.

"Lamar," gasped Corey, "is my hand healed?"

"Just about. Those bandages are due to come off any minute now."

As Lamar was letting go of Corey's hand, he felt a slight tickling sensation on his own hand. He looked down at Corey's hand, and watched as Corey's fingers began to move.

"Reno," Lamar called out, "come here and take a look!"

"What's going on?" asked Reno.

"Corey was moving his fingers! He's most certainly recovering!"

Slowly, but with some pain, Corey was indeed moving his fingers, although his thumb could barely move.

"Corey," said Reno, "it appears that you may have some stiffness in your joints. I'll have to give you some medicine."

"Medicine?" asked Corey. "What kind?"

"It's one of those deep-heating ointments; I sometimes forget what its name is—it's an unusual name, as most medicine names are."

"Come with me," said Lamar, "I'll help you find it."

Lamar and Reno went into a storeroom, where most of the medicine used by the hospital was kept. Lamar took a tube from a shelf.

"Here," he said to Reno, "this is what we need. It's called Noitacidem. It's an arthritis medicine with deep heating."

"Noitacidem," commented Reno. "I just wonder where the medicine makers come up with these weird names."

Reno was back in Corey's room a few minutes later. As he walked up to Corey, he said that he had the medicine that would relieve the stiffness in his joints.

"Let me see your hand again," he told Corey. Although Corey's arm was in a cast, he somehow found himself able to raise his arm.

"Corey!" said Reno. "You moved your arm!"

55

"What's so special about that?"

"Well," said Reno, "your recovery isn't taking as long as we thought it would!"

"Ow!" yelled Corey. "My fingers still hurt!"

"Oh, now I remember what I came here for," said Reno. "I had the medicine here in my hands, and forgot why!"

Gently, Reno began to rub some of the ointment into the palm of Corey's hand. Lamar stood at the doorway, watching.

"Reno," asked Lamar, "did I see what I think I saw?"

"What did you think you saw?" asked Corey.

"Corey," asked Lamar, "did you raise your arm?"

"Yes, I did. Finally, I'm regaining mobility."

"Oh, Corey," said Lamar, "Dr. Grayer would love to see this!"

"Where is he right now?" asked Corey.

"He won't be in this morning," said Lamar. "He had to perform an emergency operation."

"Corey," asked Reno, "does your arm hurt?"

"Except for the bone break, it feels fine. I'll probably be able to move my other arm, as soon as this IV is gone."

"Dr. McCormick?" asked Reno.

"Yes, Dr. Simmons," Lamar responded, as if trying to sound facetiously professional.

"Now that he can move his arm, isn't it about time that our patient started eating solid food?" asked Reno.

"Can he swallow yet?" asked Lamar.

"I suppose so. If he can talk, and breathe, he should be able to eat."

"I guess I'm ready," said Corey. "At least I can swallow—*ick!*—saliva!"

"Good morning, Connie," said Reno as Connie walked into the room.

"How's it going with Corey?" she asked Lamar and Reno.

"How's Jevon doing?" asked Lamar.

"I talked to him last night," said Connie. "He got back home, safely."

"Did he have anything to say to me?" asked Corey.

"Oh, yes. He told me that he thought about you while he was flying high. Someday he'll be back here again."

"I'll just sit and wait for the day," sighed Corey.

"Oh, by the way, Connie," said Reno, "did you notice anything new about Corey?"

"Not really. *Is* something new?"

"Yes," said Lamar. "Corey moved some muscles for the first time today!"

"Is he recovering?" asked Connie, in excitement. "How much longer will he be in?"

"I think I may know," said Lamar. "We'll ask our boss if it is time to start him on solid food."

"Where is Kendall?" asked Connie. "Usually he's right here right now."

"Emergency operation," said Reno. "But he didn't say exactly what it was."

Later, Connie was in the lounge, on break along with Lamar and Reno.

"Go get me a cup of coffee while you're up," Lamar said to her as she walked toward the coffeepot. "Make it a Swiss Chocolate Mint."

"And Lamar," said Reno, "would you get me a Viennese Cinnamon Cafe?"

Moving as if on a tightrope, trying to avoid spilling anything on himself, Connie brought Lamar and Reno their coffees.

"Connie," said Reno, who smelled his cup briefly, "you gave me the wrong one. This is Swiss Chocolate Mint. You gave Lamar my Viennese Cinnamon Cafe."

Lamar had Reno's mug of Viennese Cinnamon Cafe in her hand, and was about to take a sip, when she heard Reno point out Connie's mistake. Lamar and Reno then switched cups with each other.

Dr. Grayer came into the lounge, and sat down at the same table.

"Kendall," said Connie, "have you heard about Corey today?"

"No, what happened?"

"He moved some muscles for the first time," said Lamar.

"Muscles?" asked Dr. Grayer. "Which ones?"

"I was checking Corey's pulse today," said Reno, "and he just began moving his fingers around. Next, his whole arm moved."

"Is he recovered fully yet?" asked Kendall.

"Not completely," said Lamar. "He'll need to go on a solid diet, before he can be released."

"Know what I think?" asked Dr. Grayer.

"What?" asked Lamar and Reno.

"I think it's time already! Today we'll start him on solid diet. But only one question remains: Can he swallow yet?"

"Oh, yes," answered Lamar. "All he's had to swallow so far is his own saliva. Bleech!"

"Indeed," said Connie, "I can't stand the taste of that stuff."

"And Dr. Grayer," asked Reno, "what was your emergency operation this morning?"

"Gunshot wound. With a team of specialists, I fought hard to save a life today. We got the bullet out. It was lodged in the rib cage. No vital organs were in the way.

"Gunshots?" asked Lamar. "In a small town like this?"

"Domestic dispute, I think it was," answered Kendall. "Those can happen just about anywhere."

It was not long before eleven-thirty, and Connie came back into Corey's room, with an order pad and a pen.

"Corey," she asked him, "today Dr. Grayer asked that you be started on the solid diet. May I take your order please?"

"Who are you?" asked Corey, "a nurse or a waitress?"

"Sometimes I'm a little of both," said Connie. "While I was a senior in high school, I worked in a local restaurant."

She gave the pen and pad to Corey, and he marked his selections on the menu, somewhat awkwardly since his hand was a bit weak. He gave back the pen and pad, and Connie walked out of the room.

Ten minutes later, she came back with a lunch tray, and Dr. Grayer came in with her.

"Corey," said Connie, "here's your lunch. Now you can take your next step to total recovery."

"And Corey," said Dr. Grayer, "later today, we'll take out the IV that's been confining your left arm."

Corey took a fork in his hand, and was able to start eating.

"Any problems?" asked Kendall.

"No," said Corey, with his mouth full.

"So I guess you've almost recovered," said Dr. Grayer. "But what about your legs? Can you move them?"

"Barely."

"Dr. Simmons, whom you know as Reno," said Connie, "told me that your wrist felt healed. Does it?"

"I guess so. It really doesn't hurt. But I still wonder now how much longer I'll be here."

"Corey," said Dr. Grayer, "you've recovered so quickly that you should be let out tomorrow morning."

Late in the afternoon, Corey heard a knock on the door to his room.

"Who is it?" he asked.

"It's me, Lester."

"Come on in, big brother!"

Lester then walked up to his younger brother's bedside, and put his arms around Corey. Corey, in return, put his right hand behind Lester's head and pulled him closer.

"It looks as though you're recovering," said Lester.

"Just about. I'm going to be released tomorrow morning."

"Do your casts come off between now and then?"

"I don't know. I heard that I might be released with the casts still on."

"But how will you get around? And how will you get back home?"

"Know something? I never had the time to think about that."

"Is one of your doctors expected in here any moment now?" asked Lester.

"I think so."

"When he comes in," said Lester, "you should ask him. He could tell you."

As Lester was speaking, Lamar came into the room.

"I could tell you what?" asked Lamar. "And who's this man you're with?"

"This is my older brother Lester," Corey told Lamar.

"And I'm Dr. Lamar McCormick. I'm an intern."

Reno came into the room while Lamar was speaking.

"And that's my partner, Dr. Reno Simmons. Reno, that's Corey's older brother, Lester."

"How do you do, gentlemen?" asked Reno.

"Today almost never came," Lamar told Lester.

"How so?"

"Mere days ago," said Reno, "Corey nearly died. He came down with pneumonia, while he was unconscious. Lamar and I were asked to take care of him."

"Have you taken care of him?" asked Lester.

"Certainly they have," said Corey. "And so has Connie, a beautiful young substitute nurse working this shift."

"Here she comes right now," Lamar told Lester and Reno.

Connie was walking into the room, with a pair of crutches in her hands. (She was only carrying them; she did not use them to walk with.)

"Who's this big man?" she asked.

59

"This is my older brother, Lester," responded Corey. "He came all the way from Boston, just to be with me."

"Corey," Connie said, "it's now time for me to take out this 'feeding tube', as you might call it."

Carefully, she withdrew the IV from Corey's left arm.

"*Y-y-yow!*" said Corey, almost loudly. "Those sure do hurt when you take them out, but even more so when you insert them."

"Now," said Lamar, "it's time for you to do some walking."

"Walking? Already?"

"Yes," said Connie, "We'll have you practicing on a pair of crutches, until your leg fractures heal."

"That reminds me of something," said Lester. "Is Corey going to be released soon?"

"Yes. Tomorrow morning," said Reno.

"But how will Corey get back home?" asked Lester. "The only reason he rode the train was because he has a fear of flying. And he has little or no money on him."

"Besides," said Lamar, "his broken bones will still need time to heal."

"I just thought of something," said Connie, suddenly. "Corey, do you remember where Jevon stayed while his broken bones were healing?"

"Didn't he stay with you?" asked Corey.

"Yes. And while your fractures heal, you can stay with me the same way."

"You can't be serious," said Corey.

"I am. I took good care of Jevon, and I could do the same for you."

Corey was standing up, with a pair of crutches. With some ease, and chafed underarms, he could hobble around the room.

"Lester," said Connie, "if you need to reach Corey, you can call my house—the number is area code 710, 555-5639."

"And Corey, Lamar and I will be checking up on you," said Reno.

"Corey," said Lester, "eventually I'll see you back in Boston. Until then, take good care of yourself; and you, Connie, take good care of my little brother."

"All right. I will," said Connie.

"One more thing," said Lester, "When does Exbrook Cinemas get sold?"

"Whenever I can get to Denver."

"I'll be going back home now," said Lester.

"Goodbye. I'll be seeing you someday soon," said Corey. "And Lester, tell Jamie and Jeremy that I'm doing all right."

"I will," said Lester. "I feel so relieved just seeing you here today."

Lester put his arms around Corey, who did likewise, and thus ended up dropping his crutches and nearly falling to the floor. Lester then helped Corey pick his crutches up, then left the room.

"By the way, Corey," said Reno, "Either Lamar or I, maybe the both of us, will be coming by Connie's home, where you'll be staying, to check up on you."

"You make house calls?" asked Corey. "Not many doctors do that these days."

"But we do," said Lamar. "Dr. Grayer asks us to make at least one house call a year, as part of the grading procedures."

"When will you be there?"

"Tuesday afternoon, one o'clock," replied Reno.

The next morning, Connie had brought Corey out of the hospital in a wheelchair, carefully laid him down across the back seat of her car, and drove off for home.

10

Tour of the Town

It was a sunny afternoon in Pennsylvania, despite that the beginning of winter was only a few days away. Connie was driving Corey to her home in the southern part of the town of Sellecca Valley.

"How far is it to your house?" asked Corey, grumbling from the pain and stiffness he felt all over his body.

"Just six more miles," said Connie. "Sellecca Valley is a large town in terms of land area. Right now we're in the 2000 block. My address is 13059 South Hermosa Drive."

"Do you live alone?" asked Corey.

"Yes. My husband is dead. I inherited the house from him."

"You don't even have any children?" asked Corey in curiosity.

"None. Never had time to have children."

"Does traffic ever get heavy here in Sellecca Valley?"

"Sometimes, especially during football games. We've got the best college in all of central Pennsylvania."

"This is a crazy idea," groaned Corey. "Why would you have me lying down on the back seat, with my head leaning against the door?"

"Something wrong with that?"

"Not really," answered Corey. "I feel like I am in an ambulance, or even a hearse."

"Ambulances? Hearses? Why do you bring up such things?"

"I just don't know. I saw my father being loaded into a hearse, and I was recently loaded into an ambulance."

"I take it that your father is dead," commented Connie.

"Yes. That's why I ended up here. And it was an ambulance, nonetheless, that brought me here."

"We're not far from the accident site," said Connie. "The train went down just a few miles down this road from the university, slightly to the north. This is Sellecca Boulevard, which is actually Pennsylvania State Route 12."

"The way I'm seated in here," said Corey, "I can see only what's on the passenger side. Am I missing something on the driver's side, behind my head, which I can barely move?"

"Not much," said Connie. "Just a vacant lot. It used to be a drive-in theater."

"Hopefully not an *Exbrook* theater," commented Corey.

"No, it wasn't an Exbrook. Sellecca Valley has an Exbrook Cinema, inside Sellecca Valley Mall."

"Besides," joked Corey, "Exbrook doesn't own any drive-ins. Never did, and probably never will."

"Too bad," said Connie. "I used to love drive-ins. My late husband, Aaron, used to take me there all the time."

"I hate drive-ins," said Corey. "Those dinky little squawk-boxes have such poor sound."

"I agree, somewhat. Indoor theaters have far better sound."

"One more thing," said Corey. "Did Jevon love staying with you while his bones were healing?"

"Oh, yes. He loved it at my house. And I think you will too."

"I will?" asked Corey.

"Yes. You'll be sleeping in the same bedroom that he slept in. It's a special guest room I set aside, for those really special guests."

"Like me?" asked Corey.

"Yes. Just like you."

"Do you always have patients like me staying over?"

"This is only the second time," said Connie. "Jevon, who, as you may know, is my cousin, was the first. I usually don't get this opportunity because most of the time I'm in pediatrics."

"Why weren't you in pediatrics yesterday?"

"I'm only substituting. The nurse who should be in my shift is out with an injury."

"How much longer will she be out?"

"Indefinitely, I was told."

"Maybe it was mere fate, having a nurse like you."

Connie made a right turn onto a small residential street.

"We're just a block from home," she said.

After she finished speaking, she made a turn into the driveway of her home, and turned off the ignition.

"Now you're there!" she told Corey.

"Where?" he asked. "I don't have a good view."

63

"This is my home, at 13059 South Hermosa. Let me help you get out."

Connie opened the back door, and carefully pulled Corey out by his legs.

"Hopefully," said Corey, "it won't be long that I'll have to ride stretched out flat."

"Here are your crutches. You can walk all right with them, can you?"

"Yes," said Corey as he began walking toward the front door. "I can walk around perfectly on these things."

Connie opened the front door, and Corey followed.

"May I sit down?" asked Corey.

"Go right ahead," said Connie. "Make yourself feel comfortable."

"Easier said than done," said Corey. "I find it hard to do anything, now that I'm in all these casts."

Corey sat down on the living room couch and began to sigh.

"I don't know how much longer I can take this," he said to Connie. "Life has been so hard for me, now that I'm in this condition I'm in."

"Nobody said it would be easy," said Connie.

"Sometimes I think it would have been better if Jevon and I had died in the wreck. We wouldn't feel any pain, and we'd be together on our own cloud, eternally."

"Oh please don't say that!" pleaded Connie.

"What's wrong with that?" asked Corey.

"If Jevon were dead, I'd probably be dead too, and not by chance."

"How so?" asked Corey.

"He's just about my only reason for living," said Connie. "He's the relative I feel closest to now."

"Maybe someday, you can get married again, and have someone completely new to live for," said Corey.

"Good idea," said Connie. "But just give me a little time. It's hard to get over such a good marriage that ended so soon."

"When Jevon was here with you," asked Corey, "what kind of things did you two do?"

"Nothing too unusual. Every evening I'd make dinner, and we'd sit by the fireplace and chat."

"Just like Franklin D. Roosevelt?" asked Corey.

"Almost."

"Will you be making dinner tonight?"

"Yes," said Connie. "I'm going to make some Chicken Yeltaw. It's an old family recipe."

"I can smell it already," said Corey.

By seven o'clock that evening, Connie and Corey had finished dinner, and were sitting by the fireplace, watching sparks fly in the air.

"See those sparks?" asked Connie.

"Is something symbolic about sparks?" asked Corey.

"Sparks turn into flames. It's the same way with love. Two people meet, and a spark develops. Eventually, the sparks *do* become flames, and as the two are more in love, the fire grows much brighter."

"I wish it was the same way with me," said Corey.

"What do you mean?"

"Everytime I fall in love, it does become a flame, as you said, but the flame soon becomes and ember."

"Embers?" asked Connie. "Love is forever. It shouldn't become an ember."

"Are you trying to say that you love me?" asked Corey.

"I—I—don't know what to say. I'm not so certain."

"Not so certain? About *what*?"

"I'm not always certain about just what love really means to me," said Connie. "It's different things for different people."

Corey and Connie sat by the fire for about two hours, and eventually Corey began to yawn.

"Getting tired?" asked Connie.

"Yes. I feel so tired I should be brought over to my room, lest I should fall down and break more bones."

"Here," said Connie, "I'll take you there."

Connie held Corey by the shoulder, as Corey hobbled on his crutches until he got to his bed.

"You said that Jevon slept here?" asked Corey.

"Right here. I even changed the sheets for you."

Corey was able to get onto the bed and lie down without any difficulty. He set his crutches next to the headboard, and began fluffing his pillow.

"Connie," asked Corey, "would you get the light for me?"

Connie reached for a cigarette lighter that was lying on a dresser. She gave it a small flick, and a beautiful flame came out.

"Very funny!" said Corey. "Surely you don't smoke, do you?"

"My name's not Shirley, and I never have smoked!"

65

Connie pulled the sheets over Corey, and walked across the room to turn off the light. Corey was soon fast asleep.

"Oh, no!" gasped Connie as she walked out of the room. "It *is* getting late! I feel tired too."

Connie went into her bedroom, and took her clothes off. When she put her nightgown on, a seam had ripped.

"I guess that nightgown has had it," she said as she took her nightgown off, and threw it into a corner. "What else can I wear?"

Finally, after thinking it over for a while, Connie went to bed, wearing only her underwear. She slept the whole night, waking up only once to go to the bathroom. Corey was able to sleep all night long too, although he wondered how he could.

Corey woke up early, smelling something good. "Could breakfast be ready?" he thought to himself. Just then, he heard a knock on the door to his bedroom.

"Corey," said Connie while she stood at the door, "I just finished making breakfast. I made us some ham-and-Swiss omelets."

"Sounds delicious. I'll be out in a few minutes."

"Need help getting to the table?" asked Connie.

"No, I can manage."

Corey sat up on his bed, took his crutches, and began to go to the kitchen table. Once at the table, he set the crutches down, pulled a chair aside, and sat down.

"You looked like you were losing your balance," commented Connie.

"I almost did. I have a little trouble sitting down sometimes."

Corey sat down and began eating breakfast. After he took his first bite, his eyes widened.

"Is it good?" asked Connie.

"Very good," said Corey. "If only my roommate back in Boston could cook like you do."

"Aw, Corey," that makes me feel so good," said Connie. "Jevon felt the same way about me."

"I guess that makes us two of a kind, almost."

"Who are you talking about?" asked Connie. "You and me, or you and Jevon?"

"You know something," said Corey, "I never thought about it that way."

"Would you like to go touring the town today?" asked Connie.

"Why today?" asked Corey.

"Since I have today off," said Connie, "I might as well show you this beautiful town I live in."

"Where shall we go first?" asked Corey.

"Let's go to Sellecca Valley's biggest city park," Connie said. "Then we'll go through the university campus."

"It all sounds fascinating. But will I have to lie down flat like I did yesterday?"

"I don't know," said Connie. "Can you sit up by yourself?"

"Can I? I can. I am right now."

Corey found that indeed he was able to sit upright in the front passenger seat, but Connie had to help him with the seat belt and the door, since Corey could hardly move his arms. Corey felt more comfortable riding in a normal position.

Connie and Corey arrived at the first stop of their tour of Sellecca Valley: the town's largest public park. Connie was lying on the grass near a pond, while Corey was sitting next to her.

"Is it all beautiful?" asked Connie.

"I think it is beautiful," answered Corey. "I could just lie here forever, looking at ducks swimming on the pond, and the frogs jumping from lily to lily."

"Along the way here," asked Connie, "did you notice a lot about this town?"

"I'd say so," said Corey. "Sellecca Valley is like no place I've ever been to. I wonder if any of this is real."

"Real?" asked Connie. "It surely is! I'll even poke you with a pin, just to show you so."

"No, thanks, that won't be necessary," said Corey.

"Would you like to go sightseeing around the university campus now?" asked Connie.

"Yes. What's it like?"

"Just like the town," said Connie, "it's like no place you have ever been to."

"What do you mean by 'no place I've ever been to'?" asked Corey. "You speak as if I've never even been there, which I have."

Connie was then driving Corey down the streets surrounding the university.

"See that building there?" asked Connie, pointing to a large white building with many windows.

"Is that some big office building?" asked Corey. "Boston has many of those."

"No, that's the medical center!" said Connie. "That was the building where you were being treated, the very building where I work."

"I've never seen it from that view," said Corey.

"And that round building over there," said Connie, "is the University Arts Center."

"Is the University of Pennsylvania at Sellecca Valley known for fine art?" asked Corey.

"Oh, yes. And good athletics too."

"Now I remember," said Corey. "The game that my father, my brother, and I were watching on TV on Thanksgiving afternoon was the UPSV Firebirds."

"I watched that game live," said Connie. "I was there at the stadium."

"And," said Corey as he and Connie went by the stadium, "is that it?"

"That's the place!"

The next place Connie drove through was downtown Sellecca Valley. The downtown area was known locally for its artistic colonies, its shopping centers, restaurants, and street fairs.

"I never saw a downtown area like this," said Corey.

"It reminds me of a place in Arizona called Tempe," commented Connie. "Downtown Tempe has lots of these things, all along a street called Mill Avenue."

"How would I know?" asked Corey. "I've never really been outside the Boston area in my lifetime, until now."

"Do you like it out here?" asked Connie.

"Yes, even though I really shouldn't be here."

"Where should you be?" asked Connie.

"I should have been in Denver by now, selling my stock in Exbrook Cinemas Corporation. In fact, I should have been back home from Denver by now."

"But will the company ever get sold?" asked Connie.

"I don't know yet. My brother Lester said he would take care of everything while I was here."

"Has he done that?"

"I don't know. I think maybe he's trying to take over the company himself, and keep the profits. Profits that *should* be mine."

"Corey," said Connie, "don't talk so mean about your older brother!"

68

"I can't help it," said Corey. "It seems as though he has done something mean to me!"

Minutes later, Corey's guided tour of Sellecca Valley came to an end where it had begun: at Connie's house. Corey went right into the living room and sat down on the couch.

"Good trip," he told Connie. "This is a beautiful little town. Maybe I might retire here."

The telephone rang. Connie answered it.

"Hello?" she said.

"Connie? It is I, Jevon."

"How are you today?"

"I'm back in business, and doing very well," said Jevon. "Is Corey still staying with you?"

"Yes, he is. Want me to get him for you?"

"Yes. Do that."

Corey came right into the kitchen, and found the telephone receiver sitting on the table. Corey took it into his hand, but found it very difficult to get it up to his ear, because his arms were both in casts. So he set it back on the table, took a chair by the table, and leaned his head toward the phone.

"Corey," said Jevon, "how's it going?"

"All right now," said Corey angrily, "why'd you do it to me?"

"What?" asked Jevon. "What are you talking about?"

"You're trying to take over Exbrook Cinemas and keep the profits for yourself. Very dirty trick!"

"What, me? I'm doing no such thing!"

"C'mon now, Lester. I've known you all my life! You've always been playing tricks on me! You can't fool me now!"

"Hold everything," said Jevon. "I'm not Lester, I'm your old friend Jevon."

"Oh, it's you, Jevon," said Corey, sighing. "All day long I've been thinking about my big brother Lester. He said he was arranging the sale of the company, but I want to know for sure if he really is."

"And Corey, do you still have any broken bones?"

"Yes. Still. I have to lean my head on the table to talk on the telephone."

"At least I was fortunate. I had only one broken arm."

"You're more fortunate than me in so many ways."

"How has Connie been treating you?" asked Jevon.

"So well. She makes very good meals, and she helps me into bed at night."

"Does she ever kiss you good night?"

"No," said Corey. "Did she ever do it to you?"

"Every night."

"But I seriously doubt that she would do it to me."

"You never know," said Jevon. "I gotta go now. Goodbye."

"Goodbye, and may joy, love, and peace be with you now and forever."

11

House Calls

A few days later, Corey woke up, sensing that something unusual was about to happen that morning. As he stumbled out of bed, and made his way to the door, he heard some music coming from Connie's bedroom. Could it be the clock-radio, maybe? He went into Connie's room, but there was no clock-radio, nor even a radio, anywhere to be seen. He took a closer listen; the music sounded more familiar, but who was singing? In the background, he heard what sounded like raindrops. He looked out the window, and saw some snow; otherwise, it was a clear, sunny morning.

Suddenly the music stopped, and the raindrop sound he heard had stopped likewise. Connie stepped out of the bathroom and into her bedroom, dripping wet, and draped in just a towel, with another towel wrapped around her hair.

"Connie," asked Corey, "where was that music I heard coming from?"

"How dare you ask!" she said. "That was me!"

"You know something," Corey told her, "you remind me very much of a popular female singer of the late 1980's."

"Oh, yes," said Connie. "I think I do too."

"Do you remember a song called *Some Kinda Lover*? Or the song *Looking for a New Love*?"

"Oh, yes. I remember those songs very well. When they were popular, I used to lip-sync them very often."

"Sounds right," said Corey, "since you look and sound like the woman who sang those songs."

"Let me think," said Connie, "I believe I remember way back when. It was the spring of 1988, about when I started my job as a nurse. I think the woman who did those songs was a woman named Janet Watley."

"Oh, yeah," sighed Corey, "Janet Watley. I absolutely *idolized* her when I was in high school."

"And Corey," asked Connie, "did you ever see me with those five-inch-diameter round earrings?"

"I never saw you with them. But I remember Janet used to wear them too."

"Before I became a nurse," said Connie, "I used to do work as a nightclub singer. People often compared me to Watley."

"So why didn't you become a pop star?" asked Corey. "You sure do have the looks and the voice."

"I almost thought of becoming a pop star. But then I got married to a man with the last name 'Yeltaw'. That name doesn't sound too good for a pop star."

"Yes, it does sound like a good name," said Corey, "but not for a superstar."

"By the way," asked Connie, "do you remember what today is?"

"No. Ever since I've been here, I've completely lost track of the passing days."

"Today is Tuesday," said Connie. "You are going to be checked by Dr. McCormick and Dr. Simmons."

"Who are they?" asked Corey. "The two who worked on me at the hospital?"

"Yes, they're the interns, Lamar and Reno."

"I remember. They're the ones who are so inseparable, just like Tweedle-Dee and Tweedle-Dum."

"Lamar called early this morning, and said he and Reno would be here at about ten."

"Do they live far from here?" asked Corey.

"No, not at all," answered Connie. "As a matter of fact, they live just three blocks from here."

"Three blocks in which direction?" asked Corey.

"Two blocks south of here," said Connie, "is a street called Browning. Go right one block on Browning, and you'll be there."

"I was wondering if the two of them even live together," said Corey.

"Yes," said Connie, "they've been living together for a few years. Those two are inseparable friends."

"Yeah, I remember. But I can't get one thing straight," said Corey. "Which one's Tweedle-Dee, and which one's Tweedle-Dum?"

Connie was giggling about the comment Corey made. "You've been reading too much Lewis Carroll," she told him.

The telephone rang. Connie asked Corey to answer it.

"Me? No way," said Corey, "I can't hold a telephone with a cast on my arm."

"All right then, I'll answer it," said Connie.

She answered the telephone.

"Hello?" she asked.

"Connie, this is Lamar. Is Corey ready for Reno and me to come over and check up on him?"

"Yes," said Connie, "he's ready and waiting."

"I'll be there in about forty minutes," said Lamar.

"And we'll be waiting for you."

A few minutes before ten, Connie heard a knock on the door. She walked up to it and opened it.

"Oh, Lamar," said Connie. "Come right in! Will Reno be here too?"

"Yes, Reno will be here," said Lamar. "He's just getting some equipment out of the car."

"Oh, hello, Reno," Connie said as she saw Reno walking up to Lamar with some medical instruments in hand.

Corey came into the room on crutches. "Good morning, interns," he said.

"And good morning to you too," said Reno.

"Just what will you be doing to me today?" asked Corey.

"We'll be seeing if you've healed," said Lamar, "and do just a general check-up."

"How are you moving about?" asked Reno. "Do you have any mobility problems?"

"My legs can't move at all, and they tend to ache very often," said Corey. "My arms are in casts, keeping them from moving, but they do not hurt."

"Maybe it's time to take off the casts from your arms," said Lamar. "We'll need to take you down to the medical center for that. We need to take an X-ray, just to be sure."

"Uh, oh!" said Reno. "Why did we bring this along?" he asked himself, referring to a machine he held in his hands.

"What are you talking about?" asked Lamar.

"This portable sphygmomanometer here in my hands," said Reno.

"What's a sphygmoma—whatever you said?" asked Corey.

"In lay terms," said Lamar, "it's a blood-pressure meter. We'll have to wait for a cast to come off in order to take your blood pressure."

"So what are we waiting for?" asked Reno. "Shall we go right now?"

"Write a note explaining why we left," said Corey, "and stick it on the refrigerator."

"Couldn't you just tell her yourself?" asked Lamar.

73

"Not right now," said Corey. "Connie's doing her hair, and then she'll be putting on her make-up."

"We'll take my car," said Reno. "I'm driving."

"You?" asked Corey. "The day after I arrived at the hospital, you almost got into an accident in the parking garage."

"How did you know about that?" asked Reno.

"Connie told me."

Reno, Lamar, and Corey walked out to Reno's car. Reno opened the trunk, and put the portable blood-pressure meter in the trunk, next to a spare tire, a jack, and several pieces of junk.

"Don't you ever clean out your trunk?" asked Lamar.

"I never get the time," said Reno. "Most of my days, I'm preoccupied with things more important than the trunk of my car."

Lamar got into the rear seat, right behind the driver's seat. Corey set his crutches next to the front passenger door while Reno helped him get in. After Corey was seated, Reno walked around the car to get into the driver's seat. Without another word spoken, Reno started the ignition and drove off, not realizing that Corey's crutches were lying along the side of the car.

"Reno!" shouted Lamar, after Reno shifted into drive, lifted his foot off the brake, and set the car in motion. "We forgot his crutches!"

Corey's eyes opened widely, as if he were frightened. Reno stopped, shifted into reverse, and saw Corey's crutches lying on the sidewalk. After Reno brought the car to a stop, in exactly the same spot where the car was parked before, Corey opened the door, got out, got on his hands and knees, and crawled to where his crutches lay. Slowly he crawled back to the car, set his crutches behind the front seat, and asked someone to help him get back in.

Lamar slid across the back seat, squeezed his way past the bucket seat, and was able to get Corey back into the car. Lamar was then able to squeeze his way back into the rear seat.

"Are we all ready?" asked Reno.

"I am," said Lamar.

"So am I," said Corey.

"So let's go now," said Reno.

After Reno had driven about two blocks, he and Corey began having a conversation.

"Have you been enjoying yourself out here?" asked Reno to Corey.

"I guess so," responded Corey, "even though I really haven't done very much or been anywhere special."

"Do you plan to stay here a while?" asked Lamar.

"At least as long as I'm still injured," said Corey. "After then, I might come back here someday."

"Will you still be thinking of us?" asked Reno.

"Yeah, I probably will."

"And will you be thinking about the one who loves you?" asked Reno.

"Who loves me?" asked Corey. "Not 'Ms. Yeltaw'?"

"Yes," said Lamar, "indeed she *does* love you."

"That's really not what I was hoping for," said Corey. "I'm not here for finding love. I've already got that. Or so I think."

"What do you mean by 'or so you think'?" asked Lamar.

"In Boston, I've got a female roommate who loves me. But I'm not quite certain that she really does love me, or if she's just using me."

"But you know that Connie loves you," Reno told Corey.

"Where'd you get that idea?" asked Corey, resentfully.

"You should hear how she talks about you," said Lamar.

"She never said out loud that she loved me?" asked Corey.

"No, but I think she may have a crush on you," answered Reno.

"It probably won't last," said Corey. "Anyway, I sure hope it doesn't."

Minutes later, Corey arrived at the medical center with Lamar and Reno. Lamar was helping Corey get into the X-ray room. Reno and Lamar put on X-ray-proof aprons, then asked the radiologist on duty for four X-rays—one for each limb.

Within four minutes, and four clicks of the X-ray machine, all four of Corey's limbs had been X-rayed. All Corey could do was sit and wait in the waiting area for the negatives to be developed.

"I'll go with Corey to the waiting room," Lamar told Reno. "Tell me the results of the X-rays."

While Lamar waited with Corey, Dr. Grayer came into the waiting room. His eyes opened wide at the sight of Corey.

"How's Corey been doing?" Dr. Grayer asked Lamar.

"We just came out of the X-ray room," answered Lamar. "Reno will be back with the results of the X-rays."

"How do you feel?" Dr. Grayer asked Corey.

"My arms don't hurt, therefore, Lamar thought it just may be time for the casts to come off. That's why he and Reno brought me here."

Shortly afterward, Reno came to the waiting room.

"Corey," he said, "your right arm is completely healed. It's time for the cast to come off."

Corey, Lamar, and Dr. Grayer breathed a sigh of relief.

"What about my other limbs?" asked Corey.

"Your other arm should take a few more days," said Reno, "and I'd give your legs about a week or two."

The four men walked to a room down the hallway, where Corey put his right arm on a table. Dr. Grayer turned on a small drill, with a cutter attached, and in a matter of minutes, the cast was off Corey's right arm.

"Can you move your arm without any difficulty?" asked Lamar.

"Yes," Corey said, as he was moving his arm around in a circle, almost slapping Reno in the face with the back of his hand. But as he moved his arm back, he bent over slightly and let out a *YOWW*!

"Is something wrong?" asked Dr. Grayer.

"As I moved my arm," said Corey, "I felt a tingling in my spine."

"Oh, no," thought Reno. "Not *another* injury!"

"I'm afraid so," said Corey.

"What's this?" asked Dr. Grayer. "A new injury?"

"Maybe so," said Lamar. "But then, it may be an injury that existed before today, and went unnoticed."

"Could one of you check his file, and look at past X-rays?"

"I will," said Reno.

A few minutes later, Reno came back.

"I looked over every one of the X-rays," he said, "including the very first X-rays we took of you, Corey. There were no signs of any spinal injury."

"I wonder how he did it," whispered Lamar to himself. "How could he have not injured his spine in that terrible wreck?"

"Did you feel like this before today?" asked Dr. Grayer.

"No, I didn't," answered Corey. "But before today, I felt a slight numbness near my spine. But then again, since I could barely move, I really didn't pay much attention."

"This could sound serious," said Reno. "Seems like what you need is a good chiropractor."

"I really don't know of any around here," said Lamar. "Last one I remembered was Dr. Gunderson. Almost a year ago, when I had that terrible auto accident, he treated me. But three months ago, on his seventieth birthday, he hung up his gloves for good."

"You mean—he *retired*?" asked Corey.

"Exactly," said Dr. Grayer. "Nowadays, he spends almost all of his time on the links. Sometimes he leaves some rather wicked divots."

"Your statement about the auto accident brings back some haunting memories for me," said Reno, with an emotional voice, but an emotionless face. "I can picture the fear, which almost drove me to tears, that you'd be gone forever."

"Reno," Lamar said with his hand on Reno's shoulder, "There's really no need to feel so emotional. I'm here for you now, and I will always be here for you years from now."

"You know something," Reno told Corey, "working with Lamar makes me feel so good. He's what gets me up and keeps me going."

"Reno," said Corey, "that's precisely what I need in life. Someone to get me up and keep me—*OWW!*—going."

"Sounds serious," said Lamar. "We need to do something about your aching back. But what?"

Dr. Grayer, who had been listening to all this conversation, offered a suggestion.

"Maybe you could use a little Enicidem," he told Corey.

"Some what?" asked Corey.

"Enicidem. It's a prescription backache drug."

"Haven't heard of it," commented Reno.

"I'll prescribe some of it for you," said Dr. Grayer. "There is, however, one thing you absolutely, positively, *must* remember. Enicidem is *extremely* potent. According to the warning label on the package, the medication may cause severe drowsiness. So Corey, you should avoid driving or operating heavy machinery while on this drug."

"Sometimes," commented Corey, "I think of these casts and crutches as 'heavy machinery'."

"And," pointed out Lamar, "I don't think that Corey could do any driving in the condition he's in, anyway."

Reno was helping Corey hobble his way over to the exit, and just then Connie happened to come by.

"How's Corey doing?" she asked.

"Dr. Grayer just wrote him a prescription," said Reno.

"I have the slip in my shirt pocket," said Corey.

"Well," said Connie, "let's go pick it up."

Connie guided Corey out to the exit, into the parking structure, and into the passenger seat of her car.

"Gotta be cautious," said Corey, as Connie was driving along. "This medicine, Enicidem is its name, might make me extremely drowsy. But maybe it'll help me with my backache."

"I sure hope so," said Connie.

"So do I."

Connie pulled into the parking lot of a small shopping center, found a parking space, and turned the ignition off. She then walked to the passenger side, to assist Corey.

"At times like these," she said, "I kinda wish I had handicapped plates."

Connie and Corey went down a walkway, then went into Lorber's Pharmacy. The first thing Corey observed was the store's logo: the name "Lorber" with crossbars over the legs of the two R's, and a pestle sticking up from behind the B.

Corey leaned upon the counter, while the pharmacist greeted Connie and him.

"Nurse Yeltaw," said the pharmacist. "Another patient?"

"Yes," she said, "I am Ms. Yeltaw. This *is* my newest patient. His name is Corey Exbrook."

"Corey Exbrook," thought he pharmacist. "Name sounds familiar. Maybe he was the missing businessman from New England. Nahh, couldn't be. I must be dreaming."

"Here is a prescription for him," said Connie, as she handed the pharmacist the slip of paper.

Putting on his bifocals, the pharmacist appeared surprised when he read the slip.

"Enicidem," he said. "No doctor prescribes it very much. Too many are afraid to prescribe it. But not Dr. Grayer, apparently. I guess he isn't afraid of the possible side effects."

A minute or so later, the pharmacist came back to the counter with a small vial of Enicidem. Connie presented her health-care plan card, and therefore had to pay only ten dollars for the prescription. She put the vial in her purse, then walked Corey to her car, and helped him get in.

"It's starting to get cloudy," said Corey, in a gloomy voice.

"Is something wrong with that?" asked Connie.

"It's just that cloudy days sometimes depress me."

"According to today's forecast," said Connie, "it'll be cloudy until late at night."

"At least if Dr. Grayer was right, I should have no trouble getting to sleep tonight."

"What do you mean?" asked Connie.

"It's the medicine. It'll very likely make me feel so drowsy that you'll need a forklift to get me out of bed."

"I can see why it's so depressing," said Connie. "The sky is turning gray. (But isn't it always gray in Pennsylvania?)"

"How would I know?" asked Corey. "I've never been to this state before."

"This morning's newspaper," said Connie, "predicted a little rain for late at night, and maybe even some snowfall. Sometimes when the weather gets bad, I get feeling depressed too. I get to where I want to curl myself up in my cave for the rest of the winter. But right now I can't do that, especially while I'm—"

After a dog ran out into the street, Connie slammed on the brake.

"Driving," she completed her sentence.

"*OW!*"yelled Corey. "My back hurts enough already; the last thing I need now is whiplash!"

"It wasn't my fault," said Connie. "I just didn't want to run over that poor little pooch."

Connie finally arrived at her house. She parked in the garage, and opened the passenger-side door to help Corey get out.

"Sounds like role reversal," said Corey. "First time I've ever heard of women opening doors for men."

"Doesn't mean much to me," said Connie. "I do it all the time."

Connie and Corey arrived at home late in the afternoon. After Connie made dinner for two (something she hadn't done in quite a while), and she and Corey spent an evening watching television when there really wasn't much on to watch, Corey began feeling tired. He began to yawn.

"Do you need your pill now?" Connie asked him.

"Yes, I feel so tired. I feel like going to bed."

Connie walked Corey to the bathroom,and gave him a pill and a cup of water to take it with.

"Does your back still ache?" asked Connie.

"A little," said Corey. "But it should be relieved by morning, I presume."

Connie guided Corey to the bedroom,helped him get his clothes off, helped him put on a pajama top, and lifted him up into his bed. She drew the covers over him, turned the light off, and left the room.

Within minutes, Corey was sound asleep. Connie put the vial of medicine on the nightstand next to Corey's bed, quietly tiptoed out of the room, lest Corey be awakened, and went to bed herself.

12

Yeltaw in the Raw

On a farm, somewhere in the distance, a rooster had just started to crow. The sun was rising over the mountains located east of the town of Sellecca Valley.

It had been only twelve or so hours since Corey received a prescription for the potent backache drug, Enicidem. The morning after he took his first dose, somehow his backaches miraculously disappeared.

Corey had just awakened, and for the first time since arriving at Sellecca Valley he was able to put his hand on his forehead, painlessly. He looked at the palm of his hand, and saw a red smudge on it.

"Blood! I'm bleeding!" he said to himself, about to scream. "Connie!" he screamed, not knowing where she was.

"Corey?" she asked, while she was coming out of the bathroom. "Is something wrong?"

"Something wrong? I'd say something is wrong! See this red stain on my hand? I'm bleeding!" said Corey, in a panic.

"Did you cut your hand on something?"

"No," said Corey, "I just put my hand on my forehead, and it is letting blood like crazy! Hurry! Get some bandages!"

"Corey, don't be silly! That red mark is not blood; it's lipstick!"

"Lipstick?" asked Corey in confusion. "Wait a minute! Now I remember. Last night I dreamed about being kissed by the world's most beautiful woman—or so I think."

"Who *is* the most beautiful woman in the world?" asked Connie. "At least, who do you *think* is?"

"Janet Watley."

"Of course," said Connie. "Last night, I thought I heard you calling out to her in your sleep."

"I guess," said Corey, "maybe dreams really *can* come true."

"Do you know what today is?" asked Connie.

Like Fred Rogers, Corey began saying, "It's a beautiful day in Sellecca Valley...."

"Yes, it's a beautiful day in Sellecca Valley, but it's a *wonderful* day for you," said Connie. "Your leg casts are to come off today."

"But what about my *left arm*?" asked Corey.

"We'll have to see about that, too," said Connie. "Lamar called about fifteen minutes ago, and said he'll take another look, and some more X-rays."

"Here we go again with those X-rays," mumbled Corey. "My body must be radioactive already."

"And Corey," said Connie, "I'll drop you off on my way to work today."

"Hopefully," said Corey, "I won't forget my crutches again!"

"Yeah," said Connie. "I remember very well. Lamar told me all about it."

Just then, the telephone rang again. Corey, now that he could move his right arm, went to the phone and answered it himself.

"Hello?" asked Corey.

"Is this Corey?" asked the voice on the other end.

"This is he."

"And this is Dr. Grayer. Corey, tell Connie that she will have today off. We won't be needing her today."

"I'll tell her. Goodbye, Dr. Grayer."

"Hear that, Connie?" asked Corey after he hung the telephone up. "You have today off."

"I do?" she asked. "Who said that?"

"That was Dr. Grayer on the phone. Now do you think he has a crush on you?"

"Crush?" asked Connie. "He's already married. He has been for a little over six years."

Early that afternoon, Corey found himself back at the medical center lobby, with Connie by his side. Dr. Grayer and Lamar had just walked up next to them.

"Connie," asked Kendall, "what are you doing here today? I thought I gave you today off."

"It's not me," she answered. "It's Corey. He needs to be checked again. It may be just about time for the casts to come off his legs. Go get Reno, and tell him we're ready."

"Pardon me," said Lamar. "Reno should be here in about twenty minutes."

Dr. Grayer went to a telephone in the lobby, and began making a call.

"Dr. Simmons?" asked Dr. Grayer.

"Yes, this is Reno. Is there anything you'll need from me, Dr. Grayer? Is it an emergency?"

"No, it's no emergency, it's only Corey."

"What does he need?" asked Reno.

"He needs more X-rays. I'll take care of that. But I may need some help. How fast could you get here?"

"It should take me about fifteen minutes," said Reno. "I just finished lunch."

Fifteen minutes later, Reno arrived as he said that he would.

"So it's my absolute favorite patient," said Reno, as he looked at Corey, who was with Connie, Lamar, and Kendall.

Corey was later in a small room, where Lamar and Reno were holding his left arm still, while Dr. Grayer cut the cast off.

"Does your arm hurt?" asked Lamar.

"Not at all," replied Corey. "Another giant leap toward a complete recovery. Now what about my legs?"

"Oh, that's right!" said Dr. Grayer. "We forgot all about that. We'll have the X-rays in shortly."

"Yep, shortly," said an X-ray technician, bringing the developed negatives to Dr. Grayer.

"Corey," said Dr. Grayer, "your right leg is completely healed, but we may need about another day on your left leg."

In a few minutes, Corey's right leg was freed from the cast. He started to move his leg around, and nearly kicked Reno right between the legs!"

"Ready to go home now?" asked Lamar.

"Ready and willing," answered Corey.

Lamar and Reno took Corey back to Connie's house, where she was there waiting for them. Connie opened the passenger door, just as Corey was reaching to open it. After nearly stumbling out of the car, Corey, who now had only one crutch, went to the front door with a little help from Connie.

"Well, Corey," said Connie, "I see that you can move about by yourself now, just about."

"Yeah, just about is right," said Corey. "I still move around on one crutch. But tomorrow, I hope, my left leg should be free. Already I can see that my days here in Sellecca Valley are numbered."

Connie looked at Corey with a sad look in her eyes. Reno stood with his mouth gaping open, and held his hand on his left ribs, with his thumb touching where his heart supposedly was. Even Lamar let out a gasp.

"Is this a farewell?" asked Connie.

"Guess so," said Corey. "I said I'd be staying only until I was completely healed. Tomorrow may just be the day."

With his voice about to break, Reno started to say something. "I— I'm—"

"You're what?" asked Corey.

"He's getting all choked up," said Lamar. "But this time, it was not at all like our high-school graduation."

"What happened at your high school graduation?" asked Corey.

"Let me begin," said Lamar, as Reno, Connie, and Corey listened. "As I said, it was the night of our high-school graduation, nearly nine or ten years ago. I revealed to Reno that I'd been accepted by a small, faraway college in some unknown little town. Reno said the same thing, but that he thought it would be a different school in a different town."

"Could the small, faraway college in some unknown little town be UPSV?" asked Corey.

"Exactly," said Lamar. "But Reno didn't know that. I remember now his first response. He said, 'I'm sure gonna—'"

"He was sure gonna *what*?" asked Connie.

"Oh, I just got too choked up," said Reno. "I started to cry. I sobbed to him something that sounded like 'Me-shoo'."

"But later that night," said Lamar, "I told you I was going to the University of Pennsylvania at Sellecca Valley. And I asked about you."

"It surprised me to find that I'd be going there too," said Reno. "The two of us went through college together, then medical school..."

"Now we're where we are now. Just a few more months, and we could be licensed to practice," said Lamar. "Just one more thing, Reno. Just what did you mean by 'Me-shoo'?"

"Don't take it so hard," Corey told them. "You know I will be back here after I make my millions. Maybe I can find real love here, something I couldn't do in Boston."

"I hope you do," said Connie. "There are a few extraordinarily beautiful women here."

"Yeah," said Reno. "just one. You."

"I'm not the only beautiful woman in the world," said Connie. "I'm sure there are many other beautiful women here in this town."

While Connie, Corey, Reno, and Lamar were talking, they heard the doorbell ring. Standing at the door was Connie's brother-in-law, Mack Hawkins, a man with shoulder-length hair.

"Well, sister-in-law," Mack told Connie, "how are you doing tonight?"

83

"Not much going on," answered Connie. "It's just a Friday night. I don't have anything to do tonight; there's really nothing on TV tonight, and nothing good showing in the theaters."

"Speaking of theaters," interrupted Corey, "I've got to get that corporation of mine sold. I've got to get back to Boston, then get on the next train to Denver."

"You actually *own* a company?" asked Mack.

"Yes, Exbrook Cinemas. I inherited the company from my late father. I'm Corey Exbrook."

"Pleasure to meet you. I'm Mack Hawkins, Connie's brother-in-law. I'm married to her sister, Joanna," said Mack. "Your face looks slightly familiar. I think I saw you on the news not too long ago."

"You probably did," said Corey. "Was I lying in a hospital bed?"

"I think so," said Mack.

"It so happens that Connie was the nurse who attended to me."

"What brings you here tonight?" asked Connie.

"It's your sister, Joanna," said Mack. "She's too sick to make dinner tonight. So do you have room for one more?"

"Actually," said Connie, "I have enough room for three more. Would you like to stay for dinner, Lamar and Reno?"

"I guess so," said Lamar. "We originally were going to go out tonight, but then, we'll just save the money and go out another night."

During dinner that evening, Corey got to know Mack a little better. Even Reno and Lamar, who'd never met Mack, got to know him very well.

"Exbrook Cinemas?" said Mack. "I remember when I was in high school, in Chicago, I worked there one summer. The next summer, I remember, I was a dancer on a local music-and-dance show on TV. One of the women looked like Janet Watley."

"And maybe a little like me, therefore," said Connie.

"Oh, how beautiful she is," commented Corey.

"You mean me?" asked Connie.

"Actually," said Corey, "I was really talking about Watley."

"Yes, she sure is beautiful," said Reno. "I think she ought to be in pictures."

"Are you planning anything special?" Connie asked Mack.

"Oh, yes!" said Mack. "This year, I'm going to exhibit some of my art at the Downtown Sellecca Valley Festival of the Arts."

"I never knew you were an artist," said Corey.

"Indeed I am," said Mack. "But vocationally, I'm a dance instructor. Last year, Connie was one of my students."

"What's the Festival of the Arts?" asked Corey.

"During the week between Christmas and New Year's Day," said Connie, "State Route 12—Sellecca Boulevard—is closed off for three-fourths of a mile, from First to Sixteenth Streets, for a large arts fair. Artists from all over the country, and even nearby, sell their works in tents lined up all over the street. There's also live music, carnival games, and rides for the little ones."

"It's what I love best about this town," said Lamar. "Every year, Reno and I stroll down the streets of downtown together, taking in the special feeling of the Arts Festival."

"It's just like Tempe, Arizona," said Connie. "I visited a few relatives there one year not that long ago. Together we went to the Downtown Festival of the Arts, along Mill Avenue. I just loved it."

After dinner had ended, Lamar, Reno, and Mack went home. Corey began feeling tired, and Connie was also starting to yawn. Grabbing his crutch, Corey was able to get to the guest room—his temporary bedroom—by himself, but as he turned off the light once inside, he nearly tripped and fell. He got into bed, and fell asleep. He knew he would have to get a good night's sleep, for the next morning was a big day for him. His last cast was to come off the next day, and finally he'd be able to return home to Boston.

Connie was in her bedroom, looking for an extra nightgown, since her only one had a tear in it. She remembered that she had a pair of pajamas she could wear, but realized at the last minute that her pajamas were dirty, and were in with the laundry.

Then suddenly, near two in the morning, Corey woke abruptly from his peaceful slumber, and began shivering. He was holding his arms together, trying to bundle up and stay warm. Even with a heavy quilt wrapped around himself, he was still cold. He took his crutch, which had lain beside a bedside table, and went out toward the hallway. The heater was in a small closet in the hallway. He opened the door to the closet, and put his hand on the heater. It made a few sputtering noises, and felt cold as ice to the touch. He tried to turn up the thermostat, but since the heater wasn't working, the thermostat did absolutely no good.

"This is crazy!" said Corey, with his teeth chattering from the bitter cold. "I haven't been this cold since the night my late, dear old father, took Lester and me camping."

He went into the living room, walked over to the fireplace, and found an unburned log. "I'll curl up and sleep by the fire, I guess," he thought, knowing that perhaps it was the only way to stay warm. On the mantel lay a book of matches. Corey was able to grab it, but since the cold was making his hand feel stiff, striking it was rather difficult. He touched the match to the unburned log, but nearly burned his finger in the process.

"Ah, finally," he sighed in relief. Alas, as he spoke, a draft in the room blew the flame out.

"What now?" grumbled Corey. "I'll just have to wake Connie up, and tell her it's freezing cold in here and I can't get to sleep."

Limping along close to the wall in the hallway, Corey make his way to Connie's bedroom. Quietly he opened the door, and took a look at Connie, lying on her waterbed, sleeping like a baby. He then tiptoed over to her, trying not to make any noise.

"Connie," he whispered to her, still quivering.

Connie opened her eyes and woke up.

"Are you all right?" she asked.

"Yes, I'm fine," said Corey, "but cold. The heater has broken down, and I can't get to sleep when it's that cold."

"Oh, poor thing," said Connie.

"Oh, please! I wasn't looking for sympathy," said Corey. "Don't you feel cold?"

"No, not I," said Connie. "I sleep on a heated waterbed."

"Heat," remarked Corey, "I could use just a little of that."

"I've got plenty of room on my waterbed," said Connie. "Why don't you sleep right here next to me?"

"I might as well," said Corey. "I still feel a bit uncertain, but at least it would be better than lying awake on a cold bed in a cold room."

Corey groped his way around the dark room, around the bed, and got underneath the sheets.

"Feels a little better," said Corey. "But the waves may take some getting used to."

Corey rolled over onto his side, where he was facing Connie. He stretched out his arm, and he was touching Connie's back. His legs could feel Connie's legs, which were smooth and silky. He thought at first it was her nightgown. But after moving his hands down her body, he began shivering again—this time, with fright!

Connie awoke abruptly. "Corey," she groaned. "Do you mind?"

"What about you, Connie?" Corey snapped back angrily. "Do *you* mind?"

"What is it now?" asked Connie, in a slow, tired voice.

"Where's the nightgown? Where's the pajamas? Where's the underwear?"

"I had nothing to wear," said Connie, "so I decided to sleep *au naturel*."

"Now I know how beautiful you are," said Corey, "but picturing you in your birthday suit isn't exactly the 'pretty portrait' I want to see of you. Couldn't you at least put a T-shirt on?"

"I can't help it if my only nightgown has a rend in it, and my only set of pajamas are dirty," said Connie. "Could we get to sleep now? You and I have a big day tomorrow."

Connie woke up rather early that morning. Corey remained fast asleep, since he lost so much sleep in the process of trying to find a place to sleep that wasn't cold.

Within the hour, Connie was able to wake Corey up. He could barely keep his eyes open, and tended to stumble a little as he went to the kitchen table. Feeling exhausted still, he put his hand on his forehead, and again found a mysterious red stain—the same kind that he found the night before.

"Connie," said Corey with a scowl, "you haven't been—"

"I haven't been *what*?" asked Connie.

"Never mind. All of the sudden, it's started feeling warm in here. Did the heater start working again?"

"Yes, everything's back in order," said Connie. "Somehow the circuit breaker got tripped. I turned it back on this morning."

"Did you sleep well last night?" asked Corey.

"Yes, except for you coming into my room," said Connie. "And the fact that you were 'sleep-talking'."

"Sleep-talking?" asked Corey, not knowing what Connie meant.

"You know, talking in your sleep. You were calling out to some woman, I forgot her name."

"No way!" insisted Corey. "I never talk in my sleep, even when I dream."

"How would you know?" asked Connie. "You're asleep when you talk in your sleep."

Lamar asked Connie to bring Corey to the medical center for another X-ray (hopefully, this would be his last!), and, hopefully, the cast could be removed from his left leg, and he could walk finally.

Corey found himself back in an examining room, which had now become familiar to him, because he had been there so many times recently. In only minutes, Corey's left leg was free to move. It was the first time in weeks that Corey was able to walk. Corey felt so good about taking those steps that he decided to walk right over to Lamar and Reno, who were at the lobby. Lamar stood by the desk, talking with the receptionist, and Reno, who was talking with another doctor. Lamar looked over his shoulder, and took a second glance just to see if he could believe what his eyes were seeing.

"Corey?" asked Lamar, "are you walking already?"

"Yes, I'm walking," said Corey.

"You seem as excited as the day you took your first steps," commented Lamar.

After Lamar took Corey home, Connie was in the lounge, sitting on a couch next to Reno.

"Are you serious?" asked Connie. "Corey actually *walked* this morning?"

"I'm serious! He did walk!" said Reno. "He's now completely healed."

"Where is he right now?"

"Lamar's taking him back home. Meet him there."

"Will he be staying with me tonight?" asked Connie.

"I don't know yet," said Reno. "I'll have to ask him later this afternoon."

"I'd kinda like it if he didn't go back to Boston," said Connie. "Do you want to know a little secret?"

"Yes. And I won't tell anyone," said Reno. "What is it?"

"I think that I'm in love with Corey."

"*You* love Corey?" asked Reno.

"Yes," said Connie, "I do love him. I can see him and me walking down the aisle, getting caught up in a rice storm."

"You're making a big mistake," said Reno. "I just don't know. Is he in love with you?"

"I don't know. But I'll find out."

"Yeah, you'll find out, all right," said Reno, skeptically. "The hard way."

"We've been together for a little while," said Connie. "I think he's really getting to know me."

"I can remember when you had a crush on me," said Reno. "Once you had a crush on Lamar too."

"I did not!" insisted Connie. "True, I had a crush on you, but *not* Lamar!"

"But in case Corey *does* leave tonight," said Reno, jokingly, "then you should fall in love with Lamar."

"I can't stand it," murmured Connie. "I just can't stand it."

13

Looking for a New Love

While Connie was in the medical center lounge with Reno, Lamar decided to take Corey out for lunch, since as Corey had said, that day may be the last lunch he ever would have in Sellecca Valley.

"So how is the sale going?" asked Lamar.

"Sale? You mean Exbrook Cinemas Corporation?"

"Yes, that sale," answered Lamar.

"I haven't been able to think about it much," said Corey. "And I haven't seen any progress yet."

"Are you ready to go back to Boston yet?"

"Am I ready?" asked Corey. "How will I get back to Boston? I have no money on me, no credit cards, and no means of transportation."

"But I'm sure that Connie will let you stay with her for as long as you want to."

"Nice to know," said Corey, "but I'm not sure that I really want to."

"Corey!" chided Lamar. "How can you be so cold?"

"Ever since I've been staying with her, I've been finding all these mysterious lip marks on my forehead when I wake up each morning."

"Hickies?" asked Lamar.

"No, kisses. First it was Janet Watley. I guess my dream that night must have been real. Another night it was my roommate in Boston. But I think Connie's doing it herself while I'm fast asleep."

"Oh, Corey," said Lamar, "you just don't see it."

"What don't I see?"

"You're the man of her dreams."

"You mean the man of her worst *nightmares*," said Corey.

"Nightmares?" asked Lamar.

"I'll bet she feels this way about all her patients."

"Not all of them," said Lamar. "Until recently, she was in pediatrics. She loves to work with children."

"Obviously," said Corey. "She loves children. She treats me like one."

"I wouldn't say that," said Lamar. "You've been alone for too long, and so has she. People like you don't come along every day, you know."

"Yes, I know. People like me don't come along, because there is no one like me in the world."

"So when did you last hear any word on the sale of the company?" asked Lamar.

"Last time I heard anything was the day before I was released from the hospital. My older brother Lester was visiting."

"What's Lester got to do with it?"

"I heard that he was going to help take over the transfer of assets. But I'm beginning to think that he's trying to keep the profits for himself."

"I have a better idea," said Lamar. "I'll let you use our telephone. Call Lester, and ask how the sale is going. Then ask if he can get you back to Boston."

"I think that's a good idea," said Corey. "When we get to your house, I'll call then and there. I'll let you use our telephone. I'll just leave a message on his machine. I'm sure he'll respond. He always has returned my calls."

"And can you still remember your home phone number?" asked Lamar.

"Yes, I remember. I'll just have to see how my roommate is doing. She hasn't heard from me since the day I left Boston. And Lamar, would you be able to pay for all these long-distance calls?"

"No problem. I make many calls myself," said Lamar.

"Do you have family living far away?" asked Corey.

"Oh, yes. No one in my family lives out here. That may be the reason Reno and I are living together."

"By the way," asked Corey, "where's the telephone?"

"It's in the living room, next to the couch."

After Corey finished lunch, Lamar went with him to the telephone, and stood a few feet away from Corey, as he picked the phone up, and started to dial. After two rings were heard, he heard what he had intended to hear—Lester's voice. But Lester was not speaking; the voice was merely an answering machine.

"Lester," said Corey, "please call me back this evening. In case you forgot the number, it's area code 710, 555-5639. Take good care. I expect to hear from you."

"That was a quick message," commented Lamar.

"Yes, unfortunately," said Corey. "It was his answering machine. Sometimes I absolutely *hate* those things."

"And now," asked Lamar, "are you going to phone home?"

"Not now; I've decided to wait until early this evening," said Corey. "By the way, Lamar, since I've never been here at your house before, could you tell me where the bathroom is?"

"It's down the hallway, second door on the left."

After Corey came out of the bathroom, he went back into the living room, and sat down next to Lamar.

"I know of something you do better than Connie," he told Lamar.

"What's that?"

"You put the toilet paper on the roll the way I like it—from the top."

"Actually, I didn't put it on. Reno did. Usually when I put it on, I put it on from the bottom."

"Just like Connie," said Corey. "She *always* puts it on wrong."

"Reno and I had a dispute over that once," said Lamar. "But we figure that if something should ever get between us, it shouldn't be a roll of tissue."

"I can't believe it," said Corey. "How could two people have a battle over something so trivial as toilet paper? Many good marriages came to a sad ending because of it. Sounds almost like *The Butter Battle Book*."

It was almost five o'clock in the afternoon, and Corey was still at Lamar's, waiting until Connie got back home.

"I almost forgot," said Corey, "I have to phone home, exactly like E.T."

Corey dialed his home phone number, and nearly dropped the receiver in horror.

"Uh, oh!" exclaimed Corey. "I think I must have misdialed."

"Try, try again," said Lamar.

Corey hung the phone up, and lifted it off the hook again. Then he tried to place his call once more.

On the line, he once again heard a recording saying, "The number you have reached has either been disconnected, or is no longer in service. If you feel you have reached this recording by error...."

Corey hung the telephone up. He shrugged his shoulders and let out a sigh.

"My home phone number. Disconnected!" grumbled Corey.

"I think so," said Corey. "I'm going to try again."

He tried again. And once again, he heard that he had dialed a disconnected number.

"It's no use," said Corey. "My brother hasn't been home yet today, and my own home phone has been disconnected."

"Is there anybody else in Boston that you know?" asked Lamar.

"Let me think. I just remembered about my next-door neighbor, Wally Beasley. He was the one who helped me arrange the sale."

"There you go! Try him," said Lamar. "Do you remember his number?"

"No, but I might find out. I'll dial Directory Assistance."

Corey dialed Directory Assistance for the Boston area, and asked for the number of Wally Beasley. After waiting a minute, he wrote down the number.

"Now I'll try to reach Mr. Beasley," said Corey to Lamar.

Corey dialed Mr. Beasley's number. All he heard was an answering machine.

"I just remembered," said Corey. "Today's Saturday. Wally goes bowling on Saturdays. I'll try back later tonight. Until then, I'll spend the rest of today with suspense killing me."

"You mustn't give up now," said Lamar. "All is not lost."

"Maybe not," said Corey, "but I am. Now I don't even have a home!"

"Yes you do," said Lamar. "Connie has agreed to let you stay with her."

"But being with her is not quite living," said Corey. "It's more like living in hell. I just can't take it."

"Then maybe you should move out," said Lamar.

"But where do I stay?" asked Corey. "I've got no money and no job. I just don't belong here. I should be back at home, wherever that is."

"Just stay with Connie tonight, and I'll take care of the rest."

"But how, Lamar?"

"Listen. When Reno comes home, I'll ask if it would be all right for you to stay with us. Just explain, as kindly as you are able, that you'll be living with us. She'll understand."

Evening had fallen, and Corey was back at home (or what was thought to be home), with Connie. He had been having dinner, with Sellecca Valley's most beautiful woman by his side. But he had done very little speaking, thinking that maybe he just didn't care for Connie, and couldn't wait to leave her. He knew he was wrong; however, for Connie really cared for him very much, as it was her job to do so—she was a nurse. Maybe Connie was just another friend, who would just come and go like so many other friends Corey had known in his lifetime.

"Corey," Connie said, "you don't seem too talkative today."

"You wouldn't have much to say if you had lost your home."

"You lost your home?" asked Connie.

"Unfortunately, yes," said Corey. "The number to my apartment in Boston has been disconnected. Please tell me if Lester calls, since I'm expecting to hear from him tonight."

"I'll listen," said Connie. "But I myself am expecting a call tonight from Jevon."

"So how will we know who's who?"

"I guess we'll just play a guessing game," remarked Connie.

Corey sat alone in the guest room, while Connie was in the living room watching a movie on television. She could not hear the telephone ringing, but Corey could from inside the guest room, even with the door closed. Corey went straight to the phone, and answered it.

"Hello? Is this Lester?"

"No, it is I, Jevon. How are you, Corey?"

"I'm completely healed. Just like I was before the derailment."

"How's Connie doing?"

"I'm not certain if I can go on with her. I'm beginning to think that she loves me."

"Aw, how wonderful! You two are a perfect pair."

"Well, listen to this. A few nights ago, I went to bed and woke up the following morning with lipstick marks on me. She said you put them there."

"How could I? I don't wear lipstick!"

"Neither does my roommate—or ex-roommate, as she might be. Connie said once that *she* had put her lips upon me while I was asleep."

"Well then, I think Connie is doing it herself. She did it to me every night while I was staying over."

"To make matters worse," said Corey, "last night I found myself having to sleep with her just to stay warm, since the heater wasn't working."

"Anything wrong with that?" asked Jevon.

"Something is most certainly wrong!" said Corey. "She was in bed naked! It made me feel completely uncomfortable!"

"Could you please put her on the line?" asked Jevon.

Corey asked for Connie to come to the telephone. She went to the phone, and Corey walked away.

"So Connie," Jevon told her, "do you know what I'm thinking?"

"What are you thinking?"

"Now is it true that you're in love with Corey?"

"In love? Absolutely!"

"Have you ever considered getting *married* to him?"

"Not yet. But maybe now, I will. I'll tell you when I do."

Just as Connie could not hear Corey on the telephone, Corey paid no attention to anything Connie was saying. But when Corey looked up from a book he was reading, he heard Connie say something about love and marriage. He was stunned. While he listened, he started to yawn. He was getting tired, perhaps from waiting for Lester to return his call. He was just about to get undressed and go to bed, when Connie came into the room, and asked him to get the telephone.

"Hello, Lester?"

"Lester? Who's Lester? This is Reno. Is it true that you were wanting to move out of Connie's house?"

"Yes, it is true. The sooner, the better."

"Would tomorrow night be fine for you to move in with us?" asked Reno.

"Possibly. Where will I be sleeping?"

"We have a bedroom for you at the end of the hall."

"I'll call you back in the morning. Right now I have two calls I need to place."

Corey hung up the phone, reached into a shirt pocket, took out a matchbook with Mr. Beasley's number written on it, and dialed the number. After about two rings, the phone was answered.

"Wally?" asked Corey.

"Yes, this is. Who's this?"

"It's I, Corey. I lived next door to you."

"Oh, Corey. Where are you now?"

"I'm in the town of Sellecca Valley, Pennsylvania. Today, I tried to call home, but my telephone was disconnected."

"I have something to tell you," said Wally. "You're no longer my next-door neighbor. Last week, your roommate got married, and moved out. She thought you were dead. The apartment is being fixed up for new tenants."

"But what about Exbrook Cinemas? Heard any about them?"

"Not a word. I haven't spoken to Harry since the day I last saw you."

After Corey finished speaking with Wally, he tried once more to reach Lester. This time, no machine answered the phone, but a human voice instead.

"Hello, is Big Brother Lester around?"

"No, this is Jeremy. How are you doing, Corey?"

"Jeremy, this is absolutely important. Do you know anything about what happened to all my stuff from the apartment where I lived?"

"My family is making plans for you to move in with us as soon as you get back to Boston. We've set aside the guest room."

"But how will I get back to Boston? I have no money and no transportation."

"I'll talk to my father when he gets home," said Jeremy. "He should have the solution."

"I'll see you sometime soon, hopefully. Goodbye...."

"Was *that* Lester?" asked Connie.

"No, that was his son, Jeremy. Now I am in very much uncertainty. All my stuff is waiting at his house. But how will I get back home, or to what seems like home?"

"Yeah, that's a problem," said Connie. "But you can still stay here until then."

"I guess so," said Corey. "At least it's better than living on the streets."

A minute or so later, the phone rang again.

"Hello?" asked Corey when he answered it.

"Corey, this is Reno. How are you?"

"As usual, I don't know if I'm coming or going."

"Listen, you talked with Lamar this afternoon about leaving Connie's house. Is that really your plan?"

"Yes, it is my plan."

"Will you be ready to come move in with us tomorrow evening?"

"Yes, I will be ready. But now what I don't know is how much longer I can stay. My brother says he'll let me move in with him, back home in Boston."

"So will you be going back?" asked Reno.

"Not yet. Don't have the money to make the trip."

"So shall we expect you tomorrow evening?"

"Yes."

"Good. You should have a good time here with Lamar and me. Goodbye, and see you tomorrow."

"Guess I gotta start looking for a new love," commented Corey to himself after he hung up the phone.

It was so late in the evening that Connie was beginning to yawn and stretch out, and Corey began to do the same thing.

"I'm going to bed," said Connie.

"I guess I will too. I think I'll sleep in the guest room again tonight."

"Why not with me?"

"I tend, sometimes, to get scared when I sleep with beautiful women. I'm afraid I'll find more lipstick on me."

"Oh, please don't tease me!" said Connie. "Be serious."

"I am being serious. I think I'll take the guest room."

"But remember how cold you were last night?"

"But you took care of the heater, and now it's working again."

"Yes, I remember," said Connie.

"Don't *you* ever get cold sleeping nude?"

"It was just for last night," said Connie. "And I had no idea you'd even be sleeping in my bed. Besides, my waterbed is heated, remember?"

"Well, Connie, it just doesn't seem right. I think I'm much better off sleeping alone. I might keep you awake all night."

Corey walked off into the guest bedroom, and Connie went to her own bedroom, with a sad look on her face.

14

Breaking Point

"How well did you sleep last night?" asked Connie to Corey the next morning.

"No trouble at all. What about you?"

"Oh, it took some time, a little tossing and turning, but I managed to get to sleep finally."

"I just don't know," said Corey. "I don't sleep too well on waterbeds. But I don't see how you can."

"I've been sleeping on a waterbed ever since I was sixteen," said Connie. "Obviously, you've never slept on one."

"Are you working this afternoon?"

"No," said Connie, "I have dance lessons. You can handle it here alone, can you?"

"Actually," said Corey, "I won't be alone. Reno and Lamar will be coming over to help me with something."

"What will they be helping you with?"

"Oh, right now I can't say. But I'll tell you eventually."

"Why not right now?"

"You'll see."

"There's a question I just have to ask today," said Connie. "But I'll have to wait a little while, just to build up the courage."

"Do you like living alone?" asked Corey.

"I don't mind it," said Connie, "but I'm getting tired of it."

"I guess maybe I feel the same way. Now that my roommate has eloped, and left me with nothing, maybe now I need to find a love of my own. But I don't know where to start, and nor do I know how."

"I guess you could start here, in Sellecca Valley," said Connie. "There's plenty of beautiful girls here. Just look right in front of your face."

"Come to think of it," remarked Corey, "I'm standing in front of a very beautiful woman right now. But what I wonder is if she could ever love me."

"Oh, you never know. Just possibly, she might."

"Oh, Connie, how would *you* know?"

"I know by experience. Many men have loved me before."

"About how many?" asked Corey.

"Some ten or twenty."

"How long ago was that?"

"Back when I was still in school," said Connie. "Ever since I left school, I haven't had the opportunities to meet men."

"But I've always heard it said that the key to a woman's happiness is through her heart. So how could you be so content with this solitary life?"

"Well, actually," said Connie, "living solitary is not what I really want. I know I need love, and that you do too."

"That's true; I really do need love. But right now just doesn't seem to be the time. I still have a lot of work to do, and a company to sell. But after that, I'll have plenty of time for love, and marriage, and a family, and all that follows."

Connie raised her eyebrows at what Corey had said.

"Corey, I've got to get running now. I'll see you this afternoon. Goodbye."

"Goodbye to you, too. Because maybe you won't be seeing me this afternoon."

After Connie had driven away, Corey sat down on a living room couch, and turned on the TV set. Unfortunately, he had difficulty finding anything to watch, since he was in a place so foreign to him. Even though Connie's house had cable TV, there was nothing particularly appealing to him on TV, especially since Sellecca Valley had only five television stations, as opposed to the dozen or so stations on the air in Boston.

"Oh, my! I just remembered something!" thought Corey. "If this is semester break, and I think it is, Lester would probably be at home, and I'd be able to reach him. I think I'll call back, maybe right now."

Hesitantly, Corey called Lester's phone number. The telephone rang about five times, and Corey hung up.

"Maybe he's having lunch right now," thought Corey. "But what at ten in the morning? Wait a minute! Maybe nobody is at home. Why didn't he, Jeremy, or Jamie answer? That's why!"

Corey picked up the telephone, and tried to call again. Now the phone rang only three times, and there *was* an answer.

"Hello?"

"Is this Corey?"

"Yes, Jamie, this is Corey. Is Lester in the house?"

"Just a minute."

Corey breathed a sigh of relief. Finally he would get to speak with his older brother.

"Yo, Corey! How's things going?"

"Listen, Lester, do you remember having my things sent over to your house?"

"Yes. We're waiting for you to arrive. When are you going to get here?"

"Heaven only knows. I just need to find a way to get back to Boston. But it's kinda hard, with no money in my possession at the moment."

"Could you stay there at least until Tuesday?"

"No problem with that," said Corey. "But why wait until Tuesday?"

"Something unexpected came up. I have to leave town this evening."

"Where are you going?"

"North Carolina. It's a funeral."

"Funeral?" asked Corey. "Who died? Hopefully not someone in the family."

"No, it wasn't someone in the family. It was my junior high school basketball coach."

"What was he doing in North Carolina?"

"He retired there several years ago."

"Back to the original subject," said Corey. "How will I get back?"

"Tuesday morning, I'll be driving out to Sellecca Valley. Is the address where you're staying 13059 South Hermosa?"

"Yes, but I might also be staying with the interns, who live just around the corner, at 1229 East Browning."

"Interns? You mean Drs. McCormick and Simmons?"

"Yes, Lamar and Reno."

"I'll make sure to get down both addresses," said Lester.

Corey looked over his shoulder, and saw someone pulling up into the driveway.

"There's people coming to the house right now," said Corey. "When should I call you back?"

"Try late night Monday. I should be back by then."

"Goodbye."

When Corey set the phone down, he went over to open the door, just a second before Lamar was about to ring the doorbell.

"Come right in, gentlemen," said Corey. "I've been waiting for you all day."

99

"Wait no more," said Reno, with a grin.

"So, Corey," said Lamar, "are you ready to move in with us?"

"Ready?" asked Corey. "I'm ready and willing!"

"Does Connie know that you're leaving?" asked Reno.

"I'm not so sure," answered Corey. "But she'll get the hint, if maybe she hasn't already."

"You might as well tell her," said Lamar. "Otherwise, she won't know."

"You know, all along, I've waited to say something like that. But I never had the nerve."

"Corey," said Reno, "you're talking as if you actually want to leave Connie behind. Why?"

"I'll explain it the best I can. But it's gonna be hard. I have a lot of work to do in the next few weeks. I really should have been to Denver and back by now. But fate reached its hands out to me, and caused this terrible injury that left me stranded here."

"What I don't understand," said Lamar, "is what Connie has to do with this."

"I was just about to get to that. I had nowhere to stay; therefore, Connie agreed to let me stay with her, until I got better. But if you remember the agreement, I said I would stay *only* until I was healed. Do you think I'm fully recovered?"

"Last time I saw you," said Reno, "you looked as if the accident never took place."

"So now I'm back on my feet again. Or so I thought. But then, my roommate in Boston, who thought I was dead, eloped, and my apartment was vacant."

"But what about Connie?" asked Reno. "Where does she come into the picture?"

Corey cleared his throat, then continued speaking.

"It seems that every night, while I'm in bed, she comes into my room, and I wake up in the morning with lipstick on myself—and it wasn't *I* who put it there! At first I had thought it was blood. Then, on Wednesday night, when the heater wasn't working and I was feeling cold, she asked me to sleep with her, in her waterbed."

"Oh, how romantic!" commented Lamar.

"Not to me!" said Corey, bitterly. "Not only did I wake up feeling seasick, and with more lipstick marks, but she was sleeping in the buff! Does she always do that, I wonder?"

"Wow! I never knew that Connie slept naked," said Reno. "I'd love to get in bed with her one of these nights."

"Good for you, because I wouldn't," said Corey. "The thing is, she has a little crush on me, and I feel I'm trapped here. I've got to get up and go, but she doesn't seem to let me."

"She loves you," said Reno.

"Yeah, yeah, yeah," replied Corey. "Right now, however, I am not looking for love. I've got too many other things to worry about. One of those things is my corporation. I've been forgetting about it a little, because I've been sidetracked by these misfortunes shoved into my path."

"I think you're making a mistake," said Reno. "Connie has been very nice to you, hasn't she?"

"Nice? Maybe. But she really doesn't love me. She just wants to have me around. To her, I'm just a teddy bear to take with her to bed each night. Working in pediatrics has really got to her head. She really loves children. She treats me like one."

"Can I believe what I'm hearing?" asked Lamar.

"You might as well," said Corey. "I'm a very honest person, most of the time."

"What do you mean by 'most of the time'?" asked Reno.

"Just as I said: *most of the time.*"

The telephone rang again.

"Corey, I think you'd better answer that," said Lamar. "And if it's Connie, try to explain to her your reason for leaving."

"Oh, please, don't be Connie," said Corey to himself, as he walked over to the telephone.

"Hello?"

"Corey, this is Lester. I got news on the Exbrook Cinemas sale."

"What was the news?"

"CinemaStar announced that they will delay the sale until April. Their CEO heard about you, and decided that both he and you would be better off waiting a little while. At least the corporation is still financially afloat, and still bears the 'Exbrook' name."

"Will you still be coming by this Tuesday?" asked Corey.

"Yes, and I'm ready to bring you back home."

"And is the guest room ready for me?"

"Yes. Jamie just got finished cleaning it up last night."

"And you said you'd be driving me home?"

"Yes. I even have money for meals and motel rooms. I decided to use my Christmas bonus money for the purpose of bringing you back home, where you belong."

"Now, do you have the address?"

"Yes, let me take a look, there are two addresses—13059 South Hermosa, and 1229 East Browning."

"That's right," said Corey. "But I'd say try the address on Browning first."

"I got it. Goodbye."

"Who was that?" asked Reno, as Corey came into the living room and sat down on the couch between Reno and Lamar.

"That was my brother, Lester. This Tuesday, he'll be driving me back to Boston. I'll be staying with him. Then all my problems will be solved."

"Problems?" asked Lamar.

"Yes, problems with Connie. I'm getting more desperate by the day, possible even the hour, or even the minute!"

"But you're sure you'll stay with us this evening, and until Tuesday?" asked Reno.

"Sure as ever."

"Aren't you gonna miss Connie?" asked Lamar.

"Miss? No way. I'd rather live in a monastery than live with her!"

"You sound disgruntled," said Reno.

"I am disgruntled," said Corey. "And this time, I'm about to burst at the seams."

"Control yourself," said Lamar. "I don't want to have to clean up what left of you after you finally do burst. But I think that after hearing what you've said, Connie's heart just might—"

"Break?" asked Corey.

"No, burst!" said Lamar.

"I've known her for a long time. She can be very sensitive. Once or twice, I've seen her break down and cry."

"Once or twice?" asked Reno. "I've seen her cry more times that that! I'd say she's extremely sensitive."

"No, that's not true," said Lamar. "You're only exaggerating. I've known you for a long time too."

"Connie just loves to cry," said Reno.

"Naw," said Lamar, "nobody loves to cry. I think it's *you*. You just *love* to see her cry!"

"Why would a man love to see a woman cry?" Corey asked Lamar.

"Must be something about being a man," said Lamar. "Some men, but none that I know personally, would beat and brutalize their women just to see them sob their eyes out."

"I don't think so," said Corey. "Some men love to see women cry just so they can get romantic to them. But I'm not that type of man. But I might be, if the woman was someone else."

"What would you do if you saw her cry?" asked Reno.

"I'd think she was just using it as an attention ploy," said Corey. "I'd just walk away, and do nothing."

"It's almost time," said Lamar. "We're doing lunch today, with Dr. Grayer. Care to join us?"

"I guess so," said Corey. "Maybe I'll just ask Kendall what he thinks I should do."

"Good idea," said Reno. "He's an expert at lovemaking. He has been doing it for years, to the same woman."

Lamar took Reno and Corey to the medical center, where he found Dr. Grayer waiting by an entrance.

"Where are we going today?" Dr. Grayer asked Lamar.

"I don't know. Where would you like to go?" asked Lamar.

Dr. Grayer got into the back seat, next to Corey.

"Corey!" said Dr. Grayer. "I see that you're doing lunch with us."

"And I suppose I'll be doing lunch once or twice more," said Corey. "Tonight I'll be moving in with your two interns."

"Are you having problems with Connie?" asked Kendall.

"I could almost say that I am," said Corey.

"What's going on?" asked Dr. Grayer.

"She thinks I'm going to stay around forever. She's infatuated with me. I feel trapped."

"So she's in love with you," said Dr. Grayer. "It's really no big deal."

"It is to me," Corey told him. "I don't have time for love right now. I've got a company to sell, and a lot of money to be made."

"About how much money?" asked Reno.

"I'll never find out until it happens."

Lamar had pulled into the parking lot of Harland's Fried Chicken.

"Does Harland's sound good?" he asked.

"Yes," said Corey. "I used to go there quite a lot in Boston. If only I *was* in Boston now."

"Which do you guys want," asked Lamar, "Double Crispy or Classic Blue Ribbon Recipe?"

103

"I think I'll have a little of each," everyone said.

The four men walked in together. One of the cashiers gazed at Reno delightedly.

"Well, if it isn't Reno!" he said. "Has your bad knee got better?"

"Oh, yes. Now I'm back to normal. But that was nearly two weeks ago."

"I remember," said the cashier. "And I remember Lamar telling me how you were doing. How's he doing right now?"

"We just can't wait until this summer. We'll be graduating, and not long afterward, we'll open up our own practice."

"Shall it be the usual?" asked the cashier, "a little of each?"

"Yes, a little Classic Blue Ribbon Recipe, and some Double Crispy."

A few minutes later, Reno carried two buckets of chicken to the table.

"So when do you expect to be in practice?" asked Dr. Grayer.

"Even after we become licensed," said Lamar, "it may still take a little time. We have to find office space, and buy all that equipment."

"The thought kinda saddens me," said Dr. Grayer. "In the years I've been with you, I've gotten to know you so closely. I won't have any interns left."

"You might," said Lamar. "Next year, the intern from Dr. Francis' group, Benson Christoph, might be working with you. It'll be his second year."

"Dr. Christoph?" said Reno. "I haven't heard of him."

"I have," said Dr. Grayer. "Dr. Francis has told me all about Benson. He's studying to become an anesthesiologist. He did some work on Corey."

"He did?" said Corey. "I don't remember."

"Of course not," said Lamar. "You were under his spell."

"Dr. Christoph," said Kendall, "has already become one of the finest anesthesiologists in all of Stevens County, let alone all of Pennsylvania."

"Is that where we are, Stevens County?" asked Corey.

"Yes, Sellecca Valley is the seat of Stevens County," said Reno. "Some of the suburbs of this city include Ingolia, Franconero, and Concetta."

After a few minutes, and much conversation, the four men had finished lunch. As they were going back to Connie's house, to drop Corey off, Reno reminded Corey to get packed, for the move to the interns' house. Corey went to the guest bedroom, and took out a small suitcase he had brought with him on his train trip. Into it he put several days' worth of clothing, which had been stored in a dresser. As he was packing, he heard the front door opening. Connie had come home, and was calling out Corey's name. Corey felt frightened, and hastily began unpacking. Just after he put the suitcase under the bed, Connie came into the guest room.

"I wasn't disturbing anything, was I?" she asked.

"I was in the middle of doing something," Corey said, "but I can wait until this evening."

"Will you be here all afternoon?" asked Connie.

"Yes, I should," said Corey. "I don't plan to go anywhere before dark, at least."

"I have to go to my acting classes now," said Connie.

"You're taking acting?" asked Corey.

"Yes, I am. People have been telling me that I should be in a movie. That's why I'm enrolled in drama classes."

"Someday, I might like to see you in a film."

"If I don't get back by six-thirty," said Connie, "could you make dinner for yourself?"

"I might not need to. I could just call for something to be delivered."

"Yeah, really," said Connie. "Goodbye," she said, holding Corey closely and kissing him on the cheek—while she had gobs of lipstick on.

After Connie left, Corey began to murmur to himself.

"That did it! That was the straw that broke the camel's back! I'm getting out of here, and never returning. That's exactly what I'll do. And I won't even say goodbye. I've had enough! GET ME OUT OF HERE!"

15

Hasta la Vista, BABY!

For about an hour after sunset, Corey sat down on the couch, with his head in his hands. For some unknown reason, Corey was feeling a little guilty. But about what? Was he being too hard on Connie? No, for she did not yet know that Corey was going to be leaving. Corey just wondered, how would he tell her? Or should he leave without warning? He was so deeply in thought that he almost didn't hear the doorbell ring. He got up and answered the door.

"Lamar! Reno! Come in and have a seat."

As Reno sat down next to Corey, Lamar asked if Corey was ready to move yet.

"Move?" asked Corey. "Oh, yes, I just forgot all about it."

"How could you forget?" asked Reno.

"I've been in somewhat of a daze all afternoon, and I'm still uncertain about something."

"Uncertain about what?" asked Lamar. "Is your mind made up yet?"

"Yes, my mind is made up, but I wonder if I should tell her, and just *what* I should tell her."

"Just say that you've found your new love," said Lamar.

"I can't do that," said Corey. "It's not true. She would think I really did."

"So you're saying you love her," Reno told Corey.

"No, I'm not saying I love her, because I do not! I came here just for a temporary place to stay; I did not come here to find love!"

"Brrr!" remarked Reno. "I need a jacket! You make me feel so cold!"

"But that's the problem," said Corey. "I'm trying so hard not to be so cold-blooded. I just want her to know exactly how I feel."

"By the way," asked Lamar, "is Connie around anywhere?"

"No," said Corey, "she went to acting classes. She said she should be back around six-thirty. But now it's almost eight."

"Since she's nowhere around," said Reno, "let's get all your stuff and make our exodus."

"Is that how you describe it?" asked Corey. "An exodus? Just like the Israelis from Egypt?"

Corey walked down the hallway to the guest room, as Reno and Lamar followed.

"All of my clothing is in that second drawer," said Corey.

Corey took the suitcase out from under the bed. Lamar and Reno were putting clothing into the suitcase, being careful not to wrinkle anything.

"How long will you stay with us?" asked Lamar.

"Just until Tuesday. My brother will be coming to pick me up, and take me to his home."

With the suitcase fully packed, Corey carried it (and how heavy it was) down the hallway. As they entered the living room, Connie had just opened the front door.

"Lamar! Reno!" whispered Corey as he handed the suitcase to them, "Get back into the bedroom! Quick! Wait until I ask for you! Here she comes!"

Lamar took the suitcase, just as Connie came into the room and hung her coat up.

"What's the suitcase for?" asked Connie. "Is Lamar going on a trip somewhere?"

"No, not Lamar," answered Corey.

"Is it Reno, then?"

"Nope."

"Then who is it?" asked Connie, thinking she might know the answer.

"Me."

"You?" asked Connie. "You're leaving so soon?"

"Yes, so soon," said Corey. "I'll be staying with Reno and Lamar from tonight until Tuesday, when my brother will pick me up and take me back home to Boston."

"Why won't you stay with me?" asked Connie.

"Do you want to know the truth?" asked Corey, angrily.

"Yes, I do," said Connie, saying it almost like a wedding vow.

"Remember the agreement you and I made? I said I would stay here only until I was healed. And I am."

"But since I first met you," said Connie, "you've breathed new life into this empty house."

107

"Yeah, really," said Corey. "But what have I been doing? Spending so much time alone, while the days turn into months, and the weeks into lifetimes."

"But—" said Connie, "I don't see what's wrong!"

"I'll tell you! I should have been in Denver, and back in Boston by now! I don't belong here! I get into a train derailment, wind up in a hospital in a town I never heard of, and then I'm taken into the home of an immature nurse who thinks that she loves me!"

"Immature?" asked Connie. "What do you mean immature?"

"First you insist that I go to bed with you each night, just because I feel cold, and yet you have just enough decency to sleep naked!"

"But Corey, the only reason I slept nude that night was that my only nightgown had a tear in it, and I had nothing to wear."

"Yeah. But while I'm sleeping, you creep up on me and give me all those kisses, heavy on the lipstick, when I least expect them."

"Oh, it's because I love you," said Connie, trying to be convincing.

"You don't love me; you just want me around! I know just what you really are! And I can't take it! I've got to get out of here as soon as possible!"

"Oh, no!" pleaded Connie. "Don't go, don't go!"

"Oh, yes! I've made up my mind. I *am* going. You are so immature, it's unbelievable! If you want something to take to bed with you, get yourself a teddy bear. If you want love, I know someone who has it. He really does."

"Who?" asked Connie.

"I don't know his name, let alone what he looks like, but somewhere around here, there's an eligible young bachelor looking for a woman like you. Hopefully, he has more patience than I do at the moment."

"I know who you're talking about," said Connie. "Yourself."

"No, it's not me," grumbled Corey. "Why don't you just go chase down some of the men who loved you when you were in school?"

"But they didn't love me," said Connie. "They were just infatuated with me."

"Just as infatuated you are with me! You are such a small child! You've been treating *me* like one. I'm just an old rag doll that you want to drag around with you everywhere you go. And you only love me because I'm about to become a wealthy businessman. But it hasn't happened yet! And it's all your fault!"

As Corey was speaking, Connie started sniffling, and a few tears began coming down.

"Yeah, now I know that you're just a small child," snapped Corey. "You have to cry like one."

After hearing those words, Connie was crying harder.

"Just go to your bedroom, little bawlbaby," said Corey. "I'll be in the kitchen preparing your bottle. And I think your diapers will need changing too."

Connie went off to her bedroom, and slammed the door. Corey then went to the guest bedroom, and knocked on the door. Reno opened the door.

"It's—safe to come out now," Corey said.

"Are you ready yet?" asked Reno.

"I suppose so," said Corey. "All the dirty work's been done now."

"And Corey," said Lamar, "what was that slam I heard on the door?"

"It was just Connie, running off to her room."

Corey carried the suitcase into the living room, while Reno and Lamar were walking with him.

"Why'd she slam the door?" asked Reno.

"You said I should tell her the truth, as to why I was leaving, didn't you? Well, that's exactly what I did. Now she's crying, and it looks as thought she just can't stop."

"That doesn't sound good," said Reno. "I mean, I have seen Connie cry before, and it's not a pleasant sight. Once when I saw her cry, she threw an empty bottle at me. Fortunately, the bottle was plastic. She can get mean when she's upset, almost like a spoiled child."

"Spoiled child, that's just what she is," said Corey. "Now, I'm wishing I'd never even met her. She's just about messed my whole life up. I don't think I'm ever going to be the same person again."

For a moment, all was silent. Nobody spoke. But the silence was broken by the sound of Connie blubbering.

"It must be bad," said Lamar. "You've really done it! The way it sounds now, she'll probably cry her whole life away, drowning in her tears."

"Well who's gonna comfort the crying woman?" asked Corey.

"Not I," said Lamar. "You should be the one to do it, Reno. I know how much you just love to see her cry."

"I do not!" said Reno. "Why don't *you* do it, Corey?"

"It just doesn't feel right."

"All right," said Reno, "I suppose I'll do it. But it will be your fault if I come out of there in bits and pieces."

Reno went to Connie's room, and gently tapped on the door.

"Go away!" sobbed Connie loudly.

"Connie, it's only me, Reno. May I come in?"

"Go ahead," sighed Connie.

Reno came into her bedroom, where he found Connie sitting on the floor, with her head on her knees, crying. He sat down next to her, and put his hand on her shoulder.

"There, there, Connie, there's no need to cry," he said to her, sympathetically.

"I can't help it," sobbed Connie. "The only love in my life has turned around and walked out on me."

"But Connie, you'll have to find love somewhere else. Corey is just an injured traveler. You helped him become healthy again, and now it's about time for him to head home and get on with his life."

"But how can I get on with mine without any love?"

"There's love in your life," said Reno. "Lamar and I love you very deeply, and so does Dr. Grayer, and the rest of the staff at UPSV Medical Center."

"But I still feel alone and depressed, and Corey is the only man for me."

"No, he's not," said Reno. "He told me so."

Connie was sobbing forcefully. She got up off the floor and walked over to her dresser. From one of the top drawers she got out a small leather case, and sat down next to Reno, who watched curiously as she took out a small pocketknife.

"Connie, I hope you aren't going to...." said Reno, worried.

Still sobbing, she unfolded the knife and gave her wrist a hard gash.

"CONNIE!" screamed Reno.

Lamar stood at the end of the hallway, as Reno came out, about to panic.

"Lamar! Go dial 911, FAST! Connie has cut her wrist open. There's blood all over the floor!"

Lamar dashed into the kitchen, and picked up the telephone.

"Hello, 911," said Lamar, "we have someone her who has cut her wrists, and is bleeding all lover. Send an ambulance over to 13059 South Hermosa, Sellecca Valley."

Minutes later, paramedics came to the door. Reno led them into the bedroom where Connie lay in what was almost a pool of blood. Just as quickly, Corey saw the paramedics take her out of the house on a stretcher.

"Connie?" asked a bedazzled Corey. "Are you all right?"

"Don't worry," said Lamar. "It's only wrist lacerations."

"You mean—she was attempting suicide?" asked Corey.

"It appears so," said Lamar. "Form Reno's description, it looked like no accident."

Reno was walking down the hallway, trembling with fright.

"Reno," said Lamar, "would you call that a suicide attempt?"

"The only thing I can call it is scary," gasped Reno. "The first thing I saw her do was get out a small leather case. Right as I was watching, she slashed herself. I keep seeing images of it in my mind now. I might not be able to get to sleep tonight."

"Reno, it's going to be all right," said Lamar. "You did a good thing by wrapping her hand up in a tourniquet, and by getting me to dial 911. I think you may have saved a life."

"So the weepy wimp tried to kill herself, just because I don't love her," said Corey. "I wonder if she did that with any of the other men she's had a crush on."

"Not that I can remember," said Reno. "Remember I told you that once she had a crush on me?"

Dr. Grayer and Dr. Francis were working the emergency room shift that night. Connie, who lay unconscious on a stretcher, was brought into the emergency room where the two doctors were working.

"Looks familiar, doesn't she?" commented Dr. Francis.

"Connie? Are you all right?" asked Dr. Grayer.

"Must not be," said Dr. Francis. "She didn't answer."

"I guess this explains it," said Dr. Grayer, as he looked at Connie's wrist, wrapped tightly in a tourniquet. "Get her in the OR—immediately!"

Dr. Grayer could not sleep at all that night, since he had to stitch up Connie's wrist lacerations. Reno was also unable to sleep. It was about twenty minutes after midnight, and Corey, spending his first night at his new "home"—with Lamar and Reno—woke up after sleeping for only about ninety minutes. He walked into the living room, where he saw Reno sitting on the couch, watching an old movie on television.

"Mind if I join you?" asked Corey to Reno, softly.

"You can't sleep either?" asked Reno. "Here, take a seat right next to me. Make yourself comfortable."

"Was this evening's experience traumatic?" asked Corey. "Is that what's keeping you awake?"

"Yes, it is. I said I wouldn't be able to sleep, and I was right."

"But why worry?" asked Corey. "No one is to blame."

"No one?" wondered Reno. "How could someone just try to take his or her own life, and it be nobody's fault?"

111

"What would you do if Connie actually had died?" asked Corey, "Whose fault would *that* be?"

"Probably mine," said Reno. "If she were dead right now, I certainly wouldn't be sleeping. Actually, yes, I would too be sleeping. Eternally. I'd be dead too."

"You must really love her," said Corey. "I knew it! You're in love!"

"I'm not the one in love. She is!" said Reno. "And you're the one she's in love with."

"And I'm the one who's not in love with her," said Corey. "She thinks that life isn't worth living without me. Nobody's fault but her own."

Lamar, with bags under his eyes, came into the living room, and took a seat with Reno and Corey.

"I just couldn't sleep either," said Lamar. "Somehow I feel guilty about this evening. I suppose maybe it was my fault."

"I wonder why," said Corey. "I don't see anything that you did wrong."

"Somehow, I think that if I went into her room to talk to her, there might have been a different outcome," said Lamar.

"Yeah," Corey told Lamar. "She'd probably have killed herself, and maybe you too."

"Fortunately, it's only a Friday night," said Reno. "We have tomorrow off, therefore maybe we can pick up a little sleep in the morning."

As all was silent for a moment in the room, Corey raised his ear at what seemed to be a familiar sound. From the direction of Connie's house, he thought he heard a telephone ringing in the quiet calm.

"Sounds like Connie's telephone," said Corey.

"Are you sure?" asked Reno. "It could be any of the neighbors' phones. What makes you think it's Connie's?"

"It has a very familiar, very loud 'ring' to it," said Corey.

Corey stood up, went over to the closet, took out his jacket, and went out the door. By the time he got to Connie's house, the telephone had stopped ringing.

"False alarm," Corey thought to himself. As he started to walk away, the telephone began to ring again. Reaching into his pocket, he pulled out the key to her house (somehow he had managed to hold on to it), and went inside to answer the telephone.

"Hello?"

"Is this Corey?"

"Yes."

"This is Jevon. Is Connie here at the moment?"

"No, she's in the hospital. She apparently tried to commit suicide."

"Oh, no!" shrieked Jevon. "Not poor Connie! Why would she want to do that?"

"Failed love," said Corey. "She had a crush on me, and I decided I'd had just enough."

"Shame!" said Jevon. "How could you do that to such a nice, affectionate woman?"

"I really don't belong here," said Corey. "I should've been back home about a month ago. But no! That immature little baby wanted to keep me around, like an old rag doll."

"Baby?" asked Jevon. "She's not *a* baby; she's *your* baby."

"At least I don't have to put up with her tonight," said Corey. "Come Tuesday, I may never have to see her again, since my brother Lester will be taking me home."

"How is she doing tonight?" asked Jevon.

"I don't know. I haven't seen her at all."

"Is she staying at the same hospital?"

"Yes. Only hospital in this town."

"I'll call there. Goodbye...."

Corey hung up the telephone, and went back to Lamar and Reno's house. Once inside, he found the living room dark, and the TV set turned off.

"Lamar? Reno?" he called out.

"I guess they finally went to bed," he thought.

Corey looked at the clock on the living room wall.

"Egads! It's 2:35! I sure do feel tired! I think I'd better get to bed."

Corey went down the hallway, where he could see Lamar, in his bedroom, fast asleep. Reno, who was in his own room, was also asleep, finally. After Corey got into his own bed in the guest room at Lamar and Reno's house, and turned off the light, he too fell asleep.

16

You Are My Everything

It seemed to be a miracle that anybody could get to sleep that night. Even though he couldn't get to sleep until almost three in the morning, Corey woke up around ten o'clock. At first he was confused, feeling as though he was in unfamiliar surroundings. Later, he had just remembered how he decided to leave behind a beautiful nurse who decided to make him the object of all her affection. Affection, thought Corey, he really had no use for.

Just after Corey sat down at the kitchen table, and began staring into space, Lamar had just woke up, and came right into the kitchen. Corey, who was looking the other way, did not notice anything at all.

"Good morning," Lamar said softly. Corey shivered.

"Lamar," asked Corey. "did you sleep very well?"

"Yes. But it took some time. Normally, I get up long before this time. But today's only Saturday. At least Dr. Grayer is off today, and so are Reno and I."

"Do you plan to do anything special today?" asked Corey.

"I just thought about something," said Lamar. "Do you remember the reason we couldn't get to sleep last night?"

"All I remember was that something happened to Connie," answered Corey.

"Oh, yes, something *did* happen. She tried to take her life yesterday."

"I wonder why," said Corey, smugly.

"Think about it," Lamar told Corey. "Don't you feel a small bit of responsibility?"

"She's the one responsible for her actions, not I," answered Corey. "I didn't make her slash herself. She decided to do it herself."

"But why did she decide to do it?" asked Lamar. "Because you just didn't care about her. She really likes you."

"I really don't care whether she likes me or not," Corey said. "I didn't come to this faraway place to find love. In fact, I really should never have been here at all."

"But didn't the sight of blood scare you?" asked Lamar.

"I didn't see her do it. Reno did. Perhaps you should ask him about it."

"All right, I will," said Lamar.

Lamar went into Reno's bedroom, and gently touched Reno on the shoulders. Reno rolled over, but did not wake up. Then he started turning himself around, and his eyes, which were redder than a maraschino cherry, opened up.

"Lamar," grumbled Reno, "what is it now?"

"Corey and I wish to talk to you."

"By the way," said Reno, "thanks for waking me up. I was in the middle of a not-so-pleasant dream."

"What wasn't so pleasant about it?" asked Lamar.

"All I could dream about was what happened last night."

"That's what we wanted to talk to you about," said Lamar.

"Just give me a few minutes, and I'll get dressed. I'll be out after that."

Lamar stepped out of Reno's room, closed the door behind himself, and went back into the living room, where Corey was sitting on the sofa with his loins girded, ready to leave on a moment's notice, like the minutemen of colonial days.

"Wait a minute!" thought Corey. "What am I doing? I keep forgetting that I'm now at the interns' house. And it's going to be three more days before I head back home. I guess I'm beginning to go out of my mind!"

"Corey? Is something wrong?" asked Lamar.

"No, not really. Just a memory lapse."

At that moment, Reno was standing in front of his dresser, putting his wristwatch on. As he saw his right hand touch his left wrist, he suddenly began to see, in his imagination, Connie with a pocketknife, violently gashing herself. In panic, he dropped his watch. Corey and Lamar looked up, as they heard a scream.

"Excuse me, Corey," said Lamar, as he rushed over to Reno's bedroom. He opened the door, and saw his young friend, trembling with fright.

"Reno? What happened?" asked Lamar in concern.

"I can't help it. I keep having flashbacks," Reno said, with his voice in a frightened-sounding minor key.

Still scared, and still shaking, Reno threw his arms around Lamar, and hid his face on Lamar's chest. Lamar was holding his hand on the back of Reno's head.

115

"There's no need to quiver," said Lamar. "I'll get you through your ordeal."

Corey stood in the doorway.

"Symbol of true friendship," he said. "It's something we all need at one time of our life. Someone to hide our face on in times of fear. Is Reno all right? I never heard a scream like that, except in horror films."

"Nothing serious," said Lamar. "He's just having flashbacks."

"I'd probably be having flashbacks too, if I were in his shoes," said Corey.

"I think he's too worried about Connie," said Lamar. "He does kinda like her, you know."

"By the way," asked Corey, "how's she been doing?"

"I have yet to find out," said Lamar.

"She isn't dead yet, is she?" asked Corey.

"No, I doubt it," said Lamar. "If she was, the phone would have rung."

Reno was now shivering harder.

"Corey," said Lamar, "just look what you did. You scared him! Every time someone says something about death, or the attempt on Connie's life, he gets scared. But he'll probably get over it in a few days."

"I'm beginning to feel a little guilt," said Corey. "Now that I know exactly how Reno feels, I think I might feel the same in that situation. I guess maybe I should stop by the hospital sometime today."

"We'll go with you," said Lamar. "I think I'll drive. Reno is in no condition to take the wheel."

While Lamar was driving to the medical center, Reno sat with his face in his lap, still staying mute out of fear. When the three men walked to the front desk, who else should be standing there besides their supervisor, Dr. Kendall Grayer?

"Dr. Grayer," said Corey, "did you hear what happened last night?"

"What happened?" asked Kendall.

"About Connie," said Lamar. "How's she doing?"

"I haven't seen her at all today," said Dr. Grayer. "Normally, I wouldn't be here at this time. I was called in for an emergency operation."

"Remember last night, when she came here on a stretcher?"

"Of course I remember," said Dr. Grayer. "I helped stitch her wrist together."

"Reno witnessed it all," said Lamar. "Last night, she tried to commit suicide, right before his eyes. Today, he's been having flashbacks, and I even heard a horrifying scream. He hasn't said a word ever since."

"Did you come here to see her?" asked Dr. Grayer.

"Yes, we did," said Corey. "Got a moment?"

"I have all the time in the world," said Dr. Grayer. "I just completed a successful operation, and now I'm about to leave for lunch."

"Could we have a few words with you?" asked Lamar. "Let's step outside, and go to the park across the street."

"Good idea," said Corey. "That seems to be an ideal place to discuss such important matters."

Corey, Kendall, Lamar, and Reno began walking out the front door together. Reno was still silent, and still felt somewhat afraid. After they took a seat on a park bench, Corey began the conversation, feeling a slight lump in his throat.

"I guess I started it all," said Corey. "I did what I had to do, or at least—*ahem*—what I felt I had to do. Just because she took me into her house until I was nursed back to health, she thought I was in love with her. She was wrong—dead wrong!"

"Don't say that!" scolded Lamar.

"So then," Corey continued, "I stood up, and told her I wanted to get away. All she could do was plead. Then, the little baby started to cry just like one."

"Just like one *what*?" asked Kendall.

"Baby," responded Corey. "Even inside the living room, I could hear the sobs coming from inside a closed bedroom at the end of the hallway."

"Yeah, I could hear it too," said Lamar. "If you hadn't been in the living room, talking with us, I'd swear you were in the bedroom beating on her."

"Then what?" asked Dr. Grayer.

"Reno went into her bedroom, and tried to comfort her. And he saw her put a pocketknife up to her wrist, and she lacerated her wrist terribly," said Lamar.

Reno started to move his lips as if he were trying to say something.

"Well now, Reno," said Lamar, "are you about to break your vow of silence?"

"Yes," said Reno, "There's something I just must say right now."

"So what must you say?" asked Corey.

"It was all my fault," said Reno, sadly.

"*Your* fault?" asked Dr. Grayer.

"Yes, mine. I just told her that Corey isn't looking for love. I told her the truth; I guess that the truth hurts sometimes."

117

"You're right," said Corey. "But sometimes you may have no other choice."

"But she thinks that now her life is so empty. I guess that Corey must have been all she was living for," said Reno.

Corey sighed, seriously pondering what Reno had just said.

"But," said Reno, "I didn't intend to make her want to kill herself. I just don't feel so good about it."

For a moment or two, everyone fell silent—especially Reno, whose face was devoid of all expression.

"Lamar," asked Reno, in a sad, soft voice, "is your shirt waterproof?"

"Why do you ask that?"

Reno said not another word. Instead, he put his left arm around Lamar, leaned toward his very close friend, and began to cry. Lamar, who cared very much about his partner in medicine, put his hand on Reno's shoulder and gave him a friendly, gentle embrace.

"It's all right, Reno," said Lamar. "Now and then, everyone feels a weakness. Even I do. It's perfectly all right for a man to cry. But as long as you've got me by your side, there's no reason to lose all hope."

Corey took a deep breath, and exhaled suddenly.

"Is Reno always that sensitive?" asked Corey.

"Sometimes," said Lamar. "I've known Reno for almost fourteen years, and this is only the third time I've ever seen him cry."

"Now let's try to think about just what went wrong," said Corey.

"Why fret?" said Dr. Grayer. "No one is really to blame. I should know, since I've worked with Nurse Yeltaw so many times before. Yes, she can be sensitive at times. Maybe, if you'd just left everything alone, things would not have been so terrible."

"So maybe we should have just let her cry," said Corey. "Ever notice that after you cry just a little, you start feeling good afterward?"

By this time, Reno was no longer letting out tears.

"Do you feel better now?" asked Lamar.

"Very much," said Reno, with a grin. "I guess now I can face the world again."

Corey cleared his throat to begin speaking.

"I feel there is one person, just one person, to blame for all this: myself," said Corey. "It seems that ever since the start of this month, when I became heir to Exbrook Cinemas, all I've been thinking about has been the wealth that would soon be mine. But when it didn't come to pass, I unfairly blamed it on Connie, thinking she was in my way. I remember the moment she took me in, and let me stay with her. I felt so good, a special feeling I'd never known before. That first night, we sat by the fireplace, and she told me some very moving words, that sparks turn into flames. Two people meet, and a spark develops. Eventually, the sparks *do* become flames, and as the two are more in love, the fire grows much brighter. For me, unfortunately, the love fire burned out of control. Clearly I can now see that indeed she really loved me. However, I refused to see it that way. I know now that love is the most important thing in my life, and always has been. I just let something else get in the way. My inheritance still means something to me, but not as much as having someone to share it with. Specifically, I mean someone like Miss Yeltaw. I see in her more than just skin-deep beauty. I see someone who cares about me. She really does."

Reno, Lamar, and Kendall nodded in agreement.

"If," Corey went on to say, "you want to know exactly what went wrong, it was the way I treated her last night. I used some hard words. Today, I felt moved when I saw Reno cry, and Lamar show some compassion. If only I felt the same way about Connie last night. So where do I begin?"

"Just tell her how you feel about her," said Lamar. "Tell her you love her, and that you're sorry about last night."

"Hold it," said Dr. Grayer. "You do love her, is that right?"

"Yes, I can say that I do," said Corey.

"As they say," said Dr. Grayer, "love means never having to say you're sorry."

"What?" asked Reno. "Where do you get that idea?"

"Oh, I learned it from a movie, some twenty-five years ago," said Dr. Grayer.

"After all this conversation," said Lamar, "didn't we forget why we got together today in the first place?"

"It's about our beautiful young nurse," said Kendall. "We came to see how he was doing."

Together the four men went back to the medical center. Dr. Grayer went to the front desk, and asked which room Connie was staying in.

"Room 508," said the receptionist.

"That's exactly where I was staying," said Corey. "Must be a very popular room."

"We certainly remember," said Reno.

"One more thing," said Corey, "before we go see her, I have some pocket change; therefore, I'll make a stop at the gift shop. A beautiful bouquet, or something like it, may brighten her day."

119

"I'll go with you," said Reno.

Lamar and Kendall went down the hallway, while Reno took Corey into the gift shop.

"So it's Dr. Simmons," an employee of the gift shop said to Reno. "What brings you here?"

"It's Yeltaw. We're here to find something to make her feel better."

"Yeah, poor Connie," said the employee. "She really tried to do herself in last night. Everyone here has been talking about it today."

"How could I forget?" commented Reno. "I saw it happen."

A few minutes later, Reno and Corey walked out of the gift shop with a large bouquet, and a few helium-filled mylar balloons. Just down the hallway, they stood waiting for an elevator to take them to the fifth floor. Coming from behind were Lamar and Dr. Grayer.

"Lamar," said Reno, "did you talk to Connie yet?"

"No, we decided to wait," said Dr. Grayer. "She's fast asleep. We didn't want to wake her up, so we decided to wait for you two."

An elevator opened, and the four men stepped inside.

"I have an idea," said Reno. "Lamar, you go inside to talk to her. I think she'll feel much better when she hears from you."

"I guess I'm much more the sympathetic type," said Lamar. "You ought to know. I know just what to do if she starts to cry."

The elevator came to a stop on the fifth floor. Everyone stepped outside and went down the corridor.

"Room 508," said Corey, as he looked in the small window in the door. "She's even in the same bed I was in."

"You three wait here," said Lamar. "I'll go in."

So he went in. He walked up to Connie's bedside.

"Connie," he said softly as he put his hand gently on her forehead, "is everything all right?"

She said "Not really," in a low moan.

"Listen," said Lamar. "I talked to Corey just a few minutes ago. He and I, as well as Reno, lost a lot of sleep last night. All we could think about was Corey breading it off with you, and how your life nearly ended so violently."

Again, Connie began to cry.

"Why'd you have to save me?" she sobbed. "Nobody loves me. Nobody cares for me. Nobody gives a?*&¢%$#@! about me. My life is MEANINGLESS! I want to be dead."

"Don't say that," said Lamar, who now was starting to let out a few tears himself. "There is meaning in your life. And there is love too. Reno,

Kendall, and I care very much about you. That's why I came here to see you."

"But what about Corey? He doesn't care about me at all," Connie said, and continued crying.

"When we talked to him, he sounded extremely emotional. He seemed to have a feeling of guilt. From what he said, I think that maybe, just maybe, he really does care about you."

Lamar was gently stroking Connie's tear-dampened face, and gave her a small peck right underneath her eye. Now she wasn't letting out as many tears.

"Just a minute," Lamar told her, "there's someone else waiting outside to see you. I'll go bring him in."

Lamar stepped outside, and went right up to Corey, who was holding the bouquet with the balloons. Dr. Grayer and Reno were with Corey.

"Now it's your turn," Lamar told Corey.

"Give me just a minute more," said Corey. "I've got to get myself together. I've almost got down what I'm going to say."

"Well, c'mon," said Dr. Grayer. "It's now or never. This may be the only chance you get."

"You need not push me," said Corey. "I'll go in there—right now."

Corey stepped into Connie's room, and took a seat by her bedside.

"Connie, I've been thinking about something, and it's starting to burn holes in my mind."

"Corey?" asked Connie, as a tear went down her cheek.

"Yes, it is I, Corey. Are you all right?"

"I suppose so."

"This morning I started to think about all the things that you and I did together."

"Like what kinds of things?" asked Connie.

"Like," said Corey, "touring this beautiful town, and sitting together by firelight one beautiful night. Remember when you first saw me, lying on this bed right here, nearly dead?"

"Yes, now I remember that."

"I felt so alone, until I opened my eyes and saw you standing there, looking like the leading lady from a film, like the diva who steals everyone's hearts."

"Diva?" asked Connie, very much uncertain of what Corey meant.

"Yes. Not only do I think that you're the most beautiful girl in Sellecca Valley, but maybe even the whole wide world. And of course I say that because you bear so much resemblance to Janet Watley. But looks really don't mean much to me. The thing is, I know that upon meeting me for the first time, you seemed to fall in love at first sight. I must admit, I even felt a little affection for you. But the time just didn't seem right. All I felt I could do at the time was hold back. Basically, the only thing I could think about was my inheritance. I did what I really shouldn't have done. I thought only about myself. Now I can't think of anyone or anything but you."

"So now you know why I let you stay with me," said Connie.

"Yes, I do. And it wasn't just because I was injured. You must have *seriously* loved me; otherwise, you wouldn't have done that."

"That's true. I loved you then, and I still do now."

"I guess now it's all right for me to tell you this," said Corey. "And Connie, now I fully realize that I love you too. I really do."

Corey then leaned over, and his lips were touching Connie's. The two held the kiss for almost sixteen seconds, interrupted by the sound of applause. Dr. Grayer and his two interns were standing in the doorway, watching.

"I was right," Reno told Corey. "I always had a notion that somehow, you really did love Connie. Now I know for sure."

"This may be one of the best days of my life," said Connie. "Now I know what the true meaning of life is. It's a beautiful thing. And it's even more beautiful when there is love in it."

"One more thing, Connie," said Corey. "is there still room in your house, and your queen-size waterbed, for one more?"

"Oh, yes. I have plenty of space for you, inside and out."

"I guess maybe I'll be staying in this town for a while," said Corey.

Reno then presented Connie with the bouquet that he and Corey bought at the gift shop.

"Connie, we all love you too," said Dr. Grayer. "Ready to be discharged today?"

"I'm as ready as ever," said Connie. "Now I can get back to a normal life. And this time, my life will be full. Finally I have the one thing that's been missing for so long."

"What's that?" asked Lamar.

"Love. It's all I need to get by in this world."

"I wholeheartedly agree," said Reno.

"I second that emotion," said Lamar.

"So now we've found love," said Corey. "So what comes next?"

17

A Place to Call Home

It had been three afternoons and an evening since Connie had been discharged. Every evening since then, she and Corey had dinner together, sat side by side in the living room together, and even slept together in the same bed. Before Connie went to bed each night, or left the house, Corey would say to her, "Connie, lay some lipstick on me." She would do exactly that—give him a wet, juicy kiss right on his lips. (Except for one time, when she unintentionally kissed him about an inch or so below the lips.)

Now it was Tuesday morning. Connie and Corey were sitting at the kitchen table, where Corey was sipping a cup of coffee, and reading the morning newspaper.

"Oh, my! I forgot!" shrieked Corey.

"Forgot what?" asked Connie.

"Today's Tuesday! Lester's supposed to be coming over!"

"Your older brother will be coming down here from Boston?"

"Yes, but I forgot to tell him something."

"What?"

"He must still think that I'll be moving back to Boston," said Corey. "But I won't. I've found my new home."

Connie raised her coffee cup to take a sip when the telephone rang. She was so startled that she nearly dropped the cup. She got up and started running over to the phone.

"Hello?"

"Is my Uncle Corey in?"

"Corey?" said Connie, "He's right here. Is this Lester?"

"No, this is Jeremy."

"Corey," whispered Connie, holding her hand over the mouthpiece, "it's Jeremy."

Corey took the phone into his hand.

"Hello, Jeremy?"

"Uncle Corey, are you packed and ready to go yet?"

"Packed? I'm not going anywhere. This is my home now."

"I'll just have to tell that to my father. Everything of yours is packed inside a moving van, which is parked outside our house right now."

"Did you say *everything*?"

"I can't be sure about that."

"Where are you right now?"

"We're still at home. We'll be ready to go in about fifteen minutes."

"Jeremy, could you get your father on for me?"

"Yes. As a matter of fact, he's sitting right behind me."

Corey took a sigh.

"Yo, Corey!" said Lester.

"You reached me at my new home."

"So you got yourself a new home now," said Lester. "Do you live alone?"

"No, I've found a woman of my own. Remember Connie, the young, beautiful nurse form the University Medical Center?"

"How could I forget?" asked Lester. "I think she's even more beautiful than Jamie," Lester added, jokingly.

"What makes you say that?" asked Corey.

"It's true. She is."

"Listen, Lester," said Corey, "is it true you put all my stuff into a moving van?"

"Yes, everything—but the kitchen sink!"

"Even my high school basketball trophy?"

"Yes, even that too. We checked carefully. Everything that had been in your apartment is now in that van."

"How long should it take for you to get here?"

"Not over three hours," said Lester. "Remember that in New England, states are rather small."

"How soon will you be leaving?"

"After you get off the phone," said Lester, looking down at his wristwatch.

"When will that be?"

"Right—now! We've got to get going. See you in Sellecca Valley!"

Without even bothering to say goodbye, Lester hung up.

"Goodbye, gotta get going," said Connie, as she was about to walk out the front door.

"Didn't you forget a little something?" said Corey.

"Forget? What could I forget?"

"Connie, lay some lipstick on me."

"Silly me," she thought. "How could I forget *that*?"

After the brief smooch, she was quickly out the door. Corey picked up that morning's newspaper, sat down on an easy chair, and began looking at the classified ads section. It had been a while since Corey had been employed, for just about every day since his train trip—which turned out to be somewhat a trip through time and space, and into an unknown dimension—had been almost a fantasy. Corey wondered if maybe he wasn't really in Sellecca Valley—perhaps he was still unconscious, and was only dreaming. Indeed, everything sounded dreamlike to Corey. Having been a devout fan of pop singer Janet Watley during his teenage years, living with, and even loving, a woman who resembled Watley in almost every imaginable way seemed absolutely unreal. He would pinch himself, throw cold water on himself, even try to prick himself with pins, but apparently he wasn't imagining anything. Everything was real.

Corey's meditation was abruptly interrupted by the sound of the doorbell ringing.

"Lester?" he asked to himself as he jumped up for the chair and ran to the door, with his arms stretched out. After he had thrown open the door, he realized that he was about to embrace the wrong person—it wasn't Lester at the front door, but it was his young friend Lamar.

"You're—not Lester!" said Corey, feeling a bit startled.

"No, but at least my first name begins with the same letter."

"Lamar! What brings you here?"

"Reno sent me over here. He has a question, but I don't have the answer."

"What's the question?"

"Why's there a moving van parked across the street from our house?"

"Moving van?"

"Yes," said Lamar, "a moving van. A man, a tall man, was unloading furniture from the van. Accompanying him were a woman and a teenager."

"It could very well be Lester," said Corey. "Did you get a good look at the man?"

"No, I didn't see him at all. Reno was describing the people to me. I went out the front door, and saw the van, but I didn't see any people from where I was standing. I just went straight over here, never seeing the people."

While Lamar was standing in the doorway, Reno walked up from behind.

"Reno!" said Lamar. "I never expected you to come."

"I just talked to the three people with the moving van. They're our new next-door neighbors. Mrs. Dillman moved out last week, remember?"

"Indeed," said Lamar, "I do remember."

After Lamar and Reno took a seat in the living room with Corey, another moving van came by. This one parked in front of the house. Once again, a man (who was *also* about seven feet tall), a woman, and even a teenager, came out of the van. Corey couldn't be deceived, however. He could tell, by silhouette alone (it was an extremely sunny day), that the man was his older brother Lester. Just as well, the woman *was* Jamie, and the teen *was* Jeremy.

Slowly Corey crept up on Lester, who was too busy talking to his wife, Jamie, to notice his younger brother's presence. Then Corey took Lester completely by surprise, by putting his hands over Lester's eyes.

"C'mon now, you're not fooling me," said Lester. "I know it's you, Jeremy."

"Think again," said Jeremy. "I'm standing here in front of you."

Lester was able to move Corey's hands away, and quickly he caught a glimpse of Corey.

"So, little brother," said Lester gleefully, "do you still remember the last time you saw me?"

"Last time I saw you?" said Corey. "My whole body was in a cast."

"Yeah," said Lester. "To me, you looked like a mummy!"

"I was in a cast all right," said Corey. "Speaking of cast, someday I'd like to be in a cast—of a motion picture! I've gotten to see so many great films over the years, that often I tend to imagine myself in those films."

"I guess seeing all those films for free has helped you greatly," said Jamie.

"Are you ready to come home yet?" asked Jeremy.

"Home? This is my new home," blurted Corey.

"Did you buy this home?" asked Jamie. "Or are you renting?"

"Actually, neither. But i finally got me a woman. We're in love."

"Has she popped the question yet?" asked Jamie, as everyone walked into the living room.

"I—I—" stammered Corey, "don't know."

Corey went into the refrigerator, and took out a six-pack of beer. When he walked back into the living room, he asked if Lester or Jamie (but not Jeremy, who was too young) would like a beer.

"Not today," said Lester. "It might give me flashbacks of thanksgiving night."

"What about that night?" asked Corey.

126

"Do you recall how drunk you got?" asked Lester. "Remember how you had to stay overnight? *And* the fact that it would be the last night you saw our father alive?"

As Lester talked with Corey, Reno walked back into the house, carrying a videocassette in his hand.

"So this is your family," said Reno. "I see they're a lot like you."

"What brings you here?" asked Corey.

"Our VCR's on the fritz. I was wondering if I could borrow Connie's. There's a movie on TV tonight I want to record."

"Could you wait for her to get home?" asked Corey. "She should be here in about twenty minutes."

"Is that when she comes home for lunch?" asked Lester.

"No, she has Tuesday mornings off," said Reno. "She goes to classes on Tuesday mornings."

"What kind of classes?" asked Jamie.

"Dance class," said Lamar. "She can even dance like a certain female pop singer."

"Yeah, yeah, yeah," said Corey. "And to believe that she's *my* woman."

"Is it official?" asked Jeremy, with his eyes wide open.

"I guess," said Corey, "it will be sometime soon."

"I wonder how soon," commented Reno.

Connie came home a few minutes later, about fifteen minutes earlier than expected. She was wondering why a moving van was located outside her house. She walked into the house, and everyone was staring at her.

"You were right," said Jamie. "She is the most beautiful woman I've ever seen."

Even young Jeremy was tempted to let out a wolf whistle.

"Know something, Jeremy?" said Reno, "That was exactly how I reacted when I first saw her."

"So you're the woman in my little brother's life," said Lester. "I'd just love to have you for a sister-in-law."

"Would you even dream of being married to me?" Connie asked Lester.

"Don't say that," grunted Jamie.

"Shall we begin unloading?" asked Lester. "We've got all of your furniture and clothing from the storage space into the van. That, as well as some personal belongings."

"Even my high school basketball trophy?" asked Corey.

127

"Yes, even your high school basketball trophy," said Lester. "Jeremy and I spent about an hour and a half dismantling your bed before we put it into the storage space."

"All for naught," said Corey. "I won't be needing it now. Now I'm sharing a waterbed with Connie. Normally we sleep smoothly, but sometimes we make waves."

"How so?" asked Reno.

"Oh, it was just a little *double entendre*," said Corey. "Nothing too serious."

Everybody started walking outside, toward the moving van. Lester opened the rear door of the van. Corey was astounded, because everything of his that he could think of was there—even most of his clothes, which were inside the dresser. He couldn't see his high school basketball trophy, however, because he didn't know where it was hiding.

"I don't think I'll be needing the dresser," said Corey. "Connie and I also happen to share a dresser. But I *will* need the clothes inside. It occurs to me that I didn't bring along most of my favorite garb, even though my most expensive business suit was what I wore on the train. It got slightly soiled in the wreck."

"Slightly?" asked Connie. "It cost over two hundred dollars to dry-clean it."

Each of the drawers was removed from the dresser. Everyone took at least one of the drawers, brought it into the bedroom, and put it on the floor near the bed. Corey brought in the last drawer, and inside there was something that looked odd. It was something megaphone-shaped, about a foot tall, and it was wrapped in newspaper. Carefully, Corey lifted it out of the drawer, and started to unwrap it. Indeed it *was* his high school basketball trophy, still gleaming after ten or so years.

"Junior year in high school," said Corey. "I was Revere High School's highest-scoring player, and MVP that year. I led our school to the state championship that year, even though we would lose it to Worcester in a double-overtime nailbiter."

Corey put the trophy in the china cabinet in the living room.

"Anyone for lunch?" asked Connie.

"Yeah, we've got a few minutes," said Lester. "Make it something fast."

So Connie "made" something for lunch—leftovers of last night's spaghetti and meatballs. Just two minutes in the microwave was enough time for a quick lunch, as she said she'd make.

She brought the plate of spaghetti over to the table. It was just enough for everyone. As he sat down at the table, Reno realized that he still was holding a videocassette in his hand.

"I almost forgot," said Reno. "Connie, could I use your VCR tonight? Ours has gone haywire, and on TV tonight is my all-time favorite film, 'Late Night Radio'."

"I remember that film!" commented Corey. "Ken Taylor played the role of a highly controversial radio personality from south Florida. I thought it was an excellent film."

"Wait a minute," Lamar asked Reno. "Ken Taylor. The name sounds a little familiar, but I'm not sure I know exactly who he is."

"He's an actor who looks very much like Dr. Grayer," said Reno. "A few years ago, he used to host *The Top 21 Countdown* on one of the video music channels. He's also slated to star in the soon-to-be-released film version of *Sibling Riflery*."

"I remember that book," said Jeremy. "It's the first in a ten-volume series chronicling the goings-on of two families in Sangamon, Maryland."

After finishing lunch, Lester decided that his family would need to get back home before dark. Without too much ado, and not many words spoken, Lester, Jamie, and Jeremy got back into the van and were on their way back to Boston.

That afternoon, about the time Lester arrived at home, Corey realized that he had forgotten to ask his brother one rather essential question: How has the Exbrook Cinemas sale come along? Corey was still wondering just how much he would profit from the sale, and even if there was any sale at all. During his temporary stay in Sellecca Valley, which now was extended indefinitely, such troubles left Corey in a daze, wondering when it would all end, and he'd live his seemingly fairy-tale life happily ever after.

Around the house, things were back to normal. Connie was working the afternoon shift at the medical center. Alone at home, with little to do, he just picked up a magazine, trying to find something interesting to read.

Connie didn't come home until after nine o'clock that night. Earlier that evening, Corey had himself just a small sandwich for dinner. When Connie finally got home, Corey was already in bed. He was out cold. (Fortunately, he wasn't unconscious this time.) It was almost impossible for Connie to wake him up. She snuck into her desk drawer, took out a tape measure (the kind used in sewing), and wrapped it around Corey's finger. She had to hold a small flashlight to his finger, and get her eyes extremely close, in order to see what the diameter of the finger was.

R. Jermaine Schex

Amazingly, Corey stayed asleep the whole time. Connie changed into her nighties, laid some of her lipstick on Corey's face, and got into bed.

18

Festival of the Arts

A little over a month had passed since Corey found himself a place that he could call home. Even though he had known Connie for only five or six weeks, it seemed to him as though he'd known her for an eternity.

Now it was the middle of January. The giant pine tree, put up in the living room and decorated ornately and topped with a star, was now stripped of its trimmings, and was lying in the alley by the back gate, waiting for the refuse collectors to turn it into mulch. On the ground in the living room, where there had been empty boxes and wrapping paper left since the 25th day of December, now there was nothing but clean carpet. Furthermore; just a day ago, Corey helped Connie remove the strings of colored lights that decorated the house.

Exactly one week after Connie and Corey exchanged gifts, including gifts of love and other wonderful feelings, came the beginning of the new year. This New Year's Day was a special one for the town of Sellecca Valley. For the first time ever, a college football championship game was played at the University of Pennsylvania at Sellecca Valley. Sponsored by a Pennsylvania-based company that made plumbing fixtures, the game was nicknamed "The Toilet Bowl."

The day was Thursday. Nothing too unusual was going on. Since Connie was working that afternoon, Corey was at home on his own. Normally, he would make himself lunch in the kitchen, and eat it while sitting in the living room. Unfortunately, today there wasn't much to eat in the refrigerator, nor the freezer; even the cupboard was bare!

So Corey decided to go down to the corner, and get himself a sandwich at the local deli. While he was having lunch, he heard two men in the booth next to him, talking about something. What they were saying sounded somewhat familiar to Corey, but he couldn't quite comprehend what they were talking about.

"I just can't wait until Saturday," said one of the men to the other.

"Neither can I," said the other man. "The Downtown Sellecca Valley Festival of the Arts is always an uplifting time for me, too."

"Downtown Sellecca Valley Festival of the Arts?" wondered Corey. "I believe I've heard of it before, but I just can't seem to remember much about it."

It so happened that at the medical center lounge, Connie was having lunch at the same time, with three other nurses.

"Connie," asked one nurse, "will you be at the Festival of the Arts this year?"

"I plan to be there," responded Connie.

"And will you bring your new beau with you?" asked another nurse.

"I most certainly will. Having him with me will make times more special than ever before."

That evening, when Connie came home from work, Corey was there to greet her as she walked in the door, and even for her to "lay some lipstick on" him.

"Do you have any special plans this weekend?" asked Connie to Corey.

"Nothing I know of."

"This Saturday morning, I thought of taking the two of us to the Downtown Festival of the Arts."

"Festival of the Arts?" asked Corey. "Just what is that?"

"Twice each year, on the first weekend in December and the second weekend in April, the town of Sellecca Valley closes down a stretch of Sellecca Boulevard, to hold a street fair."

"I think I remember you telling me about that," said Corey. "You mentioned a town somewhere out west that has something similar."

"Exactly," said Connie. "The city of Tempe, Arizona, has a Festival of the Arts each year along Mill Avenue."

"Connie, you've got me excited already. From all I've heard about the Festival, it sounds like something special."

"Special indeed, for me," said Connie. "This time around, one of the exhibitors is my brother-in-law, Mack Hawkins. Remember him?"

"Yes, come to think of it, I do," said Corey.

"And do you know who else is showing off their wares?" asked Connie.

"Who?"

"Jasmine Grayer. She's a woodcarver."

"Grayer," commented Corey. "Any relation to Dr. Grayer?"

"That's Mrs. Grayer," said Connie. "I met her once before. She's a wonderful person."

"But—something isn't right," said Corey. "I thought you said that the Festival was supposed to be the first weekend in December. But it's the middle of January, now."

"Originally," said Connie, "the Festival of the Arts *was* to have been held in early December, but the train accident occurred just days before the Festival was scheduled, so it was postponed until this weekend."

"I wonder if I'll be haunted by being near the scene of the accident," said Corey, grinning.

A few days had passed; Saturday morning had finally arrived, though not quite with the bang Corey had expected. The day began just like any of the other six days of the week. Around six that morning, Connie and Corey were awakened by the sound of their alarm clock. Since today was Saturday, fortunately, they did not have to wake up immediately. Connie just reached out her fist, pounded on the snooze bar, and she and Corey went back to sleep, if only for a few minutes or so.

Connie found herself awake at about eight, and she woke Corey up, even though his eyes were still red and his vision was slightly blurred.

"Why so early in the morning?" groaned Corey.

"Don't be ridiculous," said Connie. "It's only eight o'clock."

"Eight o'clock on a Saturday morning," said Corey, yawning, "feels more like five o'clock on a Monday morning."

"Well, at least today isn't get-back-to-work day," commented Connie. "Today's the Festival of the Arts."

"Oh, yeah. Now I remember. What time does it begin?"

"It starts at ten, but we plan to be there by eleven or twelve."

"But what about lunch?" asked Corey.

"They'll be serving food there," said Connie. "They usually have plenty of food booths."

The time was now 10:25 a.m. Corey was looking at the festive carnival atmosphere of Sellecca Boulevard. Right then, he wanted to get out and be a part of it; but first, Connie had to find a place to park. "Parking," claimed Connie, "is the one fault I find with this festival."

After driving around for about fifteen minutes, Connie finally found a place to park. Even though it cost three dollars, she was able to park in the parking lot of a nearby shopping center, of which many stores had closed for this special event. (She found what she thought to be a good parking place earlier, on a nearby residential street; unfortunately, there was a fire hydrant there.)

"How much do we pay to get in the gates?" asked Corey.

"Nothing at all," said Connie.

As Connie and Corey walked past the gates into the festival area, the first thing they could see was children—both young and old—on small-scale amusement park rides.

"Just look at those little ones," said Corey. "I wonder if we'll have as much fun as them."

"I think we should," replied Connie.

After walking a block or so, Connie and Corey saw a row lined with tents. Under these tents were various hand-made arts and crafts, some of them made by local talent; some made by artists from elsewhere in the country. Almost any kind of art imaginable could be found—paintings, sculpture, caricature drawing, and much more.

Corey and Connie stood under a tent in which paintings were displayed. The paintings were not of actual objects, but symphonies of geometric forms and color.

"I don't understand," Corey told Connie. "What's the idea of a painting if you don't even know what it's of?"

"It's just one of those things you leave to your imagination," she replied. "It's whatever you make of it."

"These paintings are by a local artist," said Corey. "Not your brother-in-law, Mack, however."

"Uh, oh!" said Connie. "I forgot about him! I have to go find him."

She turned and walked away. Corey, however, stayed behind, and continued admiring the art.

Having no idea where anything was, since the whole area was laid out almost like a maze, Connie began looking at all the booths to find Mack, or any of his works of art.

After strolling through row after row of exhibits, Corey began to feel hungry. He thought he and Connie should stop for lunch; unfortunately, she was nowhere to be seen. Rather than wait for her to get back, Corey headed to the area where food was being served. Just like the art exhibits, there were rows of tents and trailers here as well. Many different types of fast foods were served. One tent was serving corn dogs and chili dogs. Another was serving tacos. There were also places serving Greek gyros, Chinese delicacies, barbecued ribs and beef sandwiches, and much, much more. Decisions, decisions. Corey felt hungry indeed, but having to make a decision made him feel hungrier than ever.

After a few minutes, it got to where he could no longer take it. At that moment, Corey stood in front of two different booths, one peddling Indian fry bread, and the other was selling sausage sandwiches. First, Corey ordered a fry bread with powdered sugar on top. That may have been a simple decision, but he still had to mull over what to get at the sausage sandwich booth, which had three types of sausage—bratwurst, *polska kielbasa*, and Italian sausage. Corey finally decided on Italian sausage, since he was fond of Italian food, especially at Colletto's Restaurant in Boston.

Now the problem was finding a place to sit. As expected, there was quite a crowd that day, making seating harder to come by. Fortunately, he spotted a vacant seat at a picnic table. He started to eat his fry bread, getting powdered sugar all over his face and shirt. Then he started on his Italian sausage sandwich.

"Is that Italian sausage?" asked a passer-by.

"Yes, it is," said Corey.

"Mild or spicy?"

"I decided to go for the spicy. The booth's over there," Corey told the passer-by.

After his lunch, Corey needed to go to the bathroom. "Where are the restrooms?" he asked himself. Not far in the distance, he could spot a row of turquoise-colored fiberglass booths. One by one, he looked at the doors on the booths, many of which were occupied. "That's strange," thought Corey. "If these are outhouses, why isn't there a crescent moon on the door?"

After finding one that wasn't occupied, Corey went inside and did his business.

"Phew! Never go into one of those again," he commented on his way out.

Onward Corey went. He decided to see if there was anything truly different at the festival, especially if he'd never seen anything like it before. One thing he came upon was a circus juggler. He also saw a clown making animals with balloons. To Corey, the festival was essentially a circus without the tent. (Or even the three rings, for that matter.)

Although Corey hadn't paid much attention, all the while there was music playing. At one site was a reggae band. Under another tent, an African steel-drum band, who came from Seattle, was playing. A few yards away, a New Age musician was playing, on an electronic keyboard. New Age music, thought Corey, sounded somewhat familiar, since it was like the music he became used to hearing over the speakers at the medical center.

"The medical center," thought Corey. "That reminds me—Where's Connie?"

Corey began searching frantically for her.

"That dirty rat!" he mumbled. "Why would she leave me here alone? Is she makin' love to other men?"

Corey was walking down every street and walkway within the Festival area, not quite knowing where he'd find Connie. Since he'd just remembered that she went to find her brother-in-law Mack, Corey thought maybe he should also look for Mack, whose shoulder-length hair should give him away.

"Corey?" he heard a familiar male voice call out to him. As Corey turned around, he saw a familiar face indeed—the face of Dr. Kendall Grayer.

"What are you doing here?" Corey asked Dr. Grayer.

"I decided to look around, see what's out here, maybe even get away from Jasmine?"

"Jasmine? You mean your woman?"

"Exactly. She's an exhibitor this year. She's a woodcarver."

"Oh, yes, I remember. Connie told me about her. Say, have you seen Connie anywhere?"

"I haven't even looked," said Dr. Grayer. "I didn't come here to chase down nurses."

"So let's go find her," said Corey. "Let's *cherchez la femme*."

"By any chance," asked Kendall, "have you seen Jasmine's wood works?"

"I don't think I have," answered Corey.

Corey and Kendall went to see Mrs. Grayer's artwork. Even though they looked hard, they could not see Connie anywhere.

When Corey saw Mrs. Jasmine Grayer at her booth selling wood carvings, right away he asked Kendall if that was the booth indeed.

"Is that it?" exclaimed Dr. Grayer. "Does this woman look like my better half? Of course she does!"

"Is this Corey Ex—" Jasmine started to ask.

"Shhh!!!" Corey told her. "I don't want anybody to know it's me."

"I couldn't blame you, since you're soon to be a—" Mrs. Grayer continued to say.

"Don't say that either!"

"At least I know who you are," said Jasmine, "since Kendall told me all about you. How's it going with you and Connie?"

"By the way," asked Kendall, "have you seen her anywhere?"

Corey was handling a sculpture made by Mrs. Grayer. To him, it looked like heaven only knows what. He started to giggle.

"What're you laughing about?" asked Dr. Grayer, also starting to giggle.

"What does this look like to you?" Corey asked Kendall.

"It was just something I dreamed up," said Jasmine.

"Well, could either of you help me?" asked Corey.

"Help you with what?" asked Dr. Grayer.

"Help me find Connie."

"You might want to try a lost children booth," said Mrs. Grayer.

Corey went toward a lost-children booth near one of the entrances. Surely he figured that Mrs. Grayer was only speaking in jest. Nonetheless, he knew that anywhere he went, he could always expect the unexpected.

As he stared out into space, he felt a little shiver as a woman walked up next to him. To Corey, there was something familiar about the curves of her face, and her hairstyle, but it was her earrings that made Corey do a double-take. Familiar indeed were the earrings, which were ring-shaped, and about five inches in diameter.

"C-C-Connie?" he asked this familiar-looking woman."

"Corey? Where were you?" asked this woman, who in fact was Connie R. Yeltaw.

"Whaddya mean, 'Where've I been'? Where've *you* been?"

"I've been looking all over," said Connie. "But not for you, however. I was looking for Mack. It turns out that he's not here today; he should be here tomorrow afternoon."

"Will you be bringing me here again tomorrow?" asked Corey. "I sure had a good time today, even without you standing next to me."

"But do you have a good time even when you *are* with me?" Connie asked Corey.

"Always," answered Corey. "I don't think I've ever really had a bad time with you around."

The sun was beginning to set. Connie and Corey felt that it was getting late, and that they should be getting home.

"Do you remember where you parked?" asked Corey.

"Yes," said Connie, "I parked in the shopping center, in front of a camera shop."

"I don't know why I remember that," said Corey, "but somehow I just do."

Connie and Corey went to the shopping center where they'd parked, and drove home.

The next morning, Connie and Corey were awake at seven o'clock, all prepared to go to the festival, even though the festival grounds would not open for another three hours. After breakfast, Corey heard a knock on the door. He opened it, and Mack Hawkins, the brother-in-law Connie had been searching for so frantically the day before, was standing at the door.

137

"I—remember you," Corey told Mack. "You're Connie's brother-in-law, the *artiste*."

"Come on in, Mack," Connie told him, from the back of the living room.

"Actually, I can't stay here for long," said Mack. "I've got to get going. Joanna and I have to get to the festival grounds in less than thirty minutes."

"Could you tell me something?" asked Connie. "Do you know of any good parking places nearby?"

"I could help you out on that," said Mack. "Actually, Joanna could. She said she'd take you and Corey. She'll be over here about ten o'clock. And parking will be no hassle, since she has a permit to park in the exhibitors' parking lot."

Later that morning, Connie's sister Joanna arrived, and drove Connie and Corey to the Festival of the Arts. After parking her car in the exhibitors' lot, Joanna went with Connie and Corey directly to where Mack's exhibit was set up. Along the way, they were observing various displays—sand sculptures, stained glass, batik, tie-dye, a caricature sketch artist, and even a display of clocks with unusual faces.

"Well, Corey," asked Mack, "has Connie walked away and left you today?

"I wouldn't let her," Corey replied. "I intend to take her with me everywhere I go today. And I've gotta be extra careful, since last night I almost got the hots for Jasmine."

"Jasmine?" asked Joanna.

"Jasmine Grayer," said Connie. "She's the wife of Dr. Kendall Grayer, the man who treated Corey at the hospital."

"Actually," interrupted Corey, "it was not the old shoemaker himself, but his two little elves, Lamar and Reno."

"Have you had much to eat?" asked Mack.

"Yesterday," said Corey, "I had an extra-spicy Italian sausage sandwich. Since it was so good, and I still have a little extra money, I'll have one more, later today."

"Oh, that reminds me," said Connie, "I've finally made up my mind. I've decided to buy one of your works, Mack. I'll take that one on top, in the left hand corner."

Connie handed Mack an almost-like-new hundred-dollar bill, to buy the painting, which cost $75. "Few businesses," she commented, "take $100 bills, but do you?"

"Yes," said Mack, "I'll take a photo of Ben Franklin, for a painting that costs a Ulysses S. Grant, an Andrew Jackson, and an Abraham Lincoln."

After Mack handed Connie the painting, Connie put it into a shopping bag.

"Thanks, come by again," Mack told her.

"Wanna do lunch right now?" Corey asked Connie as they walked away.

"I'm not so certain I know exactly what I want," said Connie. "There's so much here."

"As for me—" said Corey.

"Yes, another spicy Italian sausage sandwich."

"Yeah, but this time with the works!"

"I just don't know," said Connie. "My stomach couldn't take that. I don't see how yours could. I'll just have something simpler."

19

See Appendix for Details

"Connie," said Corey, while he was standing on a stepladder with the artwork they had bought at the Festival of the Arts about a week and a half before in one hand, and a claw hammer in the other, "hand me a one-inch nail."

Connie reached into the box of nails she was holding, and gave Corey a nail. After giving him the nail, she gave him a stroking on his hand with the nail of her right index finger. (She was wearing fake nails.)

"And," said Corey, "could you hold on to the picture while I'm up here? I only have two hands, but need three to do this job."

"Hold the picture?" Connie exclaimed. "I'd rather be holding you, touching you, squeezing you tightly, laying some lipstick on you," she said with a silent giggle.

"Oh, Connie, you've got all the time in the world for things like that," said Corey. "I just want to do all those things to you too."

"Even the lipstick?"

"Well, not quite."

With eight pounds of the hammer, performed in perfect 4/4 time, and a steady beat, Corey had driven a nail into the wall. Connie handed him the artwork, which he put over the nail.

"How's that look?" Corey asked Connie.

"It's a little off on the left side," Connie answered.

"Now what?" asked Corey, after making an adjustment.

"Too far right," Connie said in response.

"Now is it perfect?" asked Corey.

"Perfect '10'," said Connie. "Couldn't do any better."

"So you think it's a 'perfect 10'," said Corey. "I don't think I could call you that."

"Why not?" asked Connie. "Am I not the woman of your dreams?"

"Oh yes indeed," said Corey, as he stepped off the ladder. "But you rank more than a '10'; you run far off the scale. You're a million to me!"

"And to me," said Connie, "you're just a bit more than a million."

After the picture was hung firmly on the wall, Corey began to feel tired.

"Oh my!" said Connie. "It's almost ten o'clock. I'm starting to feel tired too."

Corey and Connie went into their bedroom, got undressed, put on their nightclothes, did their business in the bathroom, crawled into bed, made lip contact with each other, turned off their bedside lamps, laid their heads on their pillows, and were out cold in just a few minutes.

The following morning, Connie woke up somewhat early. Something was on her mind, but she just didn't know how to say it. She just sat at the kitchen table, staring into space, refusing to let anyone or anything interrupt her thinking.

But something did interrupt her—the telephone. After only one ring, she ran to pick it up before it could ring a second time.

"Hi-ya, Connie," said the voice on the other end of the line.

"Oh, hi-ya Jevon," Connie replied, since she could recognize her cousin's voice anywhere.

"Have you done it yet?" asked Jevon.

"Done what?"

"The question," said Jevon. "Have you popped it?"

"Not yet," said Connie. "I don't know when the moment's right. I'll have to think about it."

Connie looked up to see Corey coming out of the bedroom, feeling tired, and looking as though he was about to trip, stumble, and fall.

"I have to get off now," she said, "Corey's awake. I kinda want to surprise him with all this."

"Who was that?" asked Corey, after Connie hung up the phone.

"Oh, it was only Dr. Grayer. He told me I don't have to come in until noon today."

Later, Connie made breakfast. As Corey sat down to eat, Connie saw him holding his hand on his stomach.

"Is something wrong? Do you feel sick?" Connie asked Corey.

"Not really," said Corey. "Sometimes my stomach turns when I eat while tired."

After finishing his breakfast, Corey went back to bed, still feeling tired.

"I guess he must've worn himself out when he hung up the painting last night," mumbled Connie to herself after Corey left the room.

While Connie was outside watering the front lawn, Lamar walked up to her from behind, almost frightening her.

"Connie," said Lamar, who startled her so much that she almost squirted him with the hose, "—watch out with that hose! You almost got me."

"Do you need something?" she asked him.

"Yes, I do. What time do you start work today?"

"In about a half-hour," replied Connie.

"Could you drive me to work with you today? My battery is dying, and Reno has left already without me."

"Yes, I'll do it," said Connie. "Just give me a couple of minutes. First, I need to take care of a small task inside."

She went inside while Lamar waited at the door. A moment later, she was back.

"Ready to go?" she asked.

"Ready, willing, and able," said Lamar. "Let's roll."

Just after Connie backed out of the driveway onto the street, Lamar started a conversation.

"How's Corey doing today?" Lamar asked Connie.

"Oh, he's all right, just a little tired," said Connie. "I guess he overworked himself last night."

"Doing what?"

"The simple, trivial task of hanging a piece of art on the wall."

"Are there any plans in your future?" asked Lamar.

"Oh, yes," said Connie. "Hopefully, we'll go all the way."

"Whoa! You're that serious?" asked Lamar.

"That serious and more," said Connie. "And now, I'm just waiting for the right moment to present him a special surprise."

"And what could that be?" asked Lamar.

"It's a surprise. I couldn't tell you even if I would—or is that wouldn't tell you even if I should? Whatever."

"Thanks for the ride," said Lamar, as he and Connie walked into the medical center entrance. "Hopefully," he continued, as they went to the front desk, "my chauffeur will take me back home this evening."

"Your chauffeur?" asked Connie.

"Yes, there he is right there," said Lamar, pointing directly to Reno, who was walking out of Dr. Grayer's office.

"You mean—" said Reno, as he was walking up to Connie and Lamar, "I'll be driving you home tonight?"

"I guess so," said Lamar. "Connie had to bring me here today, since my engine wouldn't start. But I don't quite feel comfortable, since you drive rather aggressively, going almost over the speed limit, braking suddenly, and making wild right turns."

"If it makes you feel better," Reno told Lamar, "you could drive. Here," said Reno, passing his key ring to Lamar.

"Oh, two more things," said Reno. "Long as you two are here, I might as well tell you that Grayer is treating us to dinner on the night of January 30. He's inviting you, Connie, and Corey."

"Aw, how thoughtful!" said Connie. "That's my birthday. And it sure beats staying home, and not doing very much."

"One more thing, Connie," Reno said. "Dr. Grayer just told me that you don't have to come in until noon today. He tried to call earlier this morning, but your line was busy."

Connie was flustered. Indeed she had only *joked* with Corey, when she said she wouldn't have to work until noon that day, only to discover that she was really telling the truth all along. What the heck, she figured. If Corey were to awake by the time she got back home, she could just say that she had some kind of errand to run, or could muster just about any other excuse.

When Connie walked into her front door, she saw Corey sitting on the couch, trying to stay awake.

"Corey," said Connie, "I was just talking to Dr. Grayer. He's invited us to dinner on Friday night, for my birthday."

"Oh yeah," said Corey, "I remembered. The thirtieth of January. Where are we going?"

"Dr. Grayer hasn't told me yet. But I should find out soon."

The thirtieth day of January arrived just a few days later. The restaurant reservations were made for six (Kendall, Jasmine, Connie, Corey, Reno, and Lamar) at Chung Dynasty, which is Sellecca Valley's finest Chinese restaurant. (At least, according to a dining critic for a Philadelphia newspaper.)

Shortly after five o'clock that evening, Corey answered the door. It was Lamar and Reno.

"Are you ready to go?" asked Reno.

"I am," said Corey, "but Connie's still powdering herself. She should be out in a few minutes."

Connie came into the living room, and asked Reno and Lamar to come in.

"I don't know if we'll make it tonight," said Lamar.

"Why not?" asked Connie.

"Car troubles," said Reno. "Sound familiar?"

"Yeah," said Corey.

"And this time, it's rather ironic," said Reno, grinning. "Lamar's car is still in the garage, in need of a new fuel pump. Now mine won't start either. I guess car troubles must be some form of communicable disease."

"You can ride with us," said Connie. "We've got plenty of space. And my car hasn't been anywhere near yours, so I don't think it feels ill."

Only minutes later, Connie and Corey arrived with Lamar and Reno at Chung Dynasty, where they found Kendall and Jasmine already waiting.

"This is Grayer, party of six," said Jasmine, "and yes, we're one big, happy family. We have reservations for 6:45."

Everyone in the group started giggling.

"Right this way," said the woman at the counter, as she directed them to their table. After everyone sat down, she handed each of them a menu.

"Ever eaten Chinese before?" asked Dr. Grayer. "It's a truly unique experience. One person orders for the whole family, and the meal is eaten in several courses."

After a moment of discussion, Kendall finally was ready to order. First course was a pu pu platter (that's a Chinese hors d'œuvre tray), and a large bowl of Wor Wonton soup. Following that was an order of mu shu pork. Next came the main course dishes: cashew chicken, kung pao beef, and shrimp lo mein with fried rice.

After everyone had their fill of the first course, the mu shu pork was served. Dr. Grayer, skillful as he was with a scalpel and forceps, found himself able to use chopsticks with no difficulty. Everyone else, however, was dropping everything before they could bring their chopsticks to their mouths; they had to settle for just plain forks, knives, and spoons.

The main course came next. Everyone filled his plate with so much food that no one could see the designs painted onto the plates.

Two-thirds of the way through the main course, Corey asked to go to the bathroom.

Just after Corey got up from his seat and went to the men's room, the other five continued eating and talking. Five minutes later, Connie had something special she wanted to say to Corey.

"Corey," she said, though not looking at where he had been sitting, "I have a special question I want to ask you."

She looked to where he had been, only to find no one there.

"Corey?" she asked. "Has anyone seen my Corey? Where'd he go?"

"Last thing I know," said Lamar, "he asked to go to the bathroom."

"Maybe his zipper got stuck," said Jasmine.

"Either that, or he flushed himself down the toilet," said Kendall.

"I'll go check up on him," said Reno. "Where are the restrooms, anyway?"

"They're on the other side of the building, just by the entrance," answered Connie.

Reno got up, and walked quickly to the men's toilet. Just inside the door, he saw Corey, sitting on the floor, looking down, holding his hands over his stomach.

"Corey?" asked a concerned Reno. "Are you all right?"

"It's my stomach, I think," said Corey. "I heaved up almost all I've eaten tonight, and I feel a sharp pain. And I feel very weak, like I can barely move!"

"This sounds serious," said Reno. "I'd better get you to the medical center right away."

Reno helped Corey get up, and helped him over to the table, where Corey felt so weak that he almost fell down.

"Corey's become terribly ill!" said Reno. "I think it could possibly be food poisoning. I'm going to take him to the medical center for tests."

Reno reached into his pocket, only to find it empty. He'd just remembered that Connie and Corey drove him and Lamar to the restaurant.

"Quick!" he said, "could someone please lend me the keys to your car? We need to get there right away."

"Here," said Connie, handing him her keys, "take mine. But don't wreck it. I've heard about how you drive."

After Reno and Corey walked away, Lamar made a comment. "The way he drives, sometimes I think he should be a paramedic! He might make a perfect one."

In the parking lot, Reno helped Corey get into the passenger seat of Connie's car. Then he got into the driver's seat, started the ignition, and left the parking lot at about thirty miles an hour.

"Will I be all right? Will I make it another day?" asked a frantic Corey.

"Everything will be all right," said Reno, driving at 45 miles an hour. "Just keep calm, don't panic. I'll have you there in no time at all."

Within a few minutes, since the medical center was only four and a half miles from Chung Dynasty, Reno parked in the emergency loading zone of UPSV Medical Center. He helped Corey get in the front door.

"Welcome back," said the receptionist to Corey, since his face was so familiar to her.

"This seems critical," said Reno. "Corey got sick at the stomach, feels sharp pains, and is very weak. Get him into an ER."

After a nurse took Corey away to an emergency room, Reno got back into Connie's car, and headed back to the restaurant, this time driving not so quickly. Ahead of him, going in the opposite direction, he saw Dr. Grayer, driving Jasmine, Connie, and Lamar home. Reno sounded the horn, then made a U-turn to catch up with Dr. Grayer. He speeded up just a little, until he was running just to the right of Kendall. Connie was sitting in the rear passenger seat of the Grayers' car. She and Corey both rolled their windows down.

"Corey's in ER right now," said Reno. "They'll be doing tests on him."

"Just what I feared," said Connie. "What a birthday surprise for me! My man becomes terribly ill, and I must wait impatiently for the results of a few tests."

Kendall and Reno both stopped in the middle of the street, almost like a Chinese fire drill; Reno and Connie got out, swapped vehicles, and Connie drove off in her own car, while Reno rode with Lamar and Dr. and Mrs. Grayer.

"Is it too serious?" asked Lamar.

"He's in emergency," said Reno. "We should know by this evening what's wrong. Hopefully, it's nothing serious."

"Are you a bit frightened?" asked Kendall.

"Not as frightened as the time I saw her cut her wrist," said Reno. "That was a total nightmare!"

In a matter of minutes, the Grayers had dropped Lamar and Reno off at their home, then headed off for their own home.

Sitting alone at home, Connie waited anxiously for the telephone to ring. After almost half an hour, it finally did ring.

"Hello?"

"This is UPSV Medical Center. We've done a test on Corey. We've found the problem."

"What's wrong?" asked Connie, with a shiver in her voice.

"Corey's appendix is starting to become swollen. In another 24 hours, it might burst. Tomorrow morning, we'll need to operate, and have his appendix removed. Tell Lamar and Reno to be here early tomorrow morning."

After Connie hung up the phone, she called Lamar and Reno's house. Lamar answered the phone.

"Hello?" said Lamar.

"Lamar, I just heard from the medical center. You and Reno have to be there early tomorrow morning, about 7:30."

"Is this about Corey?" asked Lamar.

"Yes, it is. His appendix is getting inflamed. You and Reno will need to take it out."

After Lamar hung the phone up, he went into the living room, where Reno was sitting, not doing much of anything.

"Reno," said Lamar, "we need to get to bed early tonight. We have to be in OR at 7:30. We've got an appendectomy to perform."

"On Corey?" asked Reno.

"Yes, it is Corey. His appendix is beginning to swell. It's not too serious at the moment, but may get worse, or even burst, within 24 hours."

20

Cyrano De Exbrook

"B-Z-Z-Z!"

With the sound of her alarm clock, Connie woke up at 5:45. At first, she thought she set it too early, since she was still tired. Then she remembered something about having to be at the medical center by 7:30.

"Corey," she said, reaching over to where he normally slept, "time to get up—Oh my! I just remembered! Corey's to be operated on this morning."

Connie got out of bed, took off her pajamas and put on some "day clothes," and settled down in the kitchen. The first thing she remembered was that Lamar and Reno would do the operation. She thought she'd just go meet with Corey before the operation. Then, she figured, Reno and Lamar would begin the procedure. Wait a minute! How would they get there? Both of their cars were out of commission.

That exact moment, Lamar and Reno were still asleep. Their sleep was disrupted by the sound of the telephone in Reno's bedroom.

"Hello," grumbled Reno in a groggy voice.

"Reno, are you awake yet?"

"What's going on here?" asked Reno, looking at the clock. "It's just barely after six."

"In just an hour and a half," said Connie, "you two have an operation to perform."

"Oh, yeah. Corey. I'll go wake up Lamar."

Lamar was already awake, standing in Reno's doorway.

"Never mind. He's awake already."

"I'll be by in about fifteen minutes to pick you two up," said Connie.

"Oh, yeah, that's right. We've both got car troubles. Gotta get dressed now. Goodbye...."

"Let's get dressed," Reno told Lamar after hanging up the telephone. "We've got to operate on Corey. Connie'll be here in fifteen or so minutes to pick us up."

In a matter of minutes, Connie arrived at the door. Lamar answered.

148

"Are you ready?" she asked. "My car is warmed up."

"Oh, yes. Reno just has to get his shoes on, the we'll be ready to go."

After tying his last shoelace, Reno came to the door.

"We're ready," Reno said. "Let's go."

While driving along the road, Connie made a suggestion.

"Now Lamar and Reno," she said, "take good care of my baby. Make him all well again."

"We'll do everything, whatever it takes," said Lamar.

"Certainly," replied Reno. "Lamar and I work perfectly together. So far, no operation of ours has ever gone wrong."

"How many operations have you two done together?" Connie asked.

"This is only the second one we've done this year," said Lamar. "Last year, we did five."

After arriving at the medical center, Lamar and Reno were sent to the operating room to prepare for the operation. Connie went to Corey's room.

"Corey," said Connie, after she walked into the room. "I just dropped in to see what condition your condition was in."

"I feel a little better right now," Corey responded. "This IV keeps me from feeling starved, since I'm not able to stomach anything right now."

"In just a few minutes, you'll be under the bright lights. Within the hour, your troublesome appendix will be out," said Connie. "Shall Lamar and Reno begin soon? They're waiting for you in OR number 4."

"They can begin as soon as they're ready," said Corey.

"Anything more you need, before the operation?" Connie asked.

"Yes, one thing."

"What's that?"

"Connie, lay some lipstick on me."

After she finished locking lips with Corey, Connie moved him carefully onto a gurney, and wheeled him down the hallway toward the elevators, where two orderlies were waiting.

"Get this man into OR number 4," Connie told the orderlies. "I'll go with you up to the door."

After Corey was wheeled into the operating room, he saw Lamar, Reno, Dr. Grayer (who was supervising the operation), and one other doctor waiting for him. The other physician was Benson Christoph, a resident anesthesiologist. Benson snapped a mask over Corey's nose and mouth, and turned on a tank. Within minutes, Corey was out cold.

149

As the surgery was underway, Connie decided to leave for a short while, since she had a little shopping to do. The first place she went was Keystone Jewelers, a jewelry shop located just blocks from the medical center.

"May I help you?" the man behind the counter at Keystone Jewelers asked Connie.

"I need to order a pair of rings. I've found my new love."

"What sizes are your fingers? And his?"

"Just a minute. Let me look," said Connie, flipping through some slips of paper she was holding. She finally found the piece of paper with Corey's and her own finger measurements on it.

"Here you are," she said, handing the paper to him.

"We'll have them ready for you tomorrow."

"I'll be here to pick them up. Hopefully, Corey will be with me."

Three full hours elapsed. By now, the appendix which had been bothering Corey became a piece of history. It was fortunate that the appendix was removed before it worsened, or possibly even burst.

Later, Corey was in a regular hospital room, not yet fully recovered from his anesthesia. He finally regained consciousness as Dr. Grayer was checking his vital signs.

"Wh-wh-what? Wh-where am I?" asked a stammering Corey.

"You're back in the hospital," replied Dr. Grayer. "You just had your appendix removed."

"Yeah, and what a time for that to happen. During such a delicious dinner, on such a special occasion as a beautiful woman's birthday. I must have felt just like Connie, during one of her periods."

"She doesn't have periods," said Dr. Grayer. "She has exclamation points. And when she does, she leaves us all in question marks."

Corey tried not to giggle too much, lest his stomach begin to ache again so soon after an operation.

"Is she anywhere around?" asked Corey.

"No, not right now. She had a few errands to run, including a trip to the—" said Dr. Grayer, putting his hand to his mouth, realizing he was about to give away a secret.

"She went where?" asked Corey.

"I wasn't supposed to tell you," said Kendall. "She's holding a little secret she just doesn't want to let you in on—yet."

"I seem to have a little secret of my own," said Corey. "But I just can't seem to tell it, even if I try."

"What is your secret?"

"It's about Connie. I just know I love her."

"That's no secret," said Dr. Grayer. "We *all* know that."

"But I have one little problem," said Corey. "I don't think I've told her enough. And all too often, I just don't know how."

As Corey spoke, Lamar came into the room.

"What is it you don't know how to do?" Lamar asked.

"It's Connie. I just don't know how I should express my love for her."

"Just think of a way," said Lamar. "The words *will* come out, someday, someway."

"Yeah, I might as well take my time," said Corey. "Time's on my side, and I've got plenty of it."

After Lamar left the room, he saw Connie just down the hallway.

"Lamar," she asked, "how'd the operation go?"

"He's awake, and active," said Lamar, "but he shouldn't eat or drink for another hour or so. He was just talking with Kendall and me."

"I guess I'll have to wait a while," said Connie. "I saved something for him from last night."

"What is it?" asked Lamar.

"It's the fortune cookie, from Chung Dynasty," said Connie. "I just can't wait to hear what it says on it."

"Likewise, I saved Reno's," said Lamar. "I just can't wait either."

"By the way," said Connie, "you doing anything tomorrow afternoon?"

"No. Do you have anything planned?"

"Yes, I do. I need you to come with me to Keystone Jewelers. Remember, your name is Corey Exbrook."

"Why am I Corey?" asked Lamar.

"You'll have to be his proxy, since he won't be able to be there when our rings arrive tomorrow."

"Couldn't you just take Dr. Grayer? He looks more like Corey than I do."

"I don't think Jasmine would like that," said Connie. "And besides, they know the Grayers very well at Keystone Jewelers. That's where they bought their wedding rings."

"I suppose, I could go along with this," said Lamar, "but just give me back my own name after we leave."

Connie went into Corey's room, where she saw Dr. Grayer at Corey's bedside.

"How's my dear little Corey doing?" asked Connie.

151

"I'm a 'dear little' better than I was yesterday," answered Corey, "But I don't feel very talkative today. I need a little rest."

"I suppose," said Connie, "I'll let you rest. I'll be back tomorrow afternoon, after I return from K—"

"You're keeping a secret from me, I just know it," said Corey. "Grayer almost gave it away too, stopping himself at just the right moment."

"I'll come back with another surprise for you," said Connie. "You just might love it."

"Connie," said Corey, "lay some lipstick on me."

"Good night," said Connie, after the goodbye (or was it possibly a goodnight?) kiss. "I'll be back tomorrow afternoon."

"Good night? It's not even evening yet!" said Corey.

"Well, I'd like to get it in a little early, since I won't be with you when the night comes in."

"Will you be all right without me tonight?" asked Corey.

"I should do perfectly," said Connie. "Jasmine and Joanna will be coming over tonight for dinner."

"What about Mack, and Kendall?" asked Corey.

"It's—a woman thing, no place for 'Y' chromosomes."

"Except," said Corey, "for the chromosomes of Miss Y, as in Yeltaw. Soon, you'll have a new 'X' chromosome—as in Exbrook."

The next afternoon, Connie met with Lamar at the hospital cafeteria.

"Lamar," asked Connie, "are you ready to go yet?"

"Yes, and I remember that now I'm supposed to be Corey."

"Let's go," said Connie.

"All right, just let me get into regular clothes."

Within minutes, Lamar came back, wearing civilian attire instead of the aquamarine surgical uniform he had on minutes before.

"Ready to go," said Lamar. "Let's get going!"

As Connie was driving Lamar to Keystone Jewelers, Lamar was asking her just where she came up with the idea of having him pose as Corey.

"I just thought," said Connie, "that I should bring Corey with me, since this is for the two of us collectively. But in his absence, I needed someone to fill in his shoes—and what difficult shoes to fill!"

When Connie and Lamar stepped out of the car, parked in the lot at Keystone Jewelers, she reminded Lamar that now, for the time being, his name was Cornelius Vanderbilt Exbrook.

"Oh, hello, Connie and —" said the jeweler as Connie and Lamar walked in.

"Corey," said Lamar. "Cornelius Vanderbilt Exbrook, in full."

"Here they are," said the jeweler, taking two ring boxes out of the safe underneath the counter.

Connie and Lamar took a look inside the boxes at the rings.

"They're perfect," said Lamar. "Just what we were looking for."

"Aren't you going to try them on?" asked the jeweler.

"We'll wait until wedding day," said Connie.

"Sounds like a good idea to me," said the jeweler, while Connie handed him her credit card.

Lamar and Connie walked out into the parking lot, hand in hand, as if they were Corey and Connie in reality.

"All right now," said Lamar, "could I have my own name back, now that this little affair is over?"

"Very well, *Lamar*," said Connie. "Just remember, you must not tell Corey about this."

"And Connie," Lamar told her, "keep those rings very well hidden."

"Yes, I will. I'll keep the rings where Corey wouldn't even think of looking for them."

When Connie and Lamar returned to the medical center, Connie put the rings into a hidden "secret compartment" within her handbag, and then she gave Lamar the ring boxes.

"Quick! Hide these!" Connie told Lamar. "Those boxes are a dead giveaway."

"No need to worry about that now," said Lamar. "Corey can't see us from here. His room is clear on the other end of the building. I'll just put them in my glove compartment."

"How could you?" asked Connie. "You didn't drive today, remember?"

"Then I'll put them in *your* glove compartment," remarked Lamar.

"No good," said Connie. "Corey'd most surely find them there."

"All right then, I'll just put them in my jacket pocket, and hold on tight," said Lamar.

Connie went back to her nursing duties, while Lamar went to Corey's room, with the ring boxes well hidden. When Lamar came in, Reno was with Corey.

"How's Corey doing?" asked Lamar.

"He seems to be all right," said Reno. "I only got here a few minutes ago. Dr. Grayer dropped me off at the garage to pick up my car. I'll take you home today."

"You worry me," said Lamar. "I've seen how you drive."

153

"Don't be so silly," said Corey. "Reno's an excellent driver. He got me to the medical center with time to spare."

"Where were you and Connie?" Reno asked Lamar. "I heard that you two went somewhere together."

"I asked her to take me to the bank," said Lamar. "I needed to get something from my safe-deposit box."

"What was it?" asked Corey.

"I can't tell you," said Lamar, who had his hands in his pockets, just to make sure the ring boxes stayed hidden.

"Just as I thought," said Corey. "She's keeping secrets from me. I guess I'll have to find out the hard way."

Hours later, as the evening was about to begin, Reno was driving Lamar and himself home.

"Were you two really at the bank?" asked Reno.

"No, not really," said Lamar. "She and I were at a jewelry shop. She passed me off as Corey."

"So it's official?" asked Reno.

"I believe so," said Lamar. "Right now, however, Corey has a real problem."

"Yeah, I know," said Reno. "Dr. Grayer was telling me all about it. Corey just can't find the words to tell her he loves her. But we know, we just know, that he does."

That evening, after having had dinner, Reno was wondering if, and exactly how, he could help Corey express his love. He figured that maybe someone experienced with love, someone who has loved the same person for years, would be the best help he could get. The first couple that came to mind were the Grayers, who had celebrated their tenth anniversary less than a year ago. Without another word or thought, Reno made a beeline for the telephone.

"Is the doctor in the house?" asked Reno, as soon as he heard a voice on the other end of the line.

"He's working late tonight; this is his wife, Jasmine. May I take a message?"

"Oh, hi-ya, Jaz. This is Reno. Could you help me?"

"Oh, yes, Reno. My husband thinks very highly of you. What could I help you with?"

"It's Corey. He has problems expressing his love."

"Really? The *poet laureate* of Sellecca Valley, nonetheless, just can't find the words?"

"Yes, now that he's hospitalized, he certainly has plenty of time to think it over. But it's burning holes in his mind. Do you have any ideas?"

"Well," began Jasmine, "he could try a love letter."

"But the words won't come out. And physically, he's a little worn out. I think I could write one for him, however.

"Reno, that sounds good," said Jasmine. "I think I might try that myself, just like my own personal hero—other than Kendall—Cyrano de Bergerac."

"Cyrano *who*?" asked Reno.

"In a nineteenth-century French play," said Jasmine, "Cyrano de Bergerac was a Pinocchio-nosed swordsman who wrote love letters for a friend of his, to help his friend woo a beautiful woman."

"Well, get right to it," said Reno. "And I just might try one myself too. Goodbye."

While Reno had been talking to Jasmine, Lamar was in the room, listening to what Reno said. Lamar slipped out of the room and into his own bedroom, sat down at his desk, and tried to compose yet another love letter—one of his own. Reno, of course, did not know that Lamar had been listening.

Within the course of one hour, both Lamar and Reno had composed their own love letters, both being certain to sign them with the name Corey Exbrook instead of their own names.

As Lamar came into the living room, he saw Reno put his cap and jacket on.

"Going somewhere?" asked Lamar.

"Well, I've got a letter to mail," said Reno.

"So do I," said Lamar, handing Reno the love letter that Lamar had just written. "Mail this one too."

"Your pleasure," said Reno, taking the letter from Lamar. "I'll mail that one too—three, four, five, six...."

Lamar started giggling. Reno, without ever looking at the letters, went to a mailbox a block away to mail the letters.

The next afternoon, Connie came home for lunch, finding not one or two, but *four* letters in the mailbox addressed to her. She brought the letters, unopened, with her back to work, where she planned to read them to Corey.

When she came to Corey's room, she found Kendall, Lamar, and Reno already there.

"What's going on?" asked Lamar.

"It's Corey. He sent me four love letters in one night."

"Well, read some of them," said Reno.

Connie opened one envelope.

"I could tell you I love you," said Connie, reading from the letter, "but I don't know it that's enough. I just wish there were 86,401 seconds in a day, since I spend 86,400 seconds a day thinking of you."

"Eighty-six thousand, four hundred," interrupted Dr. Grayer, "is sixty seconds, multiplied by sixty minutes, times twenty-four hours."

Connie opened two more letters, reading a few passages from each. One of the letters featured the line that Connie remained Corey's power, his pleasure, and his pain. (Whatever that meant.) The other said that if Connie was a dream, Corey would never want to awaken.

"Well, what do you know? I've suddenly been bitten by the poetry bug," said Corey. "Now, Connie, read that last one."

When she opened the envelope and took the letter out, she gazed in suspicion at the upper left corner.

"Something's wrong here," Connie told everyone. "This letter has initials other than Corey's. The monogram 'RJS' appears on it. Reno, are those not *your* initials?"

"Yes they are. Corey actually did not write a single one of those letters. I wrote that one."

"Right," said Corey. "It all started hours after the operation, when I told Dr. Grayer that I just couldn't think of a way to say I love you—and I really do."

"Then," said Dr. Grayer, "after you and Lamar left, Connie, I told Reno. That first letter you read, I wrote it myself in my office last night."

"And the second letter," said Lamar, "was mine. I overheard Reno talk on the phone about love letters."

"Then who wrote the third?" asked Connie.

"Jasmine," said Reno. "When I talked to her on the phone last night, she suggested the love letters, getting the idea from some play about some French swashbuckler, I believe Cyrano was his name."

"Then," said Kendall, "after she got off the phone with Reno, Jasmine phoned me in my office. It sounded like a good idea, so I followed through on it."

"Now I know," said Corey, "that at least I have a way of expressing myself, through those resonating words, 'Connie, lay some lipstick on me'. However, the real way to say I love you is without words. It's all in my thoughts and actions."

"Corey," said Connie, reaching into her handbag, "take this. It's the fortune cookie from Chung Dynasty. Tell us what it says."

Corey took the little paper slip from the fortune cookie.

156

"You will find you new love," said Corey, reading his fortune. "And indeed you have a way to express your affection," he added.

Everyone laughed.

21

Unexpected Guests

It was only the fourth day Corey had been at the UPSV medical center since his appendix almost burst; fortunately, it would also be his last, because Dr. Grayer was releasing him at noon that day. To Corey, just like anyone else lying in a hospital bed that long, four days seemed more like four months, or maybe even four years.

A minute or two before eleven that morning, a man with a three-piece business suit and a leather attache case knocked at the front door of Lamar and Reno's house. Lamar, who was the only one at home, answered the door.

"Is this the home of Corey V. Exbrook?" asked the man.

"He doesn't live *here*," said Lamar. "His home's around the corner, at 13059 South Hermosa. You picked a good time to meet with him, since later today, he should be released from the hospital."

The man gave Lamar his business card. "About what time," he asked Lamar, "should I try to reach him?"

"I heard that he should be released sometime around noon today," said Lamar. "You might want to try sometime about one or one-thirty."

"I will," said the man. "I'll go back to my motel room and have lunch."

At noon, at the medical center, Dr. Grayer signed the paperwork to release Corey, while Reno was standing by.

"Reno," said Dr. Grayer, "take Corey home."

"Does he have his key?" asked Reno.

"Right here," said Corey, taking the key from his pants pocket.

"Now remember," Dr. Grayer was telling Corey, "you need a little extra rest today, and don't overfill yourself."

Once again, Reno found himself as Corey's chauffeur. It was too bad, Reno thought, that he couldn't have a regular job of driving Corey around. Just imagine the tips he would earn!

Corey was riding in the passenger seat of Reno's car, yawning, and stretching as far as the shoulder belt would allow. "I feel so tired," he told Reno. "I could just lean over and fall asleep."

158

"Yeah, right," said Reno, "except that a shoulder belt is holding you upright. If you were to lean over, your head would be pressing down on my right knee, causing my foot to hit the gas harder; even worse, I wouldn't be able to lift it off."

"Felt almost like that," said Corey, "when you took me to the hospital that night. You're not going *that* fast now, anyway."

"No, we're in no real hurry. We'll just take our time," replied Reno. "Let's take the long way home."

After taking the long way home, Reno pulled into Connie's driveway, and dropped Corey off.

"If you need anything," said Corey, "I'll be in bed. I really need the rest."

"Good night—I mean—oh, whatever," said Reno, not certain what expression to use at that time of day.

After Corey went inside, Reno backed out of the driveway, and headed for home, where Lamar was waiting for him.

"He's back home now, and so am I," said Reno. "He feels like sleeping right now, and right now I feel like lunch."

"I'll set out some cold cuts," said Lamar. "In a few minutes, Lamar's Deli will be open for business."

While Lamar was in the kitchen, Reno heard a knock at the front door.

"Lester?" asked Reno, thinking he recognized the face.

"Yes," said Lester. "How's Corey doing now? I heard he's in the hospital again."

"He *was*," said Reno. "He's back home now."

"I'll go over there," responded Lester, as he turned and walked away. Just then, Reno remembered that Corey was taking a snooze.

"Hey, wait!" yelled Reno out the door. Too late. Lester was gone.

By then, Lester was already at Connie and Corey's house. He knocked on the door. No answer. He rang the doorbell. Still nothing. Lester thought either that something might be wrong, or that Corey simply wasn't at home.

As Lester walked down the driveway, he was approached by a man with a briefcase—the same man who went to Lamar and Reno's house.

"Is this 13059 South Hermosa?" the man asked Lester.

"Yes, this is," said Lester. "I should know. I was here last month. I came all the way out here from Boston for the weekend. I got worried when I found out that Corey was ill."

"Boston?" gasped the man with the briefcase. "I came here from Denver, in a rental car at that. Are you Lester Exbrook?"

"Yes, I am!"

"I'm Harry Castormeier, of CinemaStar."

"I see," said Lester. "Finally, our moment is about to arrive."

"That's exactly right," Harry said. "I've come with all the paperwork."

"Will all this take a long time?" asked Lester.

"Not really. It shouldn't take too long, just long enough for you and Corey to read the forms, and for Corey to put his signature on the dotted line."

"I'm so relieved, gasped Lester. "I've got to be back in Boston the afternoon after tomorrow."

"You're more fortunate than I," Harry replied. "I need to be back in Denver *tomorrow* afternoon. I have to leave here extra early, to return my rental car, and catch my plane."

After hearing the word "plane," Lester felt a little shiver.

"I sure hope it really is today he gets out," said Lester. "Otherwise, I'll have driven all the way out here for nothing. Now I called the hospital before I left Friday afternoon, and I was told that it should be today."

Harry and Lester looked over their shoulders, to see Connie driving up the driveway.

"Maybe she could help us," Lester told Harry, pointing to Connie.

"Who's she?" Harry asked.

"That's Corey's fiancée," answered Lester. "Her name is Connie Yeltaw. She's a nurse at the hospital Corey was staying at."

"She sure is beautiful," said Harry.

When Connie walked down the driveway toward the front porch, she thought that one of the two men standing by her door looked like Lester. "Just who," she grumbled to herself, "is the other man?"

Connie walked up to the men to take a closer look at them.

"Good afternoon, Connie," Lester said.

"Oh, hi-ya, Les," Connie responded. "Who's this man with you?"

"I'm Harry Castormeier. I'm with CinemaStar. I've come from Denver, ready to close out the business deal of my career."

"And just what might that be?" asked Connie.

"We're about to finalize the sale of Exbrook Cinemas," said Lester. "I'm starting to get worried. I've been waiting here almost an hour, but I've yet to hear anything from Corey. Isn't he supposed to be here?"

"Yes," said Connie. "Reno dropped him off here earlier today. I'll go inside to find him. Come in, gentlemen, and take a seat."

For some reason, Connie thought Corey was in the bedroom, so that was where she went first. Inside she noticed that her bed, which she made that morning before she left, had a log-shaped lump underneath the covers. Gently she laid her hand on this "lump."

"Corey," Connie said softly.

Corey awoke and sat up.

"Hi, Connie. What is it now?"

"There are two men here to see you, one of whom you should recognize. Quickly, get yourself dressed."

"What should I wear?" asked Corey.

"Something—a little businesslike," was Connie's reply.

While Corey was scrambling through his drawers and wardrobe closet for something good to wear, Connie went into the living room, where Harry and Lester were talking with each other.

"May I get you two something?" Connie asked the men.

"Oh, no. That won't really be necessary," said Lester.

"I just had lunch less than an hour ago," replied Harry in turn.

Now fully dressed, Corey came into the living room, where his eyes opened widely after spotting his older brother sitting on the couch.

"So, big brother," said Corey, "what brings you this way? And who'd you bring with you?"

"I'm Harry Castormeier, of CinemaStar."

"So you're the one that my next-door neighbor in Boston, Wally Beasley, told me all about," exclaimed Corey.

"Well now," said Connie, "are you the one making the purchase of Exbrook Cinemas?"

"Exactly," said Lester. "I've been consulting with CinemaStar about the big deal. It's been of major concern to me since the day after."

"The day after what?" Harry asked.

"Thanksgiving," said Corey. "That was when our father had his heart attack."

"Good thing," said Harry, giggling. "We'd been planning a buyout of Exbrook Cinemas ever since 1987. Gordon Exbrook was our only obstacle. Now, Corey, there's only one thing we've been wondering about."

"What might that be?" asked Corey.

"Why'd it take us this long?"

"Actually," said Corey, "it has to do with fate. It was all in the draw of the cards, although the primary cause was fear."

161

"What kind of fear?" asked Harry.

"Flying," said Lester. "Even I have some fear of flying too. It all started nearly a decade ago, when a helicopter collision claimed our mother."

"She was a newswoman, for WCBV-TV, channel 6," said Corey.

"It was a good thing he ended up at UPSV Medical Center, where I'm a nurse," Connie said. "Sitting next to him on the train was my cousin. That was how I really came to know Corey."

"His ride on that train," said Lester, "left me on edge for so long, especially while he was recovering from his injuries."

"Even I heard about it in Denver," said Harry. "The news on Channel 8 even erroneously reported you, Corey, as dead!"

"We came so close," sighed Corey.

"I've never been to Denver," said Lester. "This is really the farthest I've ever traveled most of my life."

"Unlike me," said Harry. "You wouldn't believe where I've been."

"The cities and towns you've been in?" asked Corey.

"From Boston, to Denver," replied Harry.

"And every town in between?" asked Connie.

"Yes, just about every town," said Harry. "I drove all the way to Boston a couple of years ago for the wedding of my brother-in-law."

"And just who is this brother-in-law?" asked Lester.

"Wally Beasley," answered Harry. "He's the brother of my wife."

"Could we just get to the point, and get this over with?" asked Corey. "I still feel a little tired."

"Very well," said Harry, who handed Corey a folder he took out of his briefcase. "Open this up, and read it over carefully," he told Corey.

Corey began to read the paperwork in the folder, scrutinizing what was written as though he were trying to memorize it word-for-word.

"I'm starting to feel just a little road-weary," said Lester.

"Same here," said Harry. "At least this is better than sitting by a hospital bed waiting."

"It's a good thing that Jamie and I bought a beautiful new motorhome," said Lester. "It made *this* trip out here more bearable. It has sleeping quarters, a kitchenette, which neither Jamie or I know how to use yet—even a john."

"Did you come alone?" Connie asked Lester.

"Yes, all alone," he replied. "Jamie had too much work to do today, and my boy Jeremy feels a little ill."

Corey was sitting with the paperwork on his lap, but he wasn't looking at it; he had dozed off in the middle of reading a paragraph.

"Are you asleep?!" asked Connie, shaking Corey by the right arm.

"This is so long and hard," mumbled Corey. "Much of this I really can't understand."

"To put things simpler," said Harry, "turn to paragraph B, page 6."

Corey turned to page 6, and looked at paragraph B.

"I see two options here," he said. "One of them is for one lump sum; the other option seems to be installment payments."

"I'd go for installment payments," said Lester. "That would put you in a lower tax bracket."

"Yes," Harry said, "even I myself would choose that. It would be easier on the wallet, for sure."

"I agree with that," said Corey, as he signed his name.

"Now you are certain about that?" said Lester. "Absolutely?"

"Absolutely," Corey responded. "That way, I'll still have an income thirty years from now."

"Is that it?" asked Harry. "Is your mind made up?"

"Made up completely," said Corey. "I thought over everything without much haste."

Corey gave the folder back to Harry.

"Thank you for your time," Harry told Corey. "Here's my business card. Expect to receive your first check about mid- to late May."

"Why that long?" asked Connie.

"We're in the process of re-organization," answered Harry. "I could discuss it all in detail, but that would take too long. I need to leave around one-thirty, and to catch my flight at two-thirty. Take good care, you three, I hope to see you again sometime."

"It's 1:24 right now," said Lester.

"Oh, my! I gotta get going!" said Harry.

After Harry walked out the door, got into his rental car, and drove away, the telephone rang. Connie went into the kitchen to answer it.

"There is one thing I'm wondering about," said Lester to Corey.

"What's that?"

"Are you and Connie ever getting married?"

"I never thought about it," said Corey. "We've been living together for a while; we just need to get to know each other a little better."

"Do you thing that she can hear you?" asked Lester.

"I doubt it," said Corey. "She's on the telephone, and probably can't hear us. But whenever we do tie the knot, if we ever do at all, you will know. You will certainly know."

"I'll believe it when I see it," said Lester. "I seem to remember not quite a year ago, you said you'd probably be single all your life. You thought that your odds of winning the Massachusetts State Lottery were better."

"Just goes to show how times change, and people too," said Corey. "Take a look at me now. I'm not the same as I was a year ago. I'm the same person, actually; I'm only older, somewhat wiser, and soon, richer."

22

A Night for Remembering

February. March. April. May. Months passed. Seasons changed. It seemed only yesterday when Connie and Corey had to curl up by the hearth just to keep themselves warm on those icy, nippy, Pennsylvania nights. Now, Connie had put her fur—make that *fake* fur—coat on a hanger in the closet. The white drabness that formerly had covered the front yard was now a blanket of kelly green, with flower patches of yellow, red, purple, and other contrasting colors, breaking the monotony somewhat.

This mid-May Saturday morning, Connie, having little to do, decided to sit and relax in the spa in her back yard. Corey, who had just woke up, was looking for her, only to find her in the back yard, sitting in the spa, visible only from the breasts upward.

"Oh, there you are!" Corey told Connie. "I've been looking for you all over! I've never seen you in the spa before—in fact, I almost forgot you even had a spa."

"Oh, yes," said Connie. "I've had this for a while. Usually, I keep it covered during cold weather, which here, lasts two-thirds of a year. Dive in!"

"I'd better not," said Corey. "I arrived in this town very banged-up. A head injury is the last thing I need. Just give me a minute or two to get this all off, and I'll join you."

Minutes later, Corey came back, wearing only a bathing suit. Slowly he stepped into the spa, making certain that the temperature was just right as he settled down.

"Feels so good, this gentle warm water," he told Connie.

"Feels even better when there are two," Connie replied. "I see that you've got your swimming trunks on."

"Do you?" asked Corey.

"No," said Connie, "just my birthday suit. Are you shocked by that?"

"No, not at all," said Corey. "I've seen you that way before, when you get out of the shower, or even the tub."

"I remember the first time you encountered me like this, in the natural state," said Connie. "You were surely in for a shocker."

"I should really think so," said Corey. "I just didn't know what to think. Then again, I didn't actually *see* you that way, since it was so dark. I only felt you."

"That sure felt good," said Connie. "You touched me in all the right places. By the way, I must confess to you that the circuit breaker did not trip that night. I tripped it myself."

"So you planned it all along," said Corey. "You got me into your bed—right where you wanted me."

While Corey was sitting with Connie in the spa, they both looked up, after hearing what sounded like a knock on the door.

"Could there be someone at the door?" asked Connie.

"Sure sounded like it—" answered Corey, as he was interrupted by another knocking sound. "...to me," he continued.

"I'll go get it," said Corey, as he stepped out of the spa, dripping wet. (Quite ironically, he hadn't been in long enough for his skin to wrinkle.)

Wearing only a towel, Corey opened the door. Standing on the other side of the door was the postman.

"Did I interrupt your shower?" asked the postman.

"No, actually, I was in the spa," said Corey.

"I'll need you to sign this," the postman told Corey.

Corey, being careful not to drip, took a pen and signed his name on a card. The postman handed him an envelope. Corey felt that right now was not the moment to look at the envelope, so he hung it on the refrigerator door, went out into the back yard, and rejoined Connie in the spa.

"Who was that at the door?" asked Connie.

"Just the postman, asking me to sign for a letter. I put it on the refrigerator."

"Whom was the letter from?" asked Connie.

"I didn't look at it," said Corey. "The moment just didn't seem right."

"Does tonight seem like a special night to you?" Connie asked Corey.

"I really don't know," responded Corey. "Do you have anything extra-special planned?"

"I don't," said Connie, "but the Grayers do."

"What does the doctor, and his beautiful better half, have planned for us?"

"Dinner. They invited us to their house tonight," said Connie.

"I don't think I've ever been to their house," said Corey.

"You ought to love it," said Connie. "It's a big, beautiful house, but not quite a mansion, even though it's almost decorated like one."

"Are we the only ones they invited?" asked Corey.

"Not the only ones," said Connie. "Lamar and Reno will also be there, as well as Mack and Joanna."

"Must be some really special occasion," said Corey. "It sounds exciting to me already. I just can't wait until tonight."

Late that afternoon, Corey and Connie were in the living room, watching television, when the doorbell sounded.

"Lamar," said Connie, "come in."

Lamar sat down on the couch, between Connie and Corey.

"Connie," said Lamar, "tonight Reno and I were invited for dinner to the Grayers' house. Were you two invited as well?"

"Oh, yes, we certainly were," said Corey.

"Would you like us to take you two there and back?" asked Connie.

"Yeah, we might as well go together," said Lamar, "since this seems to be for all four of us."

"Six," said Connie. "Mack and Joanna were also invited."

Corey jumped up from his seat when he heard the telephone ringing.

"Is Corey far away enough that he can't see or hear us?" Lamar asked Connie.

He is," said Connie. "He's on the phone in our bedroom, at the other end of the house."

"Here," said Lamar, taking the ring boxes out of his pocket. "Get the rings, and put them in here."

"I won't need to," said Connie. "I've wrapped them in a small gift box. And I've kept them well hidden. Corey hasn't seen them yet, I don't think."

"Five," said Corey, as he came out of the bedroom.

"Five what?" asked Lamar.

"Only five people will be coming tonight," said Corey. "Jasmine just told me that Mack is sick tonight, and can't come."

Reno then arrived at the door.

"It's Reno, I just know it is," said Lamar as he opened the door.

"It most certainly is," said Reno. "Ready for tonight?"

"We are, almost," said Corey. "Is there something we're supposed to wear?"

"I'm wearing my Sunday best," said Connie.

"How could you?" asked Lamar. "Today's Saturday."

"We've decided that the four of us should all go together," said Connie. "Who's gonna drive?"

"I think I should," said Lamar. "I guess I'm the one who knows the place best, since I know the way there best."

"Sounds right to me," said Corey, "since I've never been there before."

"I've only been there once before," said Connie, "and that was quite a while ago."

"And I'm too worried about Reno's driving," remarked Lamar. "He goes too fast."

"I do not!" protested Reno, as he and Lamar went toward the door.

"We'll be back shortly," said Lamar. "We're just gonna run home, and get changed."

Some time later, when Lamar and Reno came back, Connie took the envelope from the refrigerator door, put it into her handbag, and left the house with Corey, Reno, and Lamar. Lamar got into the driver's seat of Connie's car (which she agreed to let him drive), Reno took the passenger seat, and Connie and Corey took the rear seat. (Connie remarked, after Lamar started driving, that it was only the first time she had ever ridden in the back of her own car.)

When the foursome arrived at the Grayers' house, Corey started to look around the front yard, which was adorned with several statues and a fountain.

"Only a doctor could afford a home like this," commented Corey.

"Not necessarily," said Connie. "A few years from now, you just might be able to."

When Lamar rang the doorbell, Jasmine opened the door.

"Come on in," Jasmine said. "We've been waiting for you."

In the dining area, under a small crystal chandelier, a table was set with fine china, crystal, sterling silver, and a fine lace tablecloth.

"So is everyone here?" asked Kendall.

"Everyone but Joanna," said Connie. "She didn't come with us."

Just then the doorbell rang. Corey went to open the door.

"Are you Joanna?" Corey asked.

"If I'm Joanna, you must be Corey," said Joanna.

"It should be less than thirty minutes," said Jasmine, "before dinner will be ready."

Without much haste, everyone sat down at the dinner table.

"Just what *did* you prepare for dinner?" Reno asked Kendall, who was sitting next to him.

"We made ham, turkey, and all the fixin's," said Kendall.

"Hopefully, you won't be serving cranberry sauce, or even cranberry pie, or cranberry juice," remarked Corey.

"Got something against cranberries?" asked Lamar.

"Skin rashes," answered Corey.

"That's not that unusual a condition," said Kendall.

"How would you know?" asked Corey.

"I'm a doctor, remember?" replied Kendall. "It's my job. I'm a true professional. I'm the man that Dr. Amos, the dean of UPSV College of Medicine looks up to. I was his best student some twelve or thirteen years ago."

"His cranberry troubles," said Reno, "remind me of a food problem I've had for years. When I was only eight or nine, *long* before I first met my best friend Lamar, I was on a Sunday picnic with my family. The next day, all of my family, myself included, became ill. It was discovered that we all ate tuna-salad sandwiches made with spoiled mayonnaise."

"Sounds like salmonellosis to me," said Kendall. "That's the trouble with mayonnaise. It's made from eggs; therefore, it spoils easily."

"That's why I still say, 'Hold the mayo', even to this very day," said Reno.

"Kendall?" asked Jasmine from the kitchen. "Can you help me get all this on the table?"

Dr. Grayer went into the kitchen. A minute later, he and Jasmine came out with dinner on a pair of silver trays.

"Here everything is!" said the Grayers in unison.

After Kendall and Jasmine set the trays on the table, and took their seats, everyone began to dig in..

As everybody got settled down at the dinner table, Corey began to think that there really wasn't anything all that special about that night's dinner.

"Is there any significance to this special event?" asked Corey. "What's so special about the 24th of May?"

"It's a make-up date," said Jasmine.

"This is because of the cut-short affair of the 30th of January," said Kendall.

"Isn't that your birthday?" Joanna asked Connie.

"Yes it is, as if you didn't know by now," Connie told her younger sister.

"I heard about that," said Joanna. "Corey went to the restroom at Chung Dynasty, but never came back. He must have flushed himself down the toilet, and ended up on the other side of the world, maybe in China."

As Joanna was speaking, Corey quietly got up from his seat, and walked toward the bathroom. Until a minute later, no one really noticed Corey's empty seat.

"I just wonder," said Lamar, "if that will happen again."

"If he is on the throne," commented Reno, "*will* he come back?"

"Unless," said Connie, "he's been abducted by the creature who lives under the sink, behind the shampoo, next to the hair dryer, and to the left of the toilet paper."

Corey came back into the room, and sat down at his place at the table.

"What took you so long?" asked Kendall.

"As I was washing my hands," said Corey, "I was talking to the creature who lives under the sink, behind the shampoo, next to the hair dryer, and to the right of the toilet paper."

"I thought it was the *left* of the toilet paper," said Jasmine.

"There's two creatures," said Corey. "The one on the left tried to abduct me. That's when I slammed the door shut, so *I* wouldn't end up under the sink, behind the shampoo, next to the hair dryer, and to the left of the toilet paper."

Connie looked down into her lap, and started flipping through her handbag. She found where she had the rings hidden, and took a look at the still-unopened envelope. For the first time, she looked at the address and postmark on the envelope. "Who," she thought, "would send him something from Denver?" Then she remembered. It just *had* to be CinemaStar.

"Corey," said Connie, handing him the envelope, "I think this may be of interest to you."

When he saw the Denver address on the envelope, Corey's eyes lit up.

"Is this what the postman brought me this morning?" Corey asked Connie.

"Yes it is," Connie replied.

"It felt embarrassing," said Corey, "to stand in front of the postman, dripping wet, with only a beach blanket covering me."

Corey ran his finger along the flap of the envelope. With a quick zip, he opened it. Slowly, as if to torment everyone, he pulled out a slip of paper from the envelope. After he took it out, he looked at this piece of paper. Without a word further, he handed Connie the envelope, with the slip of paper inside.

"Take a look," Corey said to Connie. "You may find this interesting."

"Whoa!" said Connie, as she looked at the piece of paper.

"Just what is it, anyway?" Jasmine asked.

"It's—a check," said Connie.

"From Exbrook Cinemas," said Corey. "The buyout has officially begun. That was my first payment of many more to come."

"How much is it for?" asked Lamar.

"I can't count that high," said Corey. "I was never good at math. I guess that's why I flunked the college entrance exam."

"Lamar and I were excellent at math and science," said Reno. "That's how we got where we are now."

"So now, what do you have planned for the future?" asked Joanna.

"I haven't had enough time to think it over," said Corey. "Right now, I have no major spending plans, or any plans for the future, be it distant or immediate."

"At least I have plans," said Connie.

"Do any of them involve me?" asked Corey.

"All of them do," responded Connie, as she reached into her handbag.

Corey had absolutely no idea what to make of what Connie had just said.

"Take a look at *this* now," said Connie, as she handed Corey what looked like a ring box.

"I wonder if this is—what I think it is," said Corey to himself just before opening the box.

"Let's see what it is," said Kendall to Corey. "You're killing us with all this suspense."

Everyone gasped after seeing the ring. Connie then showed everyone a matching ring.

"Is it official *now*?" asked Reno.

"Now do you, Connie Rolonda Yeltaw," asked Corey, "take me to be—"

"Indeed I do," said Connie, ecstatically.

The room burst with applause.

"I knew it; I just knew it," said Jasmine. "I just knew that Connie and Corey would exchange vows one of these days. I was right."

"You certainly were," said Corey and Connie together.

"Now the question is if it'll last," said Corey.

"I think it should," said Kendall. "Just more than ten years ago, I, Kendall Taylor Grayer, took the hand of this beauty here, Jasmine Lisa Canning. Almost a decade later, many nights still feel like honeymoon night."

"Connie," asked Corey, "where'd you get those rings?"

"Keystone Jewelers," answered Connie.

"And *when* did you buy them?"

"I picked them up while you were hospitalized," said Connie.

"It's quite a funny story," said Lamar. "Connie and I went together to pick up the rings. Corey, you may not believe this, but I assumed your identity that afternoon."

"But how did you know my ring size?" Corey asked Connie.

"I measured it while you slept one night. Try it on, and tell me if it fits."

"It fits perfectly," said Corey after he put the ring on. "And you fit me just as perfectly."

"To me, this seems like a special occasion, a night for remembering," said Kendall. "Jasmine, get out our fine crystal. I'll go get the wine."

"We're out of wine," said Jasmine. "We drank the last of it ten days ago, at your birthday party. All we have left is sparkling red grape juice."

"Then, we'll just have to make do with what we have," remarked Kendall.

After Jasmine set down a crystal wine glass in front of everyone sitting at the table, her husband Kendall poured sparkling red grape juice into each glass. Both Dr. and Mrs. Grayer then took their seats.

Kendall stood up, with his glass in his hand. "I would like," he said, "to propose a toast, to the Exbrooks, Connie and Corey, and to their continued health, prosperity, and success."

After Kendall finished speaking, everyone stood up and raised his or her glass. As the drinking began, things were soon going awry. After Lamar took his first sip, he let out a burp. Reno couldn't help giggling, so much that he lost his balance and nearly fell from his chair. It was almost like Thanksgiving of the past year, Corey thought. As Jasmine raised her glass to take a sip, she missed her mouth entirely, spilling her juice on her skirt.

"Ugh!" Jasmine said. "Spilling sparkling grape juice doesn't feel good, especially on a white skirt. Next time, Kendall, get *white* sparkling grape juice instead of red."

Kendall set his glass down on the table so hard that the fine crystal broke in his hand.

"Yow!" he said "Maybe we shouldn't have used our fine crystal."

Dr. Grayer went into the kitchen, his hand bleeding. Ironically, Reno, who had seen Connie cut herself and bleed much worse, was totally unfazed.

"Sounds like you and I might get off to a rocky start," Corey said to Connie quietly.

"Yeah, we just might," Connie replied. "But we've got time. We can work everything out."

23

The Longest Two Yards

My, how time seemed to fly, ever since Connie and Corey had announced their wedding plans. Although it was only Saturday, the seventh of June, it seemed more like the 25th of May, fully *one day* after the question was popped.

It was getting late that Saturday night. Corey was sitting with Connie in the living room, watching a movie on television. The film was *Love Story*, a 1970 feature film that had long been a favorite of the Grayers, who recommended that Corey see the film.

After the film ended, Connie and Corey began to feel tired.

"Very intriguing film," said Corey. "Didn't you just love its ending?"

"Sometimes, I just don't get you," said Connie. "How could one just love such tragic endings?"

"When Jasmine called late this afternoon, she told me that the ending was the best part of the film. She and Kendall have seen the film nine times now, including tonight—that is, *if* they were watching tonight, which I think they were."

"It's after eleven," said Connie. "We need to get to bed."

"Why the hurry? Tomorrow's only a Sunday. Do you have something special planned, something I was never told about?"

"I don't know of anything out of the ordinary," said Connie. "Tomorrow is just another Sunday, even though it's the week before the wedding."

"Yes, and I'm starting to feel tired," replied Corey.

Corey and Connie were in their bedroom, changing out of their day clothes, and into their nightwear.

"Just one week," commented Corey. "Somehow it seems to me like one more day. I'll have to get used to the sound of 'Mr. and Mrs. Exbrook'."

"So much in our lives will be changing in just one week," said Connie. "And so much more—things mostly unknown—will happen before then."

Corey was thinking of just what could happen in one week of the life of himself and his beautiful fiancée, while the two of them crawled into bed and turned the light out.

June 8

Somehow it seemed that Corey was awakened abruptly and could not sleep one wink more. Unusual, he thought, since normally Connie awoke first. He was so used to her making breakfast for him, all ready and at the table when he got up out of bed.

"Connie," said Corey, softly, "get up. It's daylight already."

Either Connie was not listening, or she was so fast asleep that Corey's words just drifted off into space.

"Aha!" thought Corey, as an idea just occurred to him. "I'll just make breakfast myself. Won't she just love it!"

Cooking—even breakfast—was nothing new for Corey; quite often in the past, he made full meals for himself when he lived alone, and even after his female roommate in Boston moved in with him. Everyone who even tasted his cooking liked it; no one seemed to fall ill.

After a few minutes of getting himself dusty, and slaving over a hot stove, breakfast for two was finally ready. Amazingly, Connie was still asleep.

Corey came back into the bedroom, to tell Connie that breakfast was ready.

"I don't feel so good," said Connie as she sat up in bed, holding her stomach. "But since you took the time and trouble, I'll come to the table."

Corey and Connie sat facing each other at the table; unlike most mornings, however, Connie didn't feel like saying anything. After eating more than half her meal, she said she felt too tired to eat another bite, and wanted to go back to bed.

"Was it good, anyway?" asked Corey.

"Yes, it was," replied Connie. "Any other morning, I'd have eaten just as though there were no tomorrow."

"Oh, please don't say that. It frightens me. It sounds almost as if my cooking could kill."

Corey continued with his own breakfast. "Not bad," he thought. "I'm still alive. At least I don't think I have food poisoning, or anything of that kind. If cooks could kill...."

As Corey nearly finished his morning meal, he could hear something cacophonous coming from the other end of the house, about where his bedroom was. Corey jumped from his seat, and ran toward his bedroom.

"Connie?" he asked as he went down the hallway. "Did I just hear....?"

When Corey found Connie in the bathroom, leaning with her head over the toilet, Corey was horrified by what he saw inside the toilet bowl.

"Yikes!" Corey shouted. "Are you heaving—*blood*?"

"It sure looks like it," Connie responded in a sick voice.

"This sounds terribly serious. I think we need to get you to the medical center. Something's definitely wrong."

While Connie stood at the john, just in case there was more to upchuck, Corey went to the bedside telephone, looked up the number of Dr. Kendall T. Grayer, and dialed.

"Jasmine?" asked Corey, hearing a familiar female voice on the other end of the line.

"Corey, is that you?" she replied.

"Jasmine, get your husband on the phone quickly. Connie's become terribly ill."

"He's at a board meeting this morning," responded Jasmine. "He'll be at his office shortly after two o'clock."

"I don't know if Connie can wait that long," panted Corey. "She's spitting up blood."

"That does not sound so good!" replied Jasmine, with her voice sounding like the key of B-flat minor. "Since it's so urgent, I'll just give you the number of Lamar and Reno's pager."

Corey stood idly waiting while Jasmine was looking up a telephone number. With his ear still on the phone's earpiece, he looked over his shoulder at Connie, to see if anything was wrong.

A few eye winks later, Jasmine was back on the line. "Their pager number," she said, "is 555-8329."

After Jasmine got off the phone, Corey dialed the pager of Reno and Lamar.

"Just hold on," Corey told Connie, who was sitting on the bathroom floor. "I just paged the two fine young future physicians. I hope to hear from them soon. Do you feel all right?"

"My stomach still hurts, but I don't feel like vomiting at the moment," said Connie.

"You sure gave me a scare," said Corey. "At least my appendicitis didn't make me give off blood."

"I'm a bit frightened," said Connie. "I do believe that something's very much wrong."

"That's what Jasmine told me," said Corey. "Maybe it'll get all better by the time Lamar gets here—or even Reno, or both."

"When will that be?"

"I'll have to wait until they get my page, and call back."

Corey sat, rather impatiently, holding Connie close to him. Finally, Corey heard just what he had been hoping to hear: the telephone. He ran to answer it.

"Is this Corey?" he heard Lamar ask.

"Yes it is. Something here just isn't right."

"Got something going on?" asked Lamar.

"Something very serious, I fear," said Corey. "Something in desperate need of your attention."

"Has your appendix acted up again?" asked Lamar, jokingly.

"Not mine, but maybe Connie's. This morning, I made breakfast, since I woke up earlier—"

"So just what *is* the problem?" asked Lamar.

"She felt too reluctant to eat when I woke her up, and she just couldn't finish more than half her—"

"Just skip the details," said Lamar, "and get to the point."

"Connie later threw up in the toilet," said Corey, "and it came out red."

"Maybe she's just allergic to tomatoes," said Lamar.

"It isn't tomatoes," said Corey. "It's blood!"

"I'd better get there—faster than a rolling 'O,' stronger than silent 'E,' etcetera, etcetera…" said Lamar. "I should be there in a few minutes."

"That was Lamar," Corey told Connie as he hung up the phone. "He'll be over here shortly. Just take it easy; don't panic, and he'll take good care of you. He sure took good care of me, heh, heh."

"I sure hope it doesn't take too long," said Connie, "especially since he only lives just around the block."

"I don't feel so sure," said Corey. "He may not have called from home. He may have been out on the road. But if he was at home, he should be here about—"

Ding-dong! went the doorbell.

"Now," Connie and Corey said together.

Corey went to answer the door.

"Lamar, come on in," Corey said. "Connie's in the master bathroom."

Corey walked down the hallway with Lamar. In the bathroom, he saw Connie sitting by the toilet.

177

"Do you feel all right?" Lamar asked Connie.

"My stomach still hurts, but that may only be temporary. I just don't know when I'll puke again, and if there'll be blood in it."

"This may sound like an odd question," said Lamar, "but did you, by chance, save a specimen of your stomach's contents?"

"Look inside," said Connie, pointing to the toilet.

Lamar lifted the lid and looked directly into the toilet bowl. He stepped back with his eyes wide open, gasping at what he saw.

"This is—not like anything I've seen before," gasped Lamar. "I think we may need to take you in for some tests."

"How long should that take?" asked Corey.

"I really can't say right now," answered Lamar. "I don't even know what condition she has."

"Maybe Grayer might know," said Corey. "He certainly has the experience."

"If only he wasn't at a meeting this morning," grumbled Lamar. "I'll go ask Reno to bring his car over. Is there a phone nearby?"

"Over there," said Corey. "That's the phone from which I tried to reach Kendall, but ended up talking to Jasmine, and paged you from."

"Lamar dialed the telephone, and stood waiting for Reno's reply. "Reno," he said after Reno answered, "bring the car by. We've got to take Connie to the medical center."

"How serious is it?" asked Reno.

"I don't know just what," said Lamar, "but she has been vomiting blood."

"I'll leave right now, without a word further."

Just mere minutes after Lamar hung up, Reno knocked on the front door. Lamar and Corey walked with Connie to the door.

"Ready to go?" Reno asked Connie and Lamar.

"Yes we are," replied Lamar, briskly.

"She's ready," said Corey, "but doesn't seem very eager. I wouldn't seem to be eager to go for medical testing, especially if something was gravely wrong with me, but I had no inkling just what."

"We won't leave you in suspense much longer," said Reno. "By this evening the lab *should* know for certain."

Corey looked out the front window as Lamar and Reno drove off with his woman. He had a whole day ahead of him, all alone, but what was there to do? In the afternoon, he could watch the soap operas on television; his particular favorites were *All My Children*, *Days of Our Lives*, and *General Hospital*.

The morning, on the other hand, was a whole different affair. There was nothing on TV but talk shows and tabloids, neither of which were of interest to Corey. (Neither did Connie care for them, likewise.)

Someone to talk to was all Corey really needed. But whom could he speak to? Lamar and Reno had just gone to the medical center; they took Connie with them. The only other close acquaintance he knew in Sellecca Valley was Dr. Kendall Grayer, but he was at a board meeting.

"Aha!" Corey spoke to himself. "I'll ask Jasmine what she thinks. I guess she's as good as anyone to help me break out of this lonely isolation."

Corey reached for the nearest telephone he could get his hands on. Having recently reached Jasmine on the phone, the number stayed fresh in his memory. (Occasionally, Corey had become a tad notorious for his short-term memory, which seemed rather irrelevant at the moment, since it was only a short "term" ago that he spoke with Jasmine.)

When the dial tone stopped, Corey heard an angelic voice—that of Jasmine. He sighed in relief.

"Jasmine, it's me again," said Corey.

"How's Connie doing?"

"I wouldn't know. Lamar took her to the medical center for tests. Results should be in by this evening. Ho, hum. What a long time to wait."

"Not as long as it was a decade or so ago," replied Jasmine. "I can remember waiting three days and nights for results from a blood test."

"The reason I called," said Corey, "is because I'm feeling all alone, with nothing exciting going on. Much of my life has been that way."

"Just like Milo, from *Phantom Tollbooth*," commented Jasmine.

"One of my all-time favorite films!" commented Corey.

"Mine too," said Jasmine. "Just this past school year, I showed the film to my fourth-grade class. I also like the book, even better."

"You mean, you actually had a full-time teaching job?" asked Corey.

"*Had* is exactly right. I was substituting for a teacher recovering from eye surgery."

"So is substituting the main thing you do?"

"That's just about it," said Jasmine. "It's, well, all I seem to have time for. But at least the pay isn't bad. And I get to meet new people—mostly kids."

"I guess that's my problem," grumbled Corey. "Since I've been here, I just haven't been out much."

"Sometimes I feel that way too," said Jasmine. "But having lived here sixteen years, I've had many opportunities to meet people. That's why I look forward to each year's Festival of the Arts—a perfect chance to meet some new people."

"Are you doing anything today?" Corey asked.

"During the morning," said Jasmine, "I'll have a lot of housework, and I have shopping to do this afternoon. Kendall and I are going out for dinner this evening. Would you like to come with us?"

"That would be wonderful, absolutely wonderful," said Corey. "At least tonight I won't have to dine on Spaghetti-O's."

"After dinner," said Jasmine, "we'll stop by to see how Connie's doing."

"I'll see you two tonight," said Corey. "Until then, I can keep occupied during the afternoon, anyway. I've become somewhat of a soap fanatic."

"Ten years ago," said Jasmine, "just before I got married, I auditioned for a starring role on one of the soaps. Although I was a leading contender for the role, I had to withdraw from contention, because it was too close to graduation day, and even my wedding day as well."

"You just reminded me," remarked Corey. "We're less than a week from my own wedding day."

"Hopefully, Connie will be well enough to be there. We'll probably find out this evening, after dinner."

"Where are we going for dinner?" Corey asked.

"We're going to 9th & Ash," said Jasmine. "Ever been there?"

"Oh yes. I remember them," said Corey. "Connie and I went there a few months ago. It's in old-town Sellecca Valley."

"Exactly. Kendall and I will come by to pick you up at six. I've gotta continue my housework now. Goodbye."

It was still morning. Corey still had nothing to do, but at least his conversation with Jasmine gave him something to look forward to that evening.

Finally, after having a can of Spaghetti-O's for lunch (which originally *should* have been his dinner) and four hours of being glued to the TV set watching the soaps, Jasmine came to the door.

"Gettin' hungry?" she asked Corey.

"My stomach's talkin' to me."

"Well then, let's go," said Jasmine. "Kendall's waiting in the driveway."

Corey slid through the side door of the Grayers' minivan, and Jasmine took the front passenger ("shotgun") seat.

"Do you feel comfortable?" Kendall asked Corey. "This minivan is fairly new. We bought it not that long ago, since Jasmine has volunteered to be a soccer mom next school year."

"How could that be, Jasmine?" asked Corey. "You don't even have any kids of your own."

"To me," said Jasmine, "every kid I teach seems like my own kid."

"That sounds just like Connie, in her normal pediatric work," said Corey.

"I never thought of it that way," said Kendall.

"You two sure do know good restaurants when you see them," Corey told the Grayers. "I really liked 9th & Ash that last time I was there. And it's in the part of town I like best—the old town, and on a street with some of this town's best and most historical homes—Ash Avenue."

"Do you remember what you had last time you were there?" Jasmine asked Corey.

"I'm not certain, but whatever it was, it was certainly good."

After waiting nearly ten minutes in the lobby, the doctor, his wife, and Corey were seated at a table next to a stained-glass window. A waitress handed the three of them menus. Everyone looked at the menus, trying to make a decision.

"What do you think you'll order tonight?" Jasmine asked her husband.

"I'll have the 16-ounce cut of prime rib. Tonight, I could eat that much and maybe more."

"You just reminded me of something," said Corey. "It was when I was in high school. We went to a Mother's Day dinner with my aunt and uncle. My ten-year-old cousin ordered prime rib, thinking he was getting a rack of ribs with barbecue sauce."

"What about you, Jaz?" Kendall asked.

"I'll have the Chicken Cordon Bleu," she responded.

"What's that like?" Corey asked Jasmine.

"It's a breast of chicken, stuffed with ham and Swiss cheese, breaded, and topped with white wine sauce. The name is French for 'blue-ribbon chicken.'"

"I could never *parlez* much *français*," said Corey. "As for me, I'll have the Blackened Cajun Seafood Combo. I can taste it now."

"I hope your stomach's up to it," said the doctor to his two-time patient.

"But I don't think Connie could, if she were here with us this very night."

181

"I don't know," said Jasmine. "Connie really likes Cajun cookin'."

"But with the shape her stomach's in," replied Corey, "she couldn't eat anything today."

Several ticks of the clock later, a waitress took their orders. In the next twenty minutes, she came back with the meals that each had ordered.

Everyone ate dinner, engaging in lively conversation along the way. To avoid grossing others out, no one said anything about Connie's mystery illness. After dinner the three politely declined to have dessert, while Kendall paid for their dinners with his debit card. Then they went to the medical enter, to see how Connie was doing.

"Have you seen Connie today?" asked Corey as Kendall was driving him and Jasmine to the medical center.

"I haven't been to the center today," said Dr. Grayer. "I've been at a board meeting all day. It took longer than I had expected."

The receptionist at the medical center told Corey and the Grayers that Connie was in room 613. In the corridor of the sixth floor, they came upon Lamar and Reno, who were just coming out of Connie's room.

"So how is she?" Corey asked.

"We don't know yet," said Reno.

"The lab results still haven't come back yet," said Lamar.

Corey went into the room, while everyone else came in behind him.

"Connie," said Corey, "here I am. Do you feel any better?"

"I tend to get sharp pains now and then, and I've thrown up once this evening, but I'm all right otherwise."

"So what do you think is wrong?" Corey asked Connie.

"I think there is still a possibility," said Lamar, "that this could be the next new medical discovery."

"Well, whaddaya know," said Reno. "Yeltaw's disease!"

"I don't think that's a good way to be remembered," murmured Connie. "I don't feel comfortable having a malady named after me."

June 9

For the first morning since who-knows-when, Corey slept for an entire night at home with no one else inside. All he could remember from the middle of the night was his dream about reading an article about "Yeltaw's disease" in a medical journal. He couldn't get past the first paragraph, since the rest was all written in medical jargon. He was finally relieved to awaken from the dream, but was still on pins and needles about what Connie's condition was.

After a simple breakfast of a bowl of Corn Pops and two Pop-Tarts, Corey went to a nearby street corner, where he waited for a public-transit bus to take him to the UPSV campus. On campus, he had no difficulty finding the medical center—it was the biggest building.

Corey knocked quietly on Connie's door, lest he should awaken her from her rest.

"Come in," Connie said softly.

"How are you today?" asked Corey.

"Just like yesterday. I wonder if I may be getting worse."

"What about your lab results?"

"I haven't heard yet," said Connie. "I wonder if this just might be Yeltaw's disease, whatever that may be."

Just then, Dr. Grayer walked in with Lamar, Reno, and another nurse.

"We've got it," said Lamar. "Here are our lab results, with some charts we've put together on Grayer's computer."

"Let me ask you something," said Reno. "Corey, what's your sign?"

"You mean—astrological?" asked Corey. "My birthday is February 17; that makes me an Aquarius."

"I'm also an Aquarius," said Connie.

"Yeah, that's right," said Corey. "The thirtieth day of January. What about you, Reno?"

"Being born on October 23, I'm a Scorpio," answered Reno.

"So is Jasmine," said Dr. Grayer. "Her day is November 7. And as for me, a May 12 birthday makes me a Taurus; quite fitting, since I tend to have a bullish outlook on life."

"What about me?" Lamar asked Reno. "December 3, as you ought to know by now."

"You are a Sagittarius, the sign of the archer," Reno told Lamar.

"I'm a Virgo," the nurse said. "But why this lecture on astrology?"

"We've looked over Connie's chart carefully," said Dr. Grayer, "and it reads almost like a horoscope."

"And we've found a very unpleasant sign," said Lamar.

"What's that?" asked Corey.

"Cancer," said Reno, straightforwardly.

"Cancer?" Connie shrieked.

"That's exactly right," said Dr. Grayer. "Connie, you have cancer."

"Where?" asked Corey.

Dr. Grayer set up an easel on the floor across from where Connie's bed was. Lamar placed a series of placards on the easel, while Reno held a pointer. The nurse slid away the first card, which was blank.

"The cancer is right here, in the jejunum," said Lamar, while Reno pointed to it on the diagram.

"The *what*?" asked Connie.

"The jejunum," said Reno. "It's part of the small intestine."

"It lies directly in between the duodenum and the ileum," said Lamar. "Next card, please."

Reno slid this card off the easel. "That's upside-down," said Dr. Grayer.

After turning the card around, Reno pointed to a diagram of an enlarged view of the small intestine. "This is a drawing of your small intestine, as it would look if it was healthy," he said. "Remember, this is just a computer-drawn two-dimensional image; for the full story, we'd need a three-dimensional view."

Reno then took this card away. Lamar said, "And this is a cross-section view. This red spot here—eh, Reno, right here," Lamar said as he guided Reno's pointer to the red spot, "is where the cancer was located. At the time the X-rays and MRI's were taken, the tumor was about the size of a dime."

"Unusual place for a cancer to begin," Corey commented.

"Yes, unusual indeed," said Dr. Grayer. "After reading up on this disorder this morning in my Gray's—make that *Grayer's*—Anatomy, giggle, giggle, there have been only four cases—all fatal—of this particular cancer. Fortunately, we're only in the early stage of the disease. Unfortunately, we must begin treatment without too much delay, since beyond this initial stage, the cancer spreads more quickly. Soon the tumor could grow from the size of a dime to the size of a silver dollar."

"What kind of treatment will you put her on?" asked Corey.

"Later today, we'll start by putting her on chemotherapy," said Lamar.

June 10

One more evening and one more night went by, but there was nothing special going on for Corey to remember. Ho-hum. Wake up in the morning, yawning and stretching. Sit down at the table, and eat a dull, impromptu breakfast. Get on the first bus that goes to the university, go to the medical center, and visit his beautiful bride-to-be, stopping along the way to ask doctors and nurses how she's doing. Even after only two days, such rituals began to bore Corey. How he just couldn't wait for Connie to come back home, so he could have someone to tell his wildest dreams to when he woke up each morning, and get through the rest of his day, with someone there with him, so each minute of the day didn't seem like thirty minutes.

Just after he finished yet another dull, impromptu breakfast, Corey walked out the front door, carrying enough change for a round-trip bus ride to the university campus.

"Good morning, Corey," he heard Lamar say as he walked out the door.

"Good morning—*Lamar? Reno?*" replied Corey, as he did a double-take.

"What are you doin' here?" Corey asked.

"Goin' to see Connie?" asked Reno, who was walking alongside Lamar.

"Yeah, since there's nothing else to do."

"We've got the same notion," said Lamar. "Would you like to come with us?"

"Yes, I'll go with you," said Corey. "I can just save this spare change for something a little more important."

"Like lunch?" asked Reno. "This afternoon, we three will do lunch together."

"Sounds good to me," Corey responded.

Corey, Reno, and Lamar arrived at the medical center. When they came in the front door, Reno asked Corey, "Would you like to see a shocker?"

"Shocker?" asked Corey? "What kind?"

"You'll see for yourself," said Lamar. "But I tell you now, you certainly will be in for quite a shocker."

When Corey arrived in Connie's room, along with Reno and Lamar, he couldn't see anything to be shocked about.

"What's the big idea?" asked Corey. "I'm not shocked yet. I don't get it."

"Look at Connie," said Reno. "See anything different?"

"Not really," said Corey. "Connie looks like she normally does, when she's healthy."

"Look at her head," said Lamar.

"That's—her favorite hat!" said Corey. "So that's why you asked me for it last night."

"No, no, no, take a look *under* the hat," said Reno.

"Don't you dare!" said Connie, in an ill voice, as Corey walked up to her.

"The hat, please," said Corey.

"Uh, uh," Connie moaned.

"C'mon now, off it comes."

"You mustn't do this," murmured Connie.

Corey pulled the hat off with his left hand, stepped back, and slapped his right hand over his widely opened mouth.

"See? I told you," said Lamar.

"Now THAT was quite a shocker," said Reno.

Corey put he hat back on Connie's shiny round head, which once had plenty of long, brownish-black wavy hair.

"All this time," Corey told Lamar and Reno, "I thought I had it made with the most beautiful woman I ever did see. We were even set to get married, and live as one. But now, something has gone wrong—seriously wrong."

"Just *what*?" asked Lamar, as he, Corey, and Reno were walking out the door.

"Now," said Corey, as he was walking outside the room, "she looks like Charles Barkley."

Near noon, Corey was at a restaurant with Lamar and Reno.

"I can just see the epitaph now," said Reno. "Here lies Connie Yeltaw, once the world's most beautiful woman; now, she looks like Charles Barkley."

"Oh, the things chemotherapy can do for you," said Lamar. "Makes you lose you hair, but often it cures the disease. Then again, sometimes it doesn't."

"Has her condition improved?" asked Corey.

"It's too early to tell," said Reno. "In a couple of days, we should know for sure."

Corey was back to being alone at home for the afternoon. As a complete surprise, he heard the phone ring. He was clueless about who it could be, or even what it could be about. After a few seconds' hesitation, and three rings, he picked up the phone.

"Is this Corey?" asked the person on the other end of the line.

"You must be Jevon," said Corey.

"That's right! I heard that Connie's not doing too well, and that she has a serious illness."

"Yes, she has cancer. It's somewhere in the small intestine; I think it's called the jejunum, or something like that. She's now on chemotherapy, and she's lost all her hair."

"Oh my!" shrieked Jevon. "I don't think I'd recognize her if I saw her."

"It's really got me feeling on edge this time," Corey said. "We won't know for a few days how it'll turn out. It's not known yet if the therapy will cure the disease."

"We've got to hold on tight," said Jevon. "We must hold on to whatever sparks of hope we hold in our hands now, even if it burns our fingers."

"That's what worries me," said Corey. "Who knows what could happen between now and Saturday."

"Saturday? Now I remember. That was supposed to be your wedding day."

"But I think we may have to wait indefinitely—that is, unless we want to hold the ceremony in room 613 of the Medical Center at University of Pennsylvania at Sellecca Valley."

"So does it get lonely at night?" Jevon asked Corey.

"Yes, but somehow I always get through the nights when I'm alone."

"Mind having someone join you?"

"Will you be coming over?" Corey asked Jevon.

"I'll be there in a couple of days," Jevon answered. "Got the guest room ready?"

"It's quite a mess," said Corey. "I don't think it'll be ready by the time you get here."

"I've got my round-trip tickets," said Jevon. "I *was* going to come for the weekend, and the wedding, but with Connie's condition worsening, I must come now. It may be my only chance."

"Never say maybe," said Corey. "I'm sure she'll recover. I gotta go now. It's almost time for me to put a frozen dinner in the microwave. Goodbye...."

June 12

"Whew!" gasped Corey, when he stepped off the bus after coming home from another afternoon of visiting Connie's hospital room. Feeling somewhat tired, he walked without any words or emotion, toward his house. Once inside his home, he felt like plopping himself down on the living room couch, taking a big sigh, and nodding off. But after he got himself settled down, he heard what sounded like a ringing door chime. Corey rushed over to the door, just to see if anyone was actually there. Somebody was at the door indeed; it was Jevon, carrying his luggage.

"Well, what's going on, Jevon?" Corey asked, as the two held each other closely.

187

"I'm here for you now," said Jevon, "so you won't have to be alone all the time. How's Connie doing?"

"She's getting worse," said Corey. "The cancer has now spread far beyond the jejunum—"

"The what?" asked Jevon, jokingly.

"It's part of the intestines," Corey continued. "Chemotherapy isn't working; I've also been told that it's too late to start radiation treatment. But somehow, I believe we're in for a miracle, if you really try to think about it. Remember when we arrived here by accident, and everyone had written me off as dead? I sure fooled all the oddsmakers and naysayers that time. Maybe Connie can do the same thing for us now."

"By the way, have you sold the company yet?" Jevon asked.

"Definitely yes," said Corey. "I've already received the first of a series of checks."

"I'm about to sell my business too," replied Jevon.

"I watched the news on TV today," Corey told Jevon, "and the weatherman predicted storms tonight."

"What's wrong, Corey? You afraid of thunder and lightning?"

"Not really. It's not the weather that scares me; it's having to sleep alone at night on such a night as tonight."

"I could go to bed with you," Jevon told Corey reassuringly, "since you said the guest room isn't ready yet."

"All right," Corey replied. "I guess if I could have survived having to share a sleeping bag with my older brother...."

"Sounds scary," said Jevon. "Why did you have to share a sleeping bag?"

"This was when I was five," said Corey. "I went with my parents and brother on a camping trip. We had the tailgate window on our station wagon open, apparently. I suppose what must have happened was that as we drove up a steep hill, my sleeping bag must have rolled out the back."

"So how was sharing a bag with your brother?"

"Terrible. Lester would snore, roll over and almost crush me—even stick his arm under me. I thought it might have been a *snake*!"

"You'll feel all right sleeping with me. I don't hiss, I don't bite, and most of all, I don't coil up and strike, serpentine as I may be."

Jevon and Corey spent a whole evening watching TV together. When both men began yawning and felt tired, they walked to the bedroom. Jevon went into the bathroom to change himself, while Corey switched into his nightwear from inside the bedroom. Jevon walked out of the bathroom wearing red-and-white striped pajamas, which were in stark contrast to Corey's blue pajamas with white stars all over.

"Looks like stars and stripes, forever," said Corey, giggling.

Corey turned a bedside lamp on just before he turned the ceiling light off. Corey got into bed in his usual place; Jevon got in bed at the place where Connie normally slept.

"I heard that one night, Connie was in bed nude," Jevon said to Corey after the two pulled the covers up over them. "You were shocked. But at least I won't shock you. Good night, Corey."

Corey felt quite embarrassed having a *man* tell him good night.

June 13

After a stormy night, which caused Corey to lose a small amount of sleep, Corey and Jevon awoke.

"I don't know if I should get up today," said Corey. "You know what today is? It's the thirteenth, and it's a Friday at that."

"Your luck is about to change," said Jevon.

"Probably for the worse," replied Corey.

"You never know," Jevon told Corey.

Early that afternoon, Corey and Jevon came to the medical center. It would be only the first visit to Connie made by Jevon, but the fifth straight day of such visits for Corey.

Corey walked with Jevon into room 613, where Connie, who felt gravely ill and had some difficulty speaking, looked at them.

"I just stopped by," said Jevon to Connie, "to see how you're doing. I see that you're not doing so well. I think I'll just step outside, so Corey can be alone with you. I'll be standing outside the door."

Corey walked up to Connie, putting his hand upon hers. Connie's eyes opened as far as they could.

"How're you doing?" Corey asked Connie.

"I was told this morning that 95% of the sand in my hourglass is in the bottom half."

"Well," joked Corey, "let's turn the thing upside-down."

"It's not that easy," said Connie in a tired voice.

"Friday, the thirteenth of June," sighed Corey. "Just my luck. A day before our scheduled wedding, this has to happen."

"Oh, Corey! When will you quit blaming yourself for things no one can do anything about?"

"Anyway, Connie, I'm here for you right now during these trying times, both for you, and for myself."

"Don't leave me," Connie said.

"I won't," Corey told her. "I'll stay here as long as I can."

"Now did you really love me?" Connie asked.

"Indeed I did. Even at first, when I thought I really didn't, I just knew that I did."

Corey came a little closer to Connie, holding his arm behind her shoulders.

"Do—you—" Connie began to ask, catching her breath as she spoke, "take me, Cornelietta Rolonda Starke Yeltaw, to—be—your law-ful-ly wedded wife?"

"I most certainly do!" said Corey. "Is there anything you want from me now?"

"Just hold me close, and never let go," Connie said.

And Corey did just that. While he held her body close to his, Corey heard Connie murmur, "I love you Corey."

"That's just what I wanted to hear. I love you too, Connie," Corey replied.

Moments later, Corey was still holding Connie, whom Corey thought now felt cold and numb. Corey didn't want to let go, but now he knew he had to.

Devoid of any traces of emotion, Corey walked out of the room into the hallway, where he saw Jevon pacing nervously. Corey placed his hand on Jevon's shoulder.

"The time—" said Corey, "has come, and gone."

Jevon sighed, collecting his thoughts.

"Time..." Jevon replied, "for so long, it was our ally. Now, time is all you and I have left, but the only time that is left for us is the past."

"Sometimes, it can surely seem that way," said Corey. "But all we really do have left now is the future ahead of us. Alas, at present, the future is just, well, a whole bunch of nothing. Seems not that long ago, she and I were on top of the world; now, I think we've hit rockbottom."

"That's about as low as we can get," said Jevon.

"I guess then, the only way we can go from here is up."

"But just where do we go from here?" Jevon asked, putting his finger to his eye, as if to wipe a tear away. "All we've lived and worked for is gone."

Corey sighed deeply, then looked into the eyes of Jevon, who seemed about to cry.

"Aw, Jevon, it's not that terrible. We've had each other from the beginning, and we've still got each other now, and well into the future."

Corey walked with Jevon down the hallway to the elevators. Inside the elevator when it opened were Lamar and Reno, who, like Jevon and Corey, were absolutely expressionless.

"I suppose you know by now," Corey told Reno and Lamar.

"Yes, we know," answered Lamar.

"We did everything there was that we could do," commented Reno, "but I guess it just wasn't good enough."

"Don't let yourself down," Corey told the two, while Jevon was listening silently. "I sure do love what you've done for me so far."

"And what a time for it to happen," sighed Lamar. "The day before what could have—should have—would have been the best day of your life, and maybe ours too."

When the elevator stopped on the main entry level, Reno and Lamar walked toward the reception desk, while Corey and Jevon headed to the exit. All was still and silent in the lobby. While Corey walked out the front door with Jevon, he stopped in the middle of the doorway after seeing his older brother Lester.

"So how have things been going?" Lester asked Corey.

"Things went all right, until today," Corey replied.

"Guess it's because today's the 13th, and it's Friday as well," commented Jevon.

"I've been trying to reach you all week," said Lester, "but no one's been at home. So I came here, hoping to find you. Indeed I did."

Lester looked at Corey and Jevon, seeing a telltale bit of sadness in their eyes.

"Is something wrong?" Lester asked.

"We've just had a 'code blue' in room 613," murmured Jevon.

"What?" Lester asked. "Code blue? Just what do you mean by that?"

For a moment, all was silent as Corey shrugged and sighed.

"Connie's dead," said Corey.

"I'm s—" Lester began to say, before being interrupted.

"Don't say that!" said Corey. "It's just not what I want to hear."

"When did this happen?" Lester asked.

"Less than a half hour ago," sighed Corey. "It happened while I was holding her."

"Now I know why you were gone all that time," Lester told Corey. "You two going back home now?"

"Yes," said Jevon.

"But now, it just doesn't seem like a home," replied Corey. "The one who helped me make this town my home is gone; therefore, this town just doesn't seem like home; yet I just can't get myself back to Boston—it seems nobody knows me there anymore."

Lester took Corey and Jevon to the home where Connie once lived. Everything there was exactly as Corey remembered it.

"Too many memories," said Corey. "There's too much here to remind me of the wonderful things that could, would, should have been, and never will be."

While Jevon sat down on the living room sofa, holding a framed photo of Connie and Corey, Corey was on the telephone, talking first with Connie's sister Joanna, then with Connie's closest friend, Mrs. Jasmine Grayer.

When Corey got off the phone, and came back into the living room, something looked slightly different. There sat Jevon, just where he was when they got home, except that now he'd set the photograph down on the coffee table, and was hiding his face, crying. Corey sat down next to Jevon, and leaned his head upon Jevon's; but as hard as he tried not to, even Corey could feel the stinging, burning sensation of tears in his own eyes.

June 14

What should have been the ultimate best day of Corey's life was now the day he dreaded the most. After a night of finding it so difficult to get to sleep, he had to awake to the cold, hard reality of having to live without the only true love he had ever known, for the rest of his days and nights.

With nothing else to do on this dull Saturday morning, Corey went to a neighborhood park, sat on the top row of a set of bleachers overlooking a baseball field, and just blankly stared into space. There was no future for Corey to think of, only the wonderful moments he and Connie had in past months. Unfortunately, some rather unpleasant memories came to mind (such as Connie's suicide attempt that past December), making him feel depressed. At moments he thought tears would come to his eyes, but somehow he found from within the strength to hold them back.

When Corey came home, he found that someone was parked in his driveway. He walked in the door, to find Dr. Grayer in the living room, talking with Lester and Jevon.

"So how are you today?" Kendall asked Corey.

"I'm still trying to adjust. It's oh so hard, harder than anything I've been through before that I can remember."

192

"But you'll pull through it, I just know that you will," Lester said to his younger brother.

"You know, Kendall," Corey said to Dr. Grayer, "that's what I like about you. Always, no matter what the situation, you hold yourself together, keeping your composure. I really admire that."

"It's not easy, but I somehow, some way manage to do it," Kendall replied. "I've gone through a lot of what you've been going through. Less than a year after finishing my residency, cancer claimed my first wife, at the age of twenty-five. What *can* you say about a twenty-five-year-old woman who died?"

"So when did you first meet Jasmine?" Corey asked.

"Nearly twelve years ago, in my first year of licensed medical practice. She was in her final year at the UPSV College of Education. After her first year of student-teaching, we were married. Yes, Jasmine. To me, she's the human version of Barbie, for a poor old Kendall like me. Get it? Kendall—*Ken doll*."

"And you've been happily married ever since," remarked Lester.

"She's never done me wrong," Kendall replied. "Except for last night, when she kept me awake almost all night. That's why I feel so exhausted this morning."

"Jasmine kept *you* up all night?" Corey asked.

"Yes," said Dr. Grayer, "but actually, it wasn't all night. She and I finally got to sleep—at about 3:07 a.m.!"

"Was she feeling sick?" asked Jevon.

"No, she was certainly not sick."

"So maybe she was snoring," said Lester.

"I don't think so," said Kendall. "I've never known Jasmine to snore."

"Then just what was she doing?" asked Corey.

"Crying," said Dr. Grayer. "We went to bed, and I seemed to fall asleep quickly. I had this bad dream that she lay there next to me, face down on her pillow crying. I awoke from the dream, however, to find that she actually was crying. At first, I took it easy, and just sat up with her in the living room, holding her close to me, gently stroking her, putting my cheeks against hers, and my lips under her eyes where the tears were falling. I guess that calmed her down; we went back to bed."

"So you fell asleep again," said Corey.

"Yes, but only for an hour or two," said Kendall. "Then, more of the same whine, sob, blubber, whimper. This time, unfortunately, I kinda lost my head, and started yelling at her, and telling her to go away so I could catch some Z's. Thinking it would help me fall asleep, she stormed out of the room. For two hours, I lay there alone, unable to sleep, with a guilty conscience. I got out of bed, and went around the house looking for her; later I found her curled up on the back patio, still crying. I sat down next to her, told her I just couldn't get to sleep, and found myself having to say I was sorry."

"Doesn't love mean never...." asked Corey. "Back in December, I remember you telling me that. Last week, I found out where you got the line from."

"All these years, I've been wondering about that," said Dr. Grayer. "Anyway, she and I sat under the stars, shared a romantic kiss, and came back in the house, and went to bed. What an adventurous night for me."

"As for Corey and I," said Jevon, "we did most of our wailing yesterday afternoon, when we got home. By evening, Corey helped himself and me snap out of it. Wherever Connie is now, I don't think she'd want to see us cry. Corey helped us grow stronger inside."

"Jasmine's really devastated," said Kendall. "She and Connie were best of friends, right to the end. She decided not to come with me this morning, because she felt so tired."

"But for me, it was much more," Corey commented. "We're talking here about the love of my life. Jevon and I had a little trouble getting to sleep last night too. Early in the morning, we just couldn't sleep anymore. We sat up on the couch, spending two and a half hours watching *World News Now*."

"Did I miss something?" asked Lester. "I suppose I must not have heard anything; I must have slept very well."

June 15

A television weatherman predicted rain for that Sunday afternoon; his forecast was right, as if he had some forms of hunch and ESP. And what an afternoon for a graveside memorial service!

Along with Lester and Jevon, Corey was among the first three to arrive at the cemetery. Corey glimpsed at the card he was holding.

In loving memory
Cornelietta Rolonda Starke Yeltaw
Born January 30, 1959; Chicago, IL.
Entered into rest June 13, 1997; Sellecca Valley, PA.

After reading that passage, Corey took a sigh.

While these three people sat and waited under a canopy, other guests arrived. Taking seats just behind Corey were the Grayers, Kendall and Jasmine. It made Corey feel choked up and speechless when he turned around and saw Jasmine cry, while Kendall was holding her. Next came Lamar and Reno, who, quite unusually, were not at all the youthful, radiant personalities Corey had come to know so very well. Although Corey would see a few familiar faces that day, most of the people were ones he'd never met—mostly Connie's co-workers at the medical center. Indeed Corey knew that these people could certainly not be relatives, since her sister Joanna and cousin Jevon were the closest relatives to her—Connie's mother was dead already; her father was in a nursing home, bedridden with Alzheimer's disease, and her brother was serving a lengthy prison sentence in California.

Just after the rain stopped sprinkling, Corey walked with the others to the grave, wherein the coffin had been lowered already, with a pile of dirt on the side. Corey, standing at the foot of the grave, cleared his throat and began to speak.

"Where *do* I begin? I started with absolutely nothing; now I'm— well, back where I started. Through a twist of fate, some sort of accident of nature, I find myself in a strange town, where nobody knew me. I myself was near death, never even knowing I was here. It took a beautiful young nurse—make that *pediatric* nurse—to bring me back to life. And not only did she do that, but she also breathed new life into me. She taught me not only how to love, but how to live as well. She told me she'd love me all her life. She lived up to her words. I should feel good about that. And I do. But once I've loved her, will there ever be another for me?"

Lamar handed Corey a bouquet. Corey knelt down to drop the bouquet into the grave. As Corey got up on his feet to stand up, the soft earth underneath him slid. After he got up, he lost his balance, falling forward. He found himself falling headfirst into the grave. "Somebody catch me!" he screamed. But nobody could reach him. Quite oddly, the grave seemed much deeper than the traditional six feet under, since Corey still felt as though he were falling.

Corey's arms were stretched out as far as they could go, but it just wouldn't do him any good; he was still falling, headfirst at that.

Just *how* deep was the grave anyway—six feet, or six miles? Would Corey ever stop? Would he come back alive, or join his love one in eternity? If he were to survive the fall, could he get back out again? Before Corey could ponder this awkward situation, he stopped moving with a gigantic....

THUMP!!!

June??

Corey sat up, and opened his eyes. It was dark; he could barely see anything. Very strange, he thought, that he wasn't sitting on soft earth, or even atop a hardwood coffin. He was sitting on his own bed! Looking at the alarm clock, he saw that it was only 2:36 AM. He wondered where everyone was, thinking he was all alone. But when he looked to his side, he saw Connie, fast asleep. Just to see if she was actually living and breathing, he put his hand on her breast. It seemed to rise and fall with every breath she took. She was awakened by the feel of Corey's hand.

"What are you doing?" Connie grumbled.

"Oh, Connie," said Corey, "just minutes ago, you were—literally—dead."

"You must be dreaming," she replied.

"Must have been," sighed Corey.

After a minute of looking at each other without speaking, Connie and Corey went back to sleep.

June 8

"So," Connie asked Corey while the tow were jogging around the block early that morning, "you say I was dead?"

"Exactly. This morning, the eighth of June, strangely enough, I woke up before you did, and I made breakfast. You, however, were to sick to eat—vomiting blood, even!"

"That does not sound so good!" Connie replied.

"That's just what Jasmine told me on the phone," Corey said. "But she didn't quite say it like you did. She spoke in the key of B-flat minor."

"What about me? What key am I speaking in?"

"I consider you voice to be, maybe, a C-sharp major?"

Connie and Corey sat down at the breakfast table later that morning. "So what happened next?" Connie asked.

"That evening, after Lamar and Reno took you to the medical center, the Grayers invited me out to dinner with them, at 9th & Ash."

"One of these nights," Connie remarked, "we ought to go there again. What did you have?"

"What *you* usually have, which is Blackened Cajun Seafood Combo. Kendall had prime rib; Jasmine had some French-named chicken dish."

"Chicken Cordon Bleu?" Connie asked.

"Yeah—that's it!" replied Corey.

"Just what was wrong with me?" asked Connie.

"That's just what I was getting to. The next day, I found out from Grayer and the gang. What you had was cancer, of the jejunum. All I know is it's part of the small intestine. When I returned the next day, you'd lost all your hair to chemotherapy, about which I joked to Lamar and Reno that you looked like Charles Barkley."

Connie made a sick face.

"Two days after that," Corey continued, "Jevon came over to stay with me. That day after that, which was Friday, the 13th, he came with me to the medical center. You, with what little strength you had, asked me to hold you tight, and never let go. That was precisely what I did. Right before I finally did let go, you felt cold, stiff, and numb."

Connie began to shiver. "Just how *did* you get out of this nightmare?"

"Sunday, I was at your graveside memorial service. Everyone I know here, as well as some people I didn't recognize, was there. I leaned over to toss a bouquet on your coffin, but the soft earth slid out from under me, causing me to fall in headfirst. For some odd reason, it seemed to be more like six miles, than six feet under. You know, it's what happens whenever you dream about falling—you get jerked awake suddenly," Corey said. "It may have actually been six feet, but it was the longest two yards I've ever gone."

"Ashes to ashes," remarked Connie, grinning, "we all fall down," she said along with Corey.

"Something happens whenever I watch movies," said Corey. "Sometimes, I find myself reliving them."

24

Together Forever As One

At last! Now it was officially the 14th of June. A week ago, it seemed as though this would have been the day Corey would have almost certainly dreaded; that is, if dreams really *did* come true.

According to this "early-summer-night's dream," the previous day, Friday, June 13, was to be the day Corey would be sitting in the living room with Jevon, both sobbing their eyes out, and neither one sleeping well that night. In reality, he was with Connie, having dinner at 9th & Ash, then out dancing at a nearby nightclub.

The morning was not all that unusual. Connie and Corey went through their normal routine that morning.

"Today," said Corey, "the course of our lives changes forever; hopefully, for the better."

"It better," Connie replied. "Forever's such a long time."

"Spending forever with a woman like you is so much more than a dream come true," remarked Corey.

"Just remember you're not the only one," Connie told Corey. "Since the death of my first husband, so many others—more than I can count on all my fingers and toes—have said they've loved me; none of them, however, was right for me."

"But I don't think they really loved you. All they really wanted was to touch your face, your hands, and gaze into your eyes."

"Did you already bring in the paper?" Connie asked Corey.

"No, but I'll go get it."

Corey stepped onto the driveway, bent down and picked up the newspaper. When he stood up, he saw Lamar walk by.

"Lamar!" Corey said. "This is it! This is the day!"

"Let me guess," asked Lamar, "you just can't wait. Are you starting to get anxious?"

"I'm not sure," said Corey, "if that's even *close* to being the right word."

Corey came in with Lamar.

"Good morning, Lamar," Connie said. "Like to see the dress I'll be wearing today?"

"Yeah, I'd like to see it," said Lamar, "just to see how you look in it."

Lamar followed Connie into her bedroom; Corey went into the guest room.

"Here it is," said Connie, taking the dress from a hanger placed over a doorstop.

"Is it fairly new?" Lamar asked.

"Not at all, far from it," Connie replied. "I wore exactly this same dress at my first wedding in 1983. "I've kept it preserved so very well. I haven't worn it since that day in the autumn of that year, when I went down the aisle with Aaron Yeltaw, the son of an African prince-in-exile."

"Woo! An African prince," gasped Lamar. "That sounds exotic! What was the prince's name?"

"His name—full name at birth—was Yeltaw Ydoj Evol I. Aaron's grandfather, the king, was King Evol VI; the queen was Queen Yeltaw Ydoj. In 1978, the royal family fled the country during a coup attempt; eventually Aaron, whose birth name was Yeltaw Ydoj Evol II, settled here at Sellecca Valley. We met in 1980, while he was a sophomore at UPSV, majoring in political science; I was in my third year at nursing school. We were married three years later, after he graduated."

"But whatever came of Aaron, anyway?" Lamar asked.

"In June of 1989," Connie continued, "the family was asked to come back, to help with famine relief. The rebel forces invited the queen (the king had died in the coup), the prince, and the prince's son—that's Aaron—to deliver humanitarian aid to the famine-stricken nation, as a conciliatory gesture. But as their plane entered friendly airspace, an extremely radical faction, who dissented with the rebels and opposed the delivery of aid, brought the plane down with a single missile, killing all three, plus the pilot."

"And where were *you* when this happened?" asked Lamar.

"I was left at home, the 'odd woman out.' There was room for only three on the plane."

Connie and Lamar looked up, hearing a tap-tap-tap on the door.

"Lamar? Are you in there?" Corey asked.

"Yes, I'm in here. What do you need?"

"I've got my suit on," Corey said. "I want you to take a look, and tell me what you think."

"While you're doing that," Connie told Lamar, "I'll go into the bathroom, and put this dress on."

Lamar went into the hallway, taking a look at a well-dressed Corey.

"That suit looks vaguely familiar," Lamar commented.

"It should," replied Corey. "It's the same one I wore on the train when I arrived here on a stretcher."

"I remember," said Lamar. "I remember well."

"So I guess this is going to be a hand-me-down wedding," said Corey. "And with all the money I'll be making, at that."

"I think I heard someone at the door," said Lamar. "Go get it. It must be Reno."

Corey opened the front door; it was Reno at the door, as Lamar had guessed.

"Reno! Come right in!" said Corey.

Reno came in with a pair of boxes in his hands.

"So how are you today, Reno?"

"Corey, if you're feeling good, I guess I feel good too."

"Do you feel a bit jumpy?" Corey asked Reno. "If *you* do, then I must feel the same way too."

"Where's Connie?" asked Reno.

"Last thing I know, she went into the bathroom to try her dress on," answered Corey.

"Have you seen her in her dress?" Reno asked.

"No, not yet," responded Corey. "Hopefully, I won't see her in it until she comes up the aisle."

Lamar walked in. "I saw her dress," he told Reno and Corey. "I was just with her. She told me all about her first marriage."

"I've known about it all along," said Corey. "She told me all about it a while ago."

"How'd she get through the death?" asked Lamar. "Knowing her, I find it difficult to believe she made it through something like that."

"It was hard, indeed," said Corey. "She would spend much of those first few days crying and sobbing, much like that December night, the night I tried to leave her. There was, however, someone—two people, to be specific—who helped her pull through."

"I think I might know who those two are," said Reno.

"Yes, the Grayers," said Corey. "Kendall, you may remember, lived through the passing of his first wife."

"Good ol' Dr. Grayer," said Lamar. "He's always been a person to look up to. Other than Reno, he's the man I look up to the most. Being with him just, well, makes people feel good."

"What time are we supposed to be there?" asked Reno.

"We need to get there soon!" said Corey. "It's almost 10:30 now. The ceremony starts at noon."

"What about Connie?" asked Lamar.

"I think she may need a little more time to get ready," said Corey. "Are you two ready already?"

"Yes, we're already all ready already," answered Reno. "Are you, Corey?"

"I'm as ready as you are," replied Corey.

"So let's go," said Lamar. "Reno, go put those boxes in the trunk. I'll start the car after I take a trip to the toilet."

In the bathroom, Lamar couldn't hear anything, despite that the master bath shared a wall with the bathroom in the hallway. He figured that either Connie must be asleep, or have gone somewhere. After he finished taking care of business, Lamar flushed the toilet, came out of the bathroom, and made sure to lock the front door when he left the house.

Reno and Corey were already in the car talking with each other. Rather than interrupt their conversation, Lamar just got in, started the ignition, and drove off.

"Got the butterflies yet?" asked Reno.

"Actually," Corey replied, "I've got the Africanized killer bees. I feel like making a beeline straight to the Grayers' house, right down the aisle."

"If we wanna get there that fast," commented Reno, "I guess I should be the one driving instead of Lamar."

"Reno, I really think you should start an ambulance service," remarked Corey. "Since that's the way you drive."

"Oh stop that!" said Reno, grinning. "You know I'm not that kind of driver."

"Actually," said Lamar, "Reno is a fairly good driver. He pays less for insurance than I do. Of course, I had a wreck recently."

At home, Connie was in her dress, talking on the telephone. When she ended the conversation, the only sound she could hear was the motor on the refrigerator.

"Where is everyone?" she asked. Looking out the front window, she saw no car, nor any sign of Corey, Reno, or Lamar.

"They couldn't have," Connie grumbled. "How *could* they have left without me?"

The three men arrived at the Grayers' home rather early. "How late are we?" asked Corey.

"It's—10:56," said Reno.

"That'll give us plenty of time," replied Lamar.

Corey walked to the front door of the Grayers' home, while Reno and Lamar followed behind closely. Corey rang the doorbell, which played a G-E-C melody similar to the NBC chimes.

Jasmine, wearing her best French dress and Italian shoes, answered the door.

"Good afternoon, Corey, Lamar, and Reno," she said. "I know just how you're feeling, Corey. I just can't wait either."

"Neither can we," said Reno and Lamar together. "This could be the most exciting spectacle of our lives," said Reno.

While the three walked in, Dr. Kendall Grayer was there to greet them.

"So Corey," Kendall asked, "are you building up excitement?"

"Yes, I'm building it up," replied Corey. "After I get to the end of the aisle, I'll unleash it all."

"That was pretty much the way it was with my wedding to Jasmine," said Dr. Grayer. "Our ceremony was held on the island of St. Thomas, in the U.S. Virgin Islands. Jasmine is a native of St. Thomas."

At home, Connie got into her car. She turned the key, but the ignition wouldn't start. When she looked under the dashboard, she found that the headlight control was in the on position.

"No battery," she mumbled. "I guess I'll ask my next-door neighbors, the Wiggins, if they could take me. No, wait. Today's Saturday. He works weekends, and takes the car with him when he goes."

Corey was with Jasmine in the Grayers' bedroom, standing in front of a mirror attached to the outside of the closet door. He was standing next to Jasmine, modeling his suit, and striking a few provocative poses.

"How do I look?" Corey asked.

"To be completely honest," replied Jasmine, "you make me feel like going on *Entertainment Tonight* and modeling some of the Princess of Wales' gowns."

"Only fitting," commented Corey. "Somehow, I've always thought that you looked like you should be a correspondent with *ET*."

Connie was still stranded at home, pondering her next move. "I'll take the bus," she said to herself. "No, that doesn't sound like a good idea. It could be up to an hour. And an hour is all I have. Less than an hour, in reality. I'll walk over to the Grayers' house myself. Actually, I should run. I'll put my lucky high-top sneakers on; it's murder to run while in heels. Determination. That's just what it takes. Good old-fashioned determination."

As Connie prepared to get up and running, Corey was talking with Kendall, Jasmine, Reno, and Lamar. Conversation among the five people was interrupted by the sound of footsteps at the front door. Corey opened the door. When he saw Lester, Jamie, Jeremy, and Jevon standing there, he felt as though his eyes would jump out of their sockets and his jaw drop to the floor, just like a character in a Tex Avery cartoon.

"Jevon! How'd you get here?" Corey asked.

"Lester picked me up at the airport," Jevon answered. "I flew to Boston, and went to Lester's home last night. This morning, we drove up here."

Corey started thinking of what to say next.

"You've got something to say," said Lester. "I just know you do."

"At least today has turned out differently from what I imagined last week," said Corey.

"Whaddaya mean?" asked Jeremy.

"It was a dream, the strangest dream I'd ever had," replied Corey. "It involved you, Lester, Jevon, the Grayers, the interns, and Connie, who disappeared from the whole thing quickly."

"Speaking of disappearing," commented Jevon, "where's Connie?"

"She didn't come with me," said Corey. "Last time I saw her, she went into the bathroom to try the wedding dress on. I just hope she wasn't nabbed by the creature who lives under the sink, behind the shampoo, next to the hair dryer..."

"...and to the left of the toilet paper," said Kendall and Jasmine, joining in.

Now that her dress and veil were on, along with high-top sneakers, Connie left the house. In order to build up energy, she had decided just to walk the first mile or so.

"I'm starting to get worried," Lamar said. "It's getting closer to noon. I'd think she should be here by now."

Somehow Connie felt she should take it easy, and just keep walking at a moderate pace. Unfortunately, she was afraid that a moderate pace would not get her there on time.

"It's almost midnight," Corey told Kendall, "and Cinderella's coach may soon become a pumpkin again."

203

"I just remembered!" Kendall shrieked. "I was supposed to pick her up, but when I called the house, the line was busy."

Down a major arterial street of Sellecca Valley ran Connie, holding onto her gown so she wouldn't trip over it. It was late morning, quite warm, with a clear sky. After walking almost two and a half miles, then jogging one more mile, she was now running at full steam, with less than four miles to go. She was breathing at an average rate, and was not sweating heavily. All the while, she hoped she'd have enough energy to make it down the aisle.

From the phone in his home, Dr. Kendall Grayer called Connie and Corey's house. The phone rang six times; there was no answer.

"No one's at home," Kendall said while Corey and Jasmine were standing by him. "I'll go over there and pick her up. Jaz, go get me my car keys. They should be on the dresser."

After Jasmine came back and gave her husband his car keys, Kendall told her he was going to go pick Connie up. Saying no more, he kissed Jasmine and ran out the door. Seeing the lips of Kendall and Jasmine gently stroke each other made Corey more anxious to feel Connie's lips gently stroke his.

Kendall had driven less than a mile, when on the side of the road, he saw someone dressed in a white gown and a veil seated on a bench. The person appeared to be tired and frustrated. "Could that be Connie?" Dr. Grayer wondered, as he pulled onto a side street.

As Kendall left his car, he walked toward the bench. The woman sitting on the bench looked at him.

"Can I help you with something?" the woman asked.

Dr. Grayer looked at her; just by her voice, he knew that she was not Connie Yeltaw.

"Oh no," he said. "You're not who I thought you were." He just walked back to his car and drove away.

Into the Grayers' home walked Connie, tired and gasping. Everyone was excited to see her, but they were also eager to run up and catch her if she were to faint and fall down.

"I need somewhere to sit down," she said. She found herself a seat next to Jevon; Corey was sitting on Jevon's other side.

"Unusual way to dress," Jevon commented. "What's with the turban?"

"It's no turban," said Connie, unfolding it. "It's the veil. I had to fold it into a turban while I was making a run for it. Running with a veil on makes you less aerodynamic."

"Running, indeed," mumbled Corey. "I guess that's why you wore your favorite high-top sneakers to your wedding."

"It was terrible," said Connie. "The car wouldn't start, there were absolutely no buses running locally, and it was a mad scramble. I'd walk two miles, then jog one, then walk two more, then run hand and fast the rest of the way."

"You surely do look exhausted," said Jevon. "I think we'd better wait a little while."

"Looks like we must," remarked Jasmine. "I wouldn't quite say we're ready yet. Kendall isn't back yet."

"Where'd he go?" Connie asked.

"He went to get you," Jasmine replied. "I just wonder, did he take his cell phone with him?"

Jasmine ran right to the telephone. She dialed the number to her husband's cellular telephone.

At this time, Dr. Kendall T. Grayer was inside the home of Connie R. Yeltaw—soon to be *Exbrook*, R.N., when he faintly heard the sound of a telephone. He went to the kitchen, where he saw the nearest phone, but when he picked it up, all he could hear was a dial tone. Meanwhile, he felt his waist vibrating unusually. He looked down, and saw that it was his own cellular phone ringing indeed.

"Hello, Dr. Kendall T. Gra—"

"Never mind the formal intro," said Jasmine.

"Jasmine?" he asked.

"Connie's here already," Jasmine replied. "Everyone's waiting for you."

"How'd she get there?" Kendall asked in wonder.

"She just—ran. Anyway, get back over here fast. Don't leave Corey and Connie waiting too long."

Several minutes later, Kendall finally returned home, walking right to the back yard, where everyone was waiting, even Connie and Corey, standing at the foot of the aisle.

"Is everyone prepared?" Dr. Grayer asked.

"We two have been prepared quite some time," answered Connie. "I'm certain we've got our vows memorized. We practiced them all week."

Music started playing. After Jevon and Jasmine handed a bouquet to Corey and Connie, the groom and bride somewhat casually strolled to the makeshift altar set up at the end.

"Dear thee beloved," the presiding judge spoke, "we are gathered here today to witness the union, in matrimony and life, or Cornelius

R. *Jermaine Schex*

Vanderbilt Exbrook and Corneli-e-e-*ahem*-Cornelietta Rolonda Starke Yeltaw. Our bride and groom have chosen to write their own vows for this ceremony. I now turn the microphone over to the groom, Mr. Exbrook."

Corey cleared his throat, stepped to the microphone, and prepared to speak.

"I've always know that he could speak so eloquently," Reno said to Lamar.

"Love and life," said Corey. "Besides being part of the title of a defunct CBS soap opera, they are, in my opinion and that of many others, the two most beautiful words in the English language. These two words may not be synonyms, but to us, they certainly mean the same thing. Now it may be true that there can indeed be love without life, but there can never be life without love. Both Connie and myself have experienced thus forehand. In nearly three decades as one of the children of Good Mother Earth, I've never experienced what it truly means to be alive. All those years in Boston were just day-to-day, same-old-grind, year in, year out. It wasn't until a reprieve of fate took me away from this so-called life, and placed me here in Sellecca Valley. Just what was waiting for me here? Someone who had so much life to live, and so much love to give. The fact that this same hand of fate has also given us wealth and prosperity seems not to make any real difference. Love is all I need to get by in this time on the face of the earth. I've found my new love."

As the judge looked on, Corey and Connie placed rings on each other's fingers.

"Now do you, Cornelietta Rolonda Starke Yeltaw, take this man, Cornelius Vanderbilt Exbrook, to be your lawfully wedded husband?" the judge asked Connie.

"I do; indeed I do," Connie answered.

"Same here, for me," said Corey.

"Thanks for helping me out," said the judge. "In less than two hours, I have another wedding to perform. I've got to rest my voice; my throat is starting to feel a bit scratchy. So by the authority vested in me by the State of Pennsylvania, I now pronounce you husband and wife."

"Connie," said Corey, "lay some lipstick on me."

Corey and Connie's lips were now locked together. It was now official. Now the atmosphere was a little more festive. Corey ducked when he felt rice falling upon him. "If only I knew there would be such a storm," he told Connie, "I'd have brought my umbrella."

By four o'clock, the big three-tiered cake was now almost completely eaten, and some guests had left already. The two newlyweds, along with the Grayers, Lester, Jeremy, Jamie, Jevon, Lamar, and Reno, stayed behind and were talking with each other.

"So what do you think the future holds for you?" Jasmine asked Connie and Corey.

"This fall," said Corey, "I'm set to enroll in business classes at nearby Stevens County Community College; eventually Connie and I plan to start a new chain of movie theaters with the 'Exbrook' name; indeed, the return of a familiar name, because all the existing 'Exbrook' signs will have been replaced by 'CinemaStar' signs by this year's end."

"And you, Lamar and Reno?" asked Connie.

"Now that we've completed our second-year internship," answered Reno, "we've decided to put in a year of residency in family practice."

"As for myself," said Jevon, "so much has gone on in my life the past few months, with so much more in the not-too-distant future."

"Now let's hear about it," said Corey. "And start from the beginning."

"Two months ago, I finally got my business sold off," Jevon began. "This joyous moment, alas, was overshadowed by a very messy breakup. I wasn't fortunate enough to get to where you two are now. But at least I've got a couple more things to look forward to."

"What 'cha lookin' forward to?" asked Connie.

"First, within this next month, I'll be doing some charitable volunteer work for the Young Citizens' Leadership Fund."

"You mean, the YCLF?" asked Lester. "I've worked with them before.

"Even more so," said Jevon, "after that, I'm scheduled to make a small appearance in an independently produced feature film. A former classmate of mine, from junior high, wrote and is directing this film. Sure has an eye for talent, this guy. For the lead role, he chose a classmate of ours—someone who made his big debut in 1984, on the stage at our school, doing impersonations of Michael Jackson."

"And what else do you have planned?" asked Corey.

"I've got all my belongings loaded," continued Jevon, "and I'm headed out to St. Louis to do my time with YCLF; then off to Phoenix to do the film, where I'll be staying with a few friends. When I put this all together, I figure I should be gone 'til November, when filming is expected to be completed. After that, I'll find a place to live out here."

As hours went by, newlyweds Connie and Corey were alone at home for the evening. Even though it was a warm night in June, they decided to sit next to the hearth in front of a crackling fire.

"Isn't it romantic?" asked Connie.

"I can't believe it," sighed Corey. "I *still* can't believe it. On our silver, golden, or even *platinum*, anniversary, I still might not believe it's real."

"Can you feel the passion?" Connie asked.

"B-r-r!" said Corey, shivering. "You chill me whenever I think about it."

"I think it was all in the draw of the cards," Connie remarked. "It was mere fate that brought us together."

"Yeah, like a train crash," said Corey.

"That, plus the fact that I wasn't originally supposed to work the shift I was on when I came upon you," Connie replied. "I was just filling in for an injured nurse."

"Really doesn't make any difference now," said Corey. "All that matters now is that here we are now, and here we'll stay forever. And forever's such a long, long, time."

It was getting late; Corey and Connie felt tired. The two were sitting in the living room looking at each other contently.

"Connie, lay some lipstick on me," Corey sighed.

Connie and Corey shared one last intimate kiss before retiring for the night. Then they continued gazing into each other's eyes. In Connie's eyes, Corey saw a face that reminded him so much of his own. Connie stared into Corey's eyes, envisioning a visage of herself. Without saying anything, they were still looking into each other's eyes. There was something unusual, they thought to themselves. But it wasn't odd at all. All they saw was real. They were together forever as one.